IMAGES
of Rail

ROCK ISLAND RAILROAD IN ARKANSAS

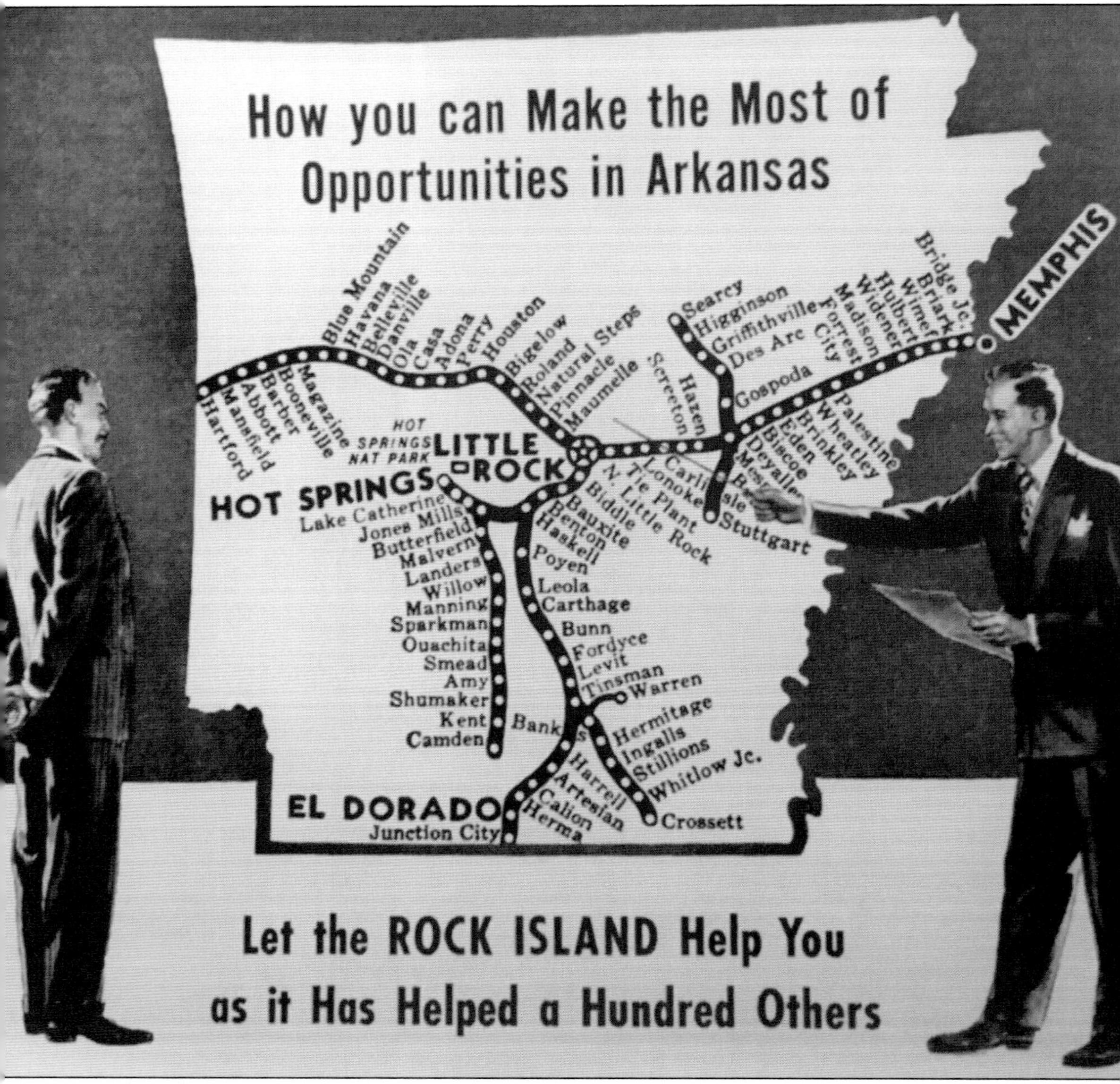

This advertisement, likely from the 1950s, features a map of all the communities served by the Rock Island in Arkansas at that time and encourages industrial development along its tracks. Service would later be scaled back on some less profitable branch lines. (Author's collection.)

ON THE COVER: Rock Island employees pose alongside Locomotive No. 425 at the company's rail yard in what is today North Little Rock. This c. 1905 photograph was taken after the Rock Island had acquired the Choctaw, Oklahoma & Gulf Railroad in a hostile takeover. Note that three of the men are filthy from probably having worked on the steam engine while the other two, most likely managers, are well dressed. (Courtesy of the North Little Rock History Commission.)

IMAGES
of Rail

ROCK ISLAND RAILROAD IN ARKANSAS

Michael E. Hibblen

ARCADIA PUBLISHING

ISBN 978-1-4671-2538-3

Published by Arcadia Publishing
Charleston, South Carolina

Printed in the United States of America

Library of Congress Control Number: 2016962058

For all general information, please contact Arcadia Publishing:
Telephone 843-853-2070
Fax 843-853-0044
E-mail sales@arcadiapublishing.com
For customer service and orders:
Toll-Free 1-888-313-2665

Visit us on the Internet at www.arcadiapublishing.com

To the employees who kept the Rock Island running through great adversity until a judge eventually shut down the struggling railroad.

Contents

Acknowledgments

This book would not have been possible without the assistance of Dr. Bill Pollard, an Arkansas railroad historian who shared many incredible photographs from his collection as well as his deep knowledge of railroad history. He is to be commended for capturing on film the last breaths of the Rock Island in the state, including the last westbound passenger train in 1967 and the final hours of the railroad's existence in 1980. Bill has shared his passion for railroads his whole life by taking photographs, writing histories, promoting passenger rail service, and advocating for the preservation of historic structures.

Thanks also go to others who helped connect me with historical images of the Rock Island, including David Stricklin and Glenn Whaley of the Butler Center for Arkansas Studies; Shannon Lausch with the University of Arkansas at Little Rock Center for Arkansas History and Culture; Cary Bradburn with the North Little Rock History Commission; Barry Arthur with the *Arkansas Democrat-Gazette*; and Skip Rutherford, dean of the Clinton School of Public Service, which is housed in the building that was the Rock Island's Little Rock station.

The passion many photographers clearly felt for the Rock Island still radiates from their images here, including those taken by Clifton Hull, Earl Saunders, and Rock Island company photographer and employee magazine editor Edward Wojtas. Information has come from a broad range of sources, including company publications; the now defunct Rock Island Technical Society; past issues of the *Arkansas Railroader* magazine, published for decades by Ken Ziegenbein; and the Laman Library's Railroad Room in North Little Rock.

Finally, a thank-you is owed to the many former Rock Island employees who have shared stories with me about their decades of working for the railroad at a time of great change in the industry. Some have since passed away, but their voices and incredible experiences live on in the interviews I have recorded over the years, starting in 1988. L.T. Walker, Joe P. Rook, Al Dodson, Guy Winters, Jerry Oates, and too many others to list here, please know how much I appreciate the sharing of firsthand accounts of working for the Rock Island.

INTRODUCTION

When the Rock Island was shut down in 1980, it was an incredible blow for Arkansas. The railroad had a huge footprint in the state and was an institution in the communities it served. For nearly 80 years, its trains were a familiar sight and had been important to the economy by moving goods and people. It was never the biggest railroad in Arkansas but was impressive in many ways. Despite the railroad serving parts of 13 states, employees described the Rock Island as a family operation. Some said they did not fully appreciate just how much of a family it was until they ended up working for different railroads.

Getting hired and beginning to build seniority with the Rock Island were considered good ways to provide a secure future for oneself and his or her family. It was competitive to get that opportunity. Employees bonded during the long hours together doing work that could be grueling or dangerous. Sometimes, several generations within one family worked for the Rock Island. They saw each other through the good or mundane times, but they really came together during the bad times. The bad times included horrific accidents, or in the final decades, bad management decisions and just unfortunate circumstances that led to a slow decline in the railroad that was painful to watch. Uncertainty at the end was nerve-wracking for employees, as well as the industries and communities that depended on the railroad.

When the last trains ran in March 1980, the railroad was in ragged condition. With the operation having not earned a profit in 15 years, it was a struggle for employees to keep it running. A lot of factors put the railroad in this condition. The rapid growth of automobiles and the airline industry after World War II cut deeply into passenger service. Improved highways and the interstate system made it easier for people to get around and led to more freight being carried by trucks. Onerous federal regulations imposed on the railroad industry had also not kept up with the times.

An argument can be made that if the Rock Island had been allowed to continue just a few more years, it would have greatly benefited from the deregulation that occurred in the 1980s. The Staggers Rail Act replaced a regulatory structure that had been in place more than a century and allowed shippers and railroads to work out more mutually beneficial agreements. Deregulation was credited with helping railroads reverse the loss of traffic to trucks and profits finally began to rise. Deregulation also made it easier for railroads to merge operations and become more efficient.

But decades earlier when the Rock Island proposed merging much of its operations with Union Pacific in 1964, it started the longest and most complicated merger case in the history of the Interstate Commerce Commission. The plan divided up the railroad, with the Southern division, which included the Arkansas trackage, to be bought by Southern Pacific. At that time, the Rock Island essentially stopped investing money to maintain its tracks and equipment. When the deal was finally approved a decade later, the Rock Island was in such bad shape that the other railroads walked away from the deal saying the cost to rehabilitate the infrastructure and union obligations were not worth what they would get in return.

The Rock Island filed for bankruptcy protection on March 17, 1975. While employees realized the dire condition the railroad was in, there was the belief from many that the government would not let such a big rail network fail. Either it would be propped up with government subsidies and eventually emerge as it had done twice in the past, or it would be purchased by another railroad. Many employees even agreed to give the railroad a "loan" of 10 percent of their wages. That March, about 130 employees in Little Rock are reported to have agreed to the pay deduction.

The Rock Island attempted a reorganization, but conditions did not improve. When employees never received their back pay and labor agreements expired, the Brotherhood of Railway and Airline Clerks and the United Transportation Union called for a strike in August 1979. About 700 of the railroad's roughly 800 employees in Arkansas took part. It was a difficult situation for employees, many of whom felt for the precarious situation the railroad was in but also disagreed with some management decisions and felt an obligation to stand with their unions.

It was a time of incredible tension as management attempted to keep trains running. There were reports of vandalism to tracks, including suspected arson to a trestle west of Booneville, which halted the movement of trains on that key artery that crossed Arkansas from east to west. The strike was pretty much the final blow for the Rock Island.

The situation was a major concern for then Arkansas governor Bill Clinton, who was serving his first term in office. Files kept by his office show Clinton and his staff devoted a great deal of time to looking at developments during the strike and getting comments from Rock Island employees, shippers who were worried about the movement of freight, and union representatives. When the end of the Rock Island was clearly in sight, they also considered what was in the best interest of the state.

The Interstate Commerce Commission (ICC) eventually declared a transportation emergency and ordered the Kansas City Terminal Railway to take over operations to ensure the movement of agricultural commodities. Creditors, like Henry Crown, had long argued the Rock Island was worth more dead than alive and wanted the assets liquidated. On January 24, 1980, Judge Frank McGarr went along with that request and ordered the shutdown of the railroad to take place two months later.

Frank B. Newell, an administrative assistant to Governor Clinton, spoke at an ICC hearing in Little Rock on October 31, 1979, saying he was taking the opportunity "to put the Governor's Office on record in support of a liquidation plan calling for sale of the Arkansas portion of the Rock Island as a core system or two core systems" and said the commission "must do its utmost under the law to prevent a piecemeal disposition of Rock Island Railroad assets."

Despite talks involving several different railroads, a buyer for the Rock Island's trackage as a whole in Arkansas could never be found. It was not just the poor condition of the track, and in one memo to the governor dated January 29, 1980, Newell writes that attorneys for other railroads are concerned about potential labor problems like having to pay severance, back wages, or hire Rock Island employees.

There was then a proposal for the state to buy the trackage and lease it to another railroad, which had been done in other states, but that failed in the legislature. In the end, except for a few stretches operated by different railroads, most of the Rock Island rails in Arkansas were removed and sold for scrap. It was an ugly ending for a once proud railroad with a storied history.

The irony was that while Clinton as governor was not able to preserve what had been the Rock Island's Arkansas division, he would later enshrine two of the Rock Island's proudest properties after serving as president of the United States. He chose the grounds along the Arkansas River that had once been owned by the Rock Island to build his presidential library. Part of that complex today includes the 1899 passenger station and Arkansas River bridge.

One

The Rock Island Takes Over in Arkansas

Formally known as the Chicago, Rock Island & Pacific (CRI&P), the railroad entered Arkansas at a time of aggressive nationwide expansion by the company. It acquired more than 700 miles of tracks in the state that had been parts of 32 different railroads. Key was the hostile takeover of the Choctaw, Oklahoma & Gulf (CO&G) Railroad. In May 1902, the Rock Island purchased a controlling interest in the CO&G, which officially became part of the Rock Island on March 24, 1904. The CO&G and its subsidiary, the Choctaw & Memphis (C&M) Railroad, had made major investments in the state with a goal of linking coal mines in what was then Indian Territory (today Oklahoma) with Memphis, Tennessee. It also handled lucrative shipments of lumber and agricultural commodities.

The Choctaw & Memphis had purchased many existing lines, including what had been the first chartered railroad in Arkansas, the Memphis & Little Rock (M&LR), which was incorporated January 11, 1853. It then made plans to expand west. In 1899, the C&M built an impressive bridge over the Arkansas River and a nearby passenger station in Little Rock, both of which still exist today. Track was simultaneously laid west from Little Rock and east from Indian Territory (Oklahoma), meeting near present-day Roland. It is easy to see why this infrastructure was so enticing for a larger, growing railroad like the Rock Island.

The following decades were a time of tremendous growth for the Rock Island. It outgrew some of the original Choctaw facilities, built a larger freight yard, and constructed many passenger depots and stations in Arkansas in the 1910s that are still around today. But in 1915, the railroad had its first brush with bankruptcy protection. It would emerge and grow with the economic boom of the 1920s.

After oil was discovered at El Dorado in 1921, it was reported that the Rock Island transported 90 percent of the barrels of oil produced that first year. But the railroad was impacted by the Great Depression and by what some considered mismanagement, and by 1933, it was again in receivership, from which it emerged in 1948.

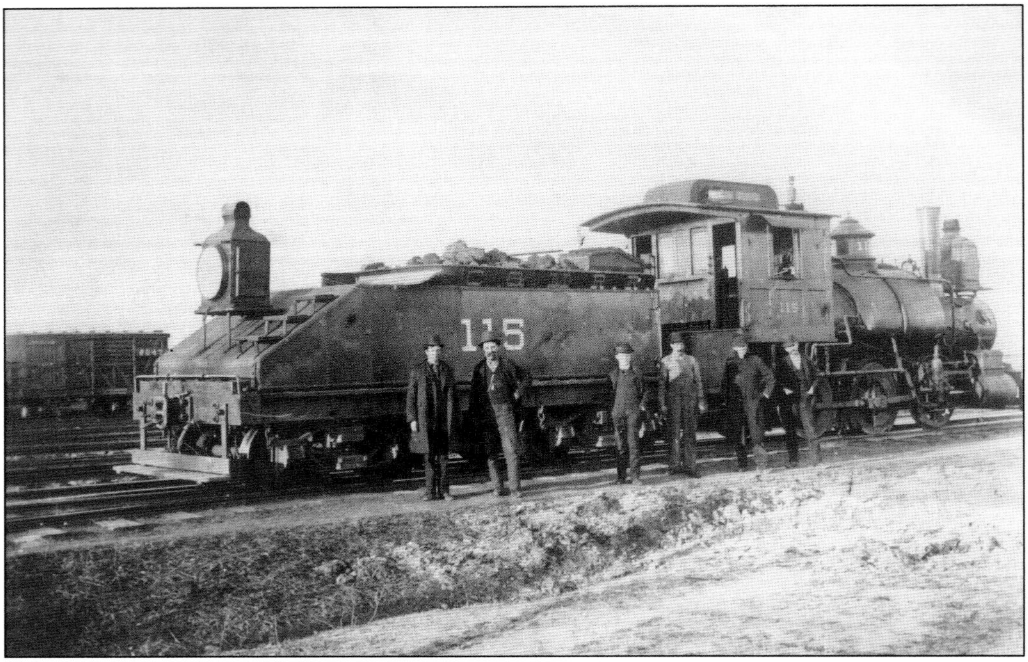

This c. 1899 photograph shows a Choctaw & Memphis locomotive and employees in an area that is in present-day North Little Rock. This had originally been a rail yard for the Memphis & Little Rock Railroad. The name Choctaw was a reference to the Native American tribe in what was then Indian Territory (Oklahoma), where the railroad wanted access to coal resources. (Courtesy of the North Little Rock History Commission.)

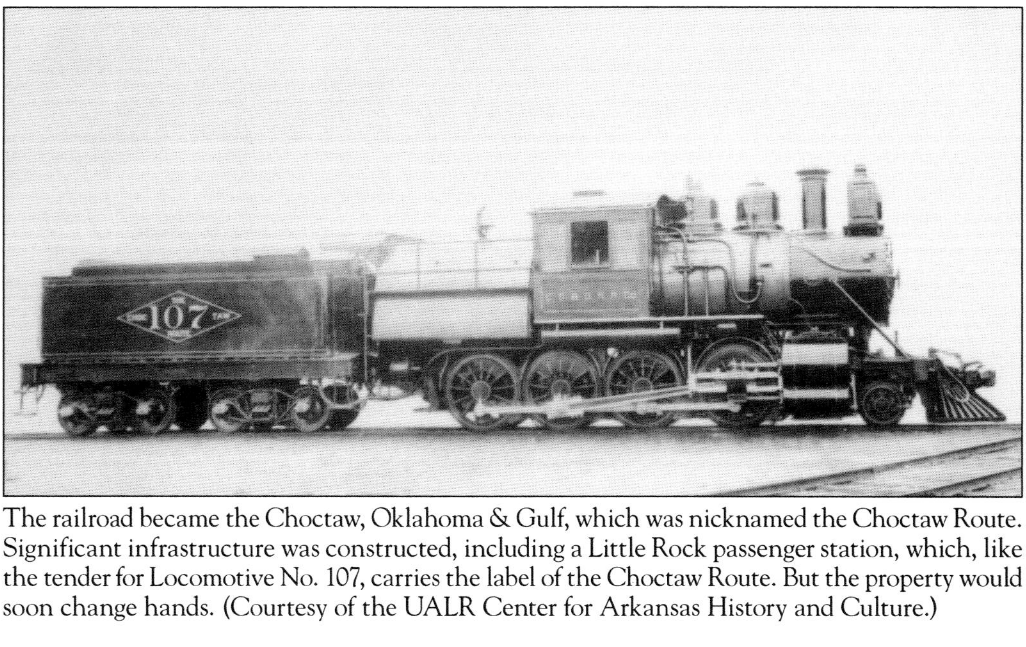

The railroad became the Choctaw, Oklahoma & Gulf, which was nicknamed the Choctaw Route. Significant infrastructure was constructed, including a Little Rock passenger station, which, like the tender for Locomotive No. 107, carries the label of the Choctaw Route. But the property would soon change hands. (Courtesy of the UALR Center for Arkansas History and Culture.)

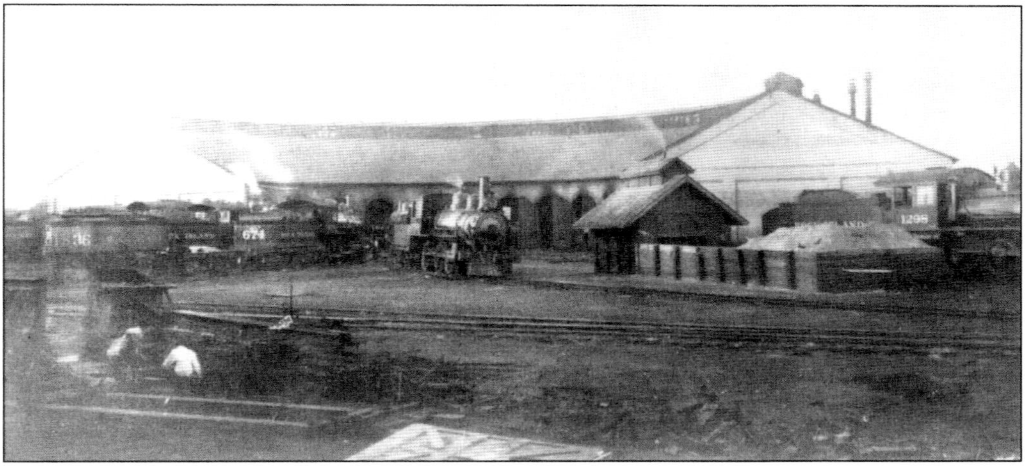

In 1904, the Rock Island completed its acquisition of the Choctaw, Oklahoma & Gulf. Among the facilities it acquired in Arkansas was this roundhouse in the city then known as Argenta, located in an area that is present-day East Fourth Street between Hazel and Beech Streets in North Little Rock. (Courtesy of the North Little Rock History Commission.)

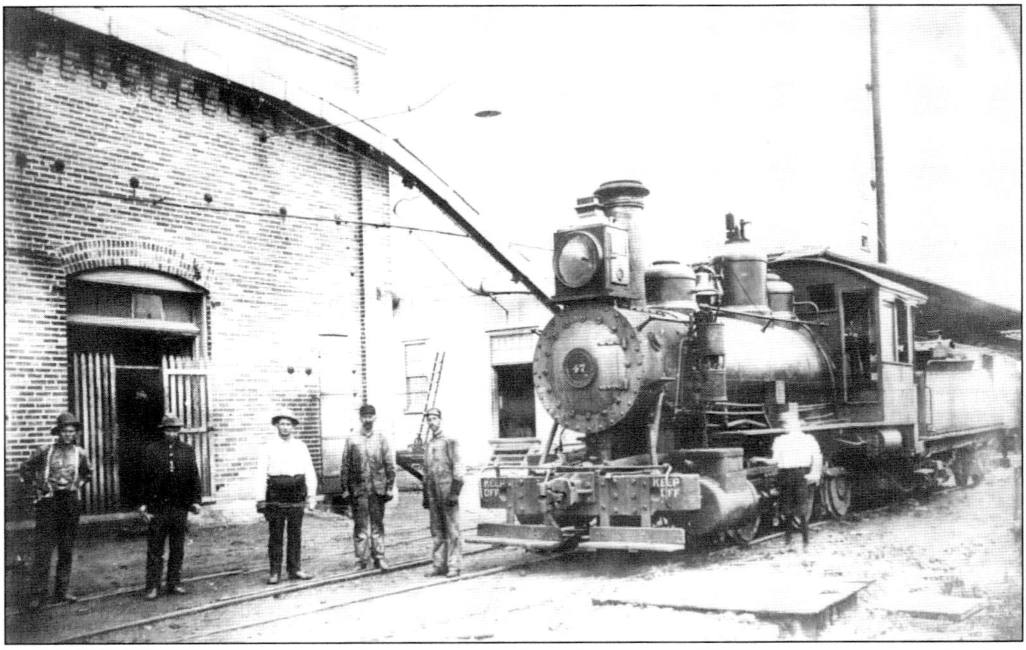

Rock Island workers are seen in the Argenta rail yard around 1905. A notation on the back of the photograph identifies four of the five along with their titles as Tom Mitchell, helper; Bill Harvey, helper; Tab Mackey, fireman; and Harry Sharp, fireman. (Courtesy of the North Little Rock History Commission.)

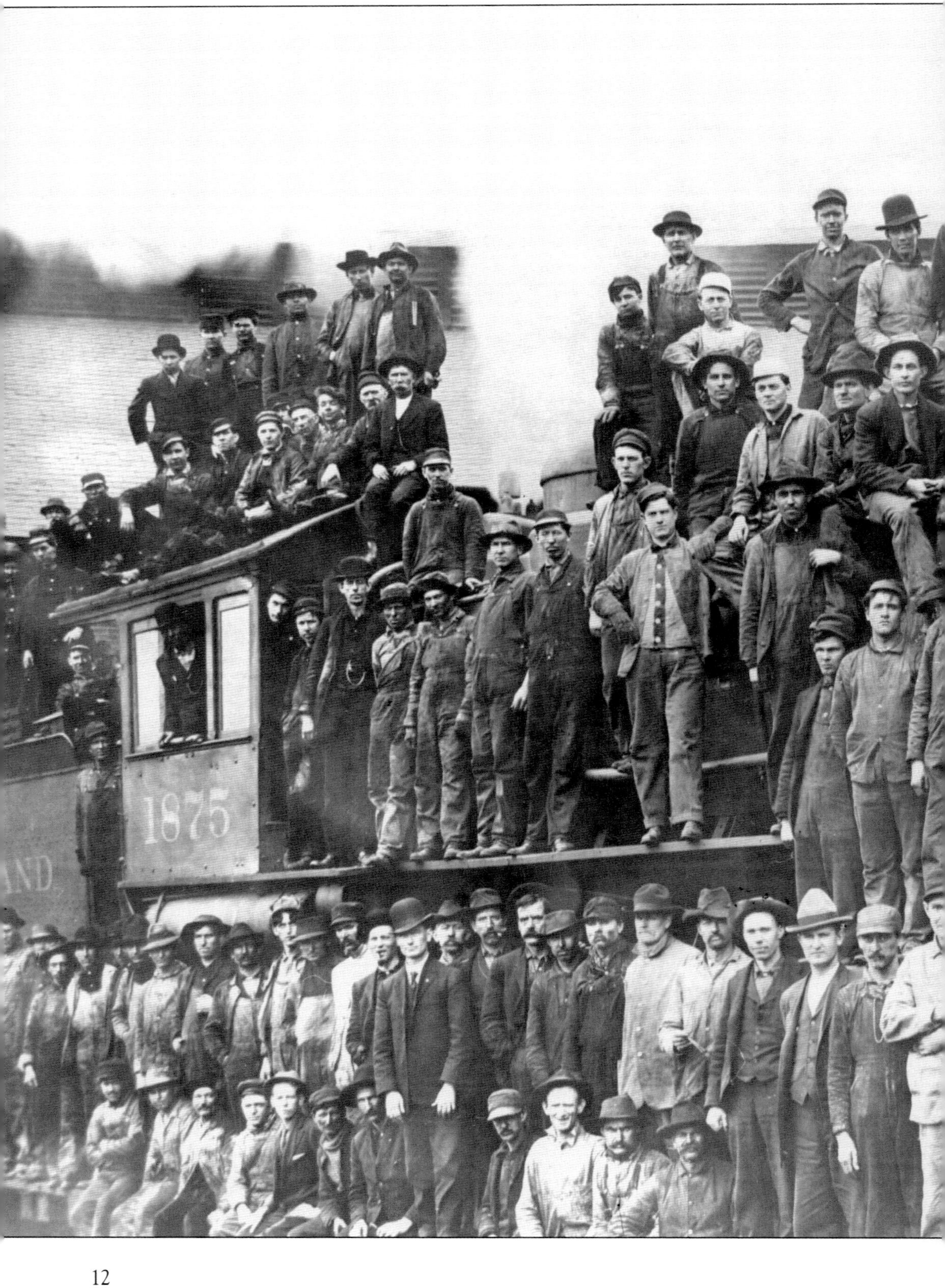
1875
AND

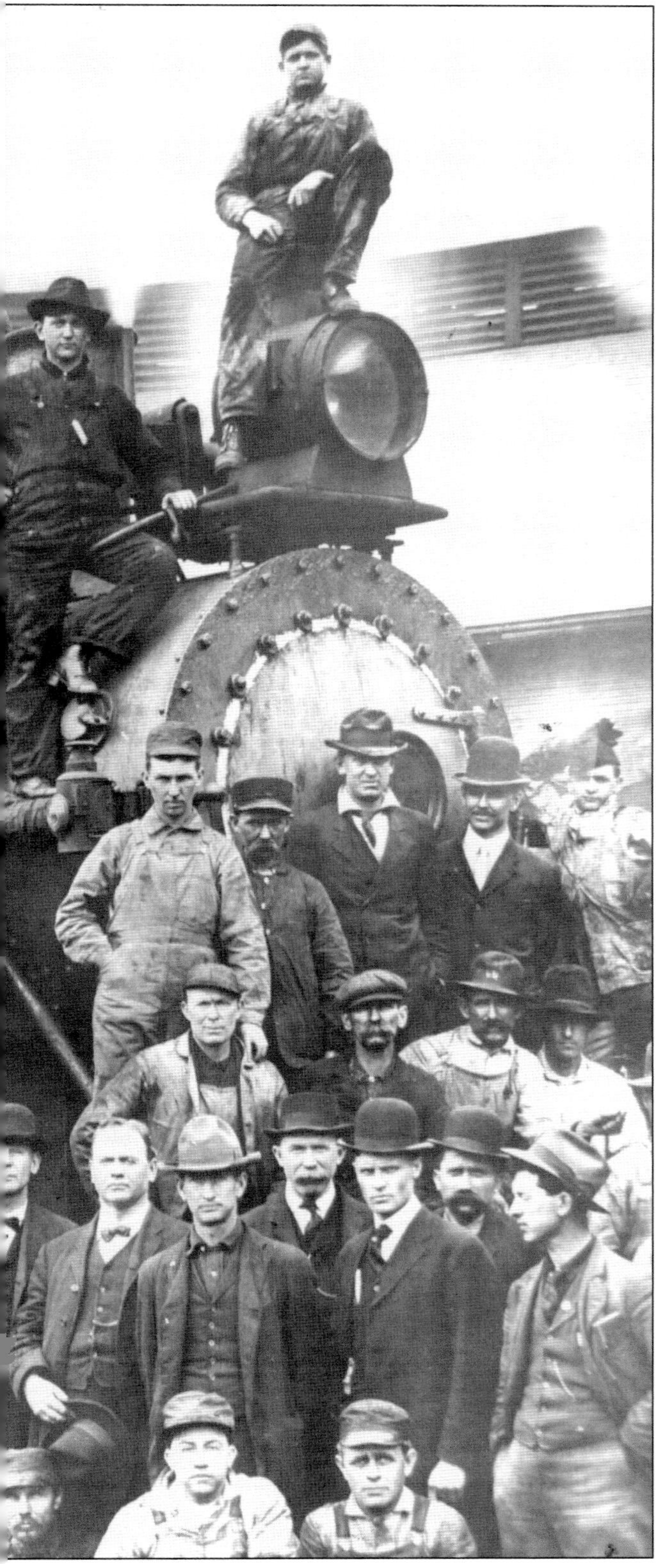

Employees crowd onto every possible place to stand or sit on Locomotive No. 1875 shortly after the Rock Island took over the CO&G in 1904. This was in the company's yard in Argenta, which changed its name to North Little Rock in 1917. The hierarchy of each employee is clear based on his clothes, with executives in suits and clean, white shirts and workers covered in grime. One cannot help but wonder how the worker with his foot on the headlight secured that prominent spot. (Courtesy of the North Little Rock History Commission.)

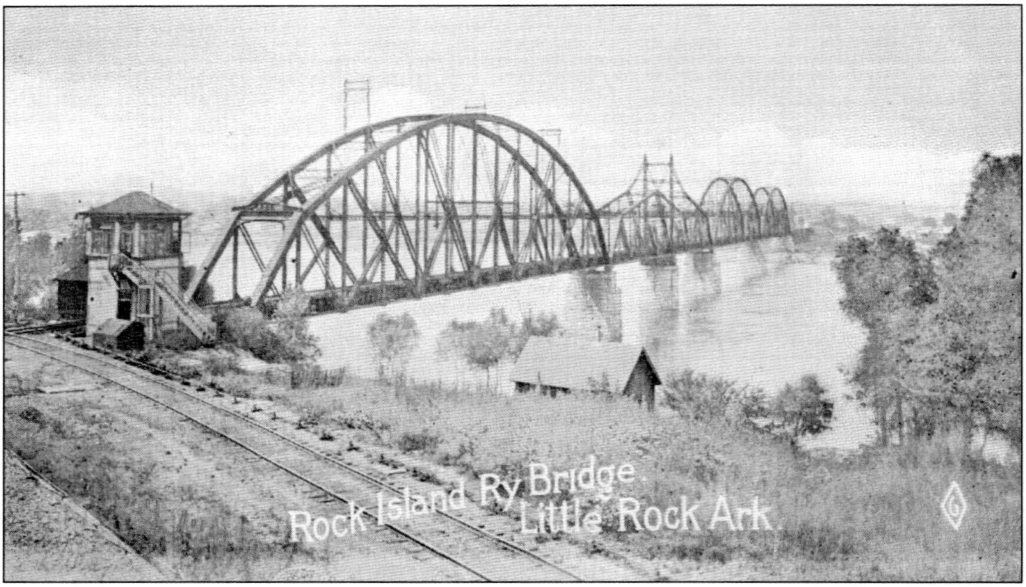

The 1899 construction by the Choctaw & Memphis of this bridge crossing the Arkansas River was necessitated by a competing railroad, which had allowed the Memphis & Little Rock Railroad to use its Baring Cross Bridge, no longer wanting to allow access to a growing competitor. Transfer boats had originally carried freight and passengers from one side of the river to the other. This postcard is from shortly after the Rock Island took over the bridge. (Author's collection.)

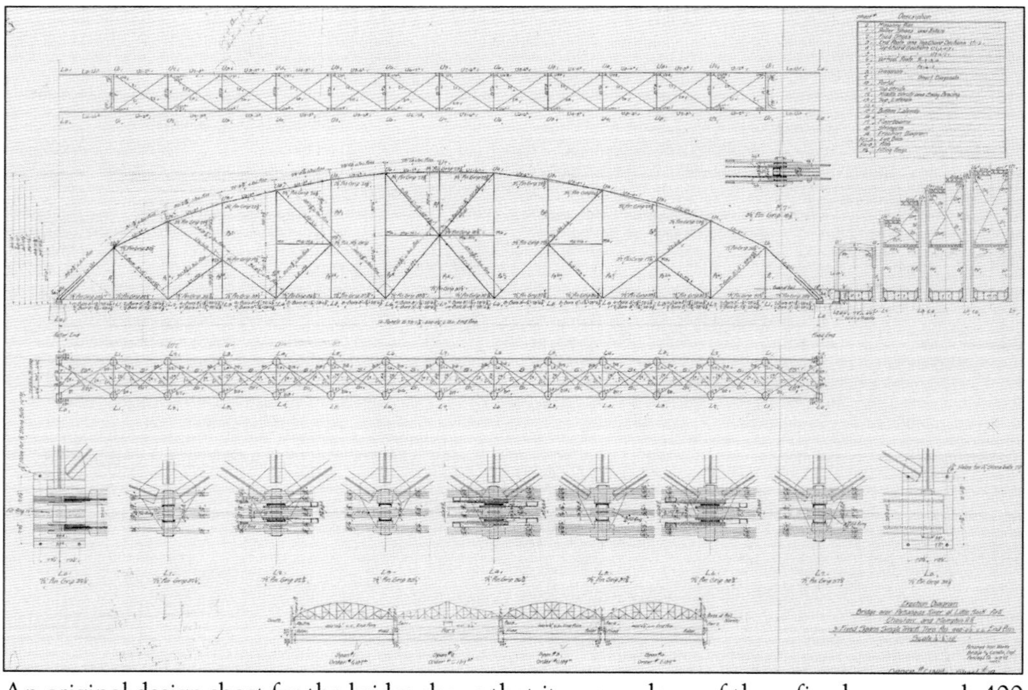

An original design sheet for the bridge shows that it was made up of three fixed spans, each 400 feet long, and a swing span to allow river traffic to pass. It featured through-truss spans with a design that had been pioneered by the Pennsylvania Railroad. In 1970, the swing span was replaced with a lift span that would allow barge traffic to pass underneath. (Courtesy of Union Pacific Railroad.)

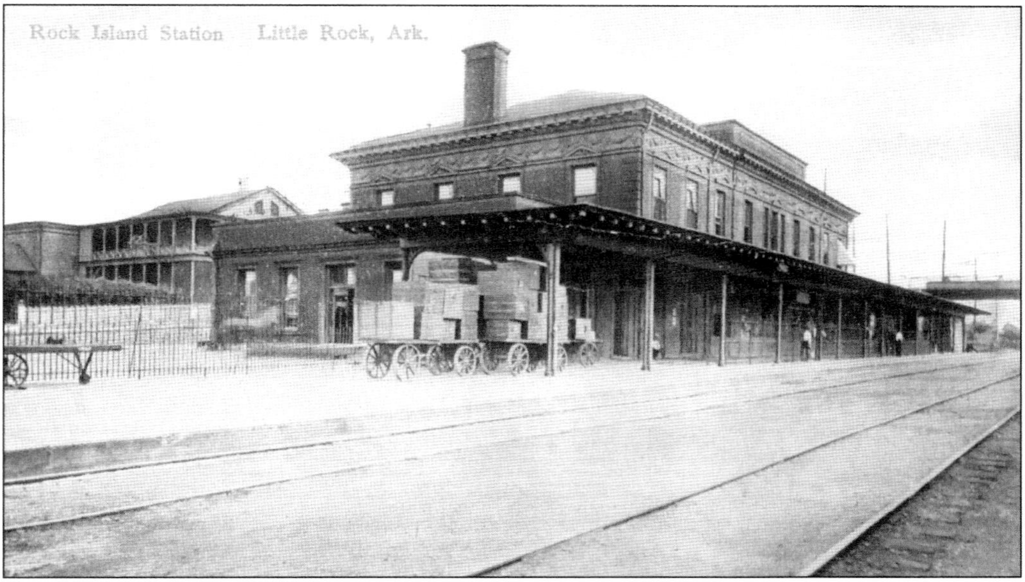

A postcard depicts the two-story Little Rock train station built for the Choctaw, Oklahoma & Gulf Railroad, completed in 1899. It featured a highly decorative terra-cotta frieze toward the roof, and lettering on dormer-like structures on the front and back of the building reads "the Choctaw Route." The structure included segregated waiting rooms for different races, a baggage room, and a restaurant. A postmark on the back of the postcard indicates it was mailed in 1909. (Author's collection.)

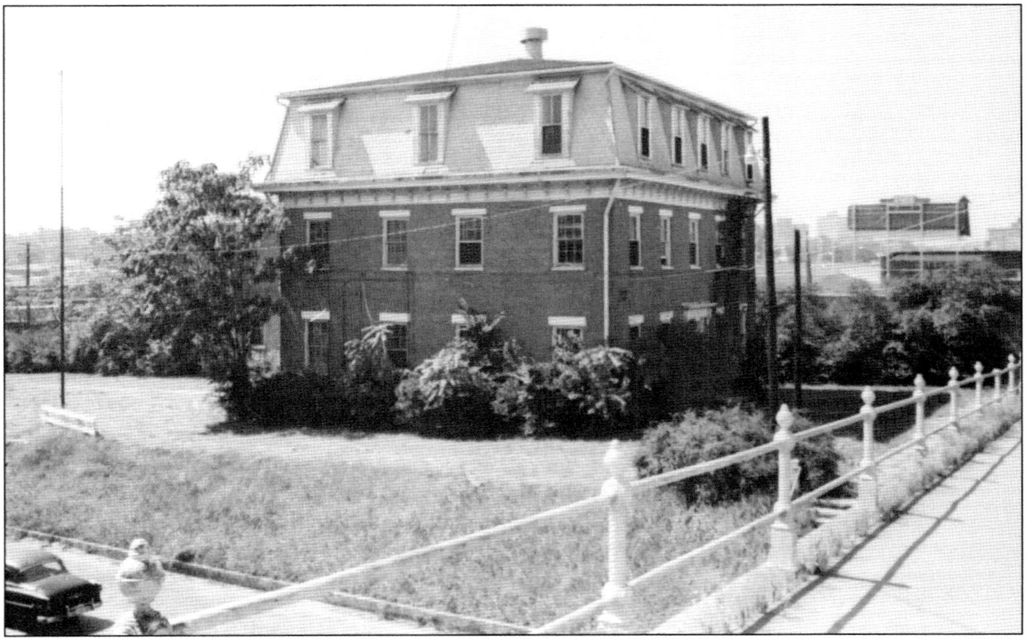

Beside the train station to the west was the Alexander George House, which served as headquarters for the Choctaw, Oklahoma & Gulf, then Arkansas division offices for the Rock Island. It was originally the home of Alexander George, who was one of Little Rock's wealthiest residents in the 1800s. It later housed the state's first Catholic hospital before the railroad came through, acquiring the property in 1900. (Courtesy of Bill Pollard; photograph by Clifton Hull.)

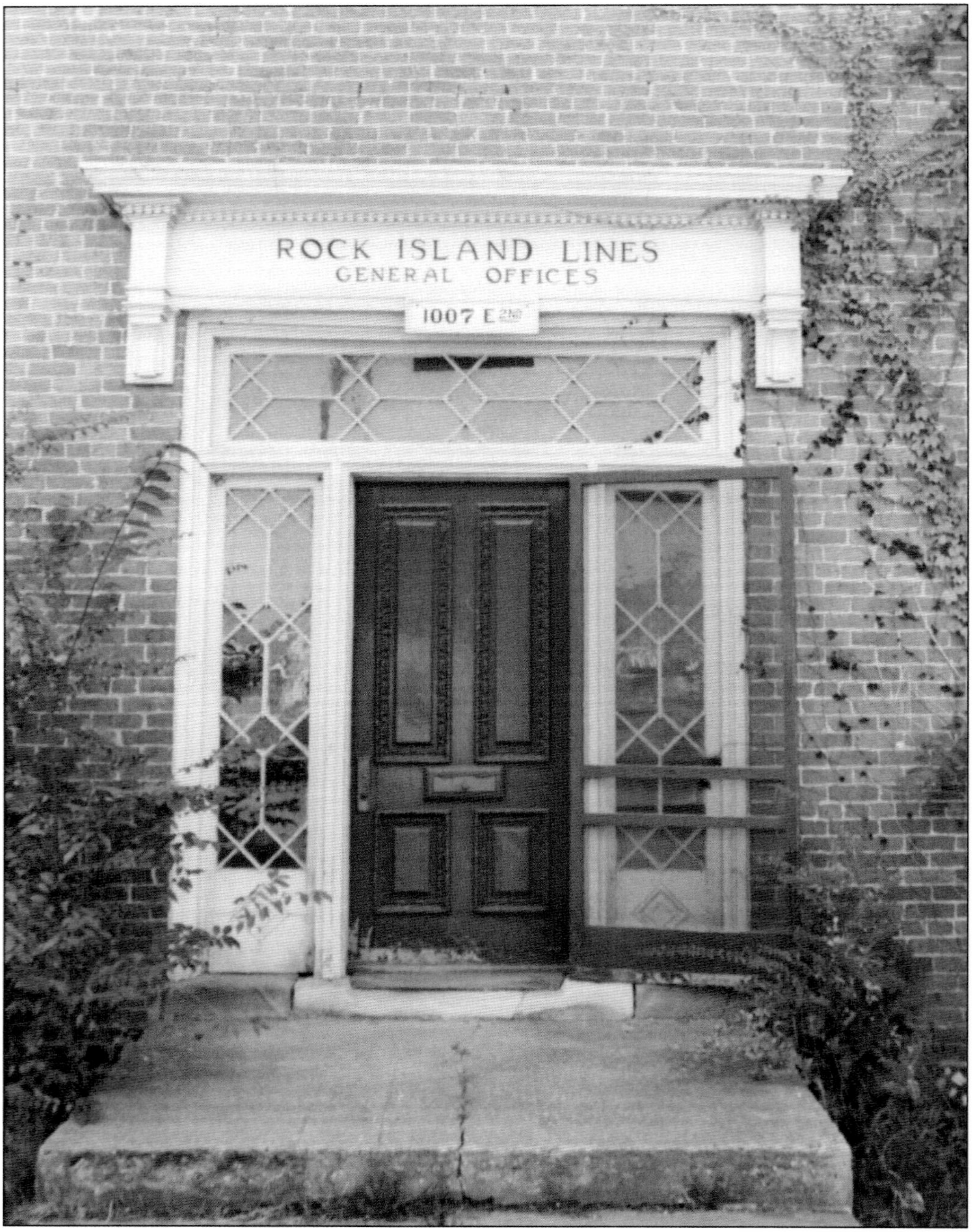

The entrance to the railroad's offices in the George House faces the Arkansas River. This photograph was taken in September 1966 by Clifton Hull, who wrote that it was believed that most if not all of the Rock Island's offices had been relocated to the passenger station by this time and the building was likely vacant. The relocation occurred in 1964, and the building remained empty until being town down in 1994 after various preservation attempts failed. (Courtesy of Bill Pollard; photograph by Clifton Hull.)

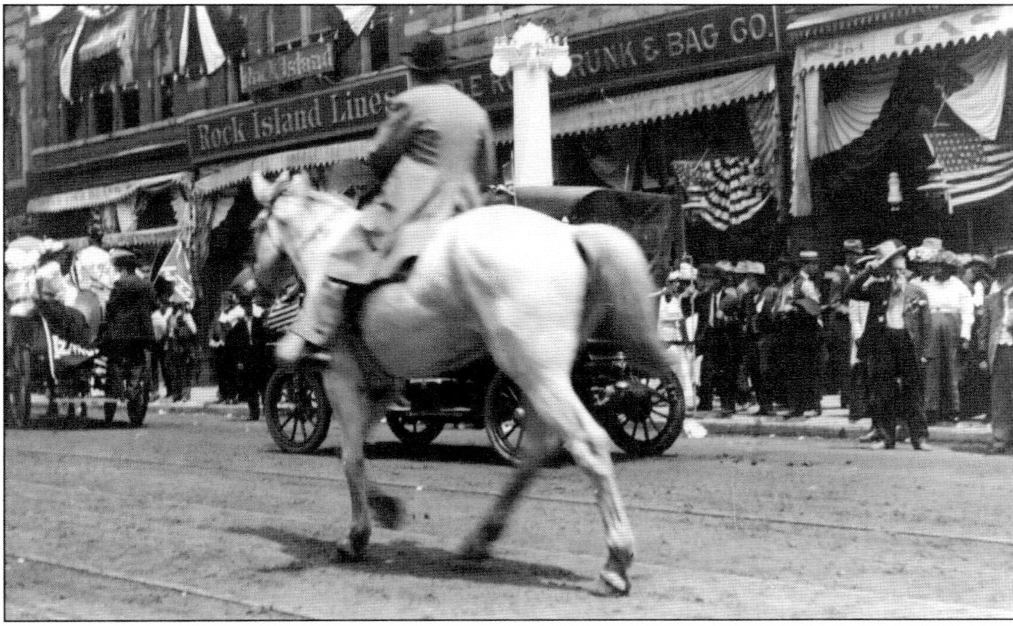

For three days in 1911, Little Rock hosted a reunion of former Confederate veterans, which drew a record number of visitors to the city. About 90,000 people above the regular passenger load are said to have come through the Rock Island station. The railroad added 108 special trains before, during, and after the gathering. A parade was held during the reunion on May 18, 1911, with the downtown ticket office for the Rock Island seen in the background at 211 Main Street. (Courtesy of the Butler Center for Arkansas Studies.)

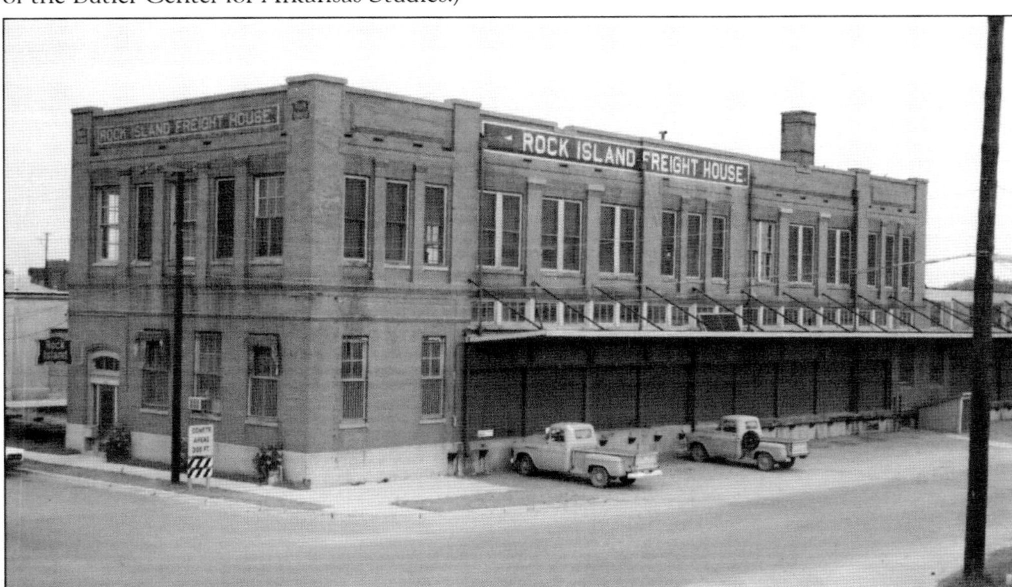

The Choctaw, Oklahoma & Gulf had built an ornate freight depot across the tracks from the Little Rock passenger station, but the Rock Island quickly outgrew that. In 1911, this larger facility for freight was opened a couple of blocks down the tracks on East Fourth Street. By 1962, when this photograph was taken, most less-than-carload freight was moved by truck rather than rail. (Courtesy of Bill Pollard; photograph by Clifton Hull.)

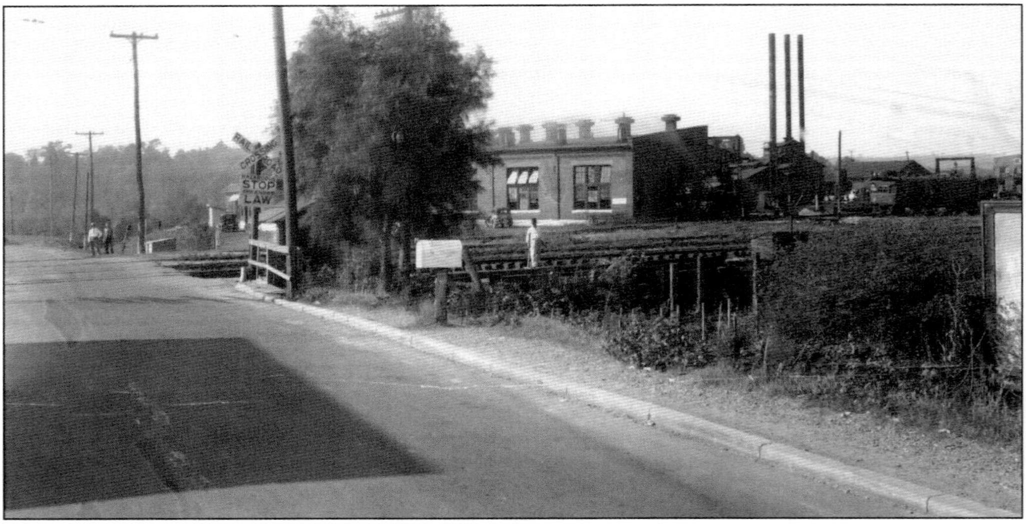

Completing a process that began in 1907, the Rock Island in 1917 closed its Argenta roundhouse and consolidated all shops in the new Biddle Yard in south Little Rock. Perhaps as an appeasement to its departing city, the Rock Island built a relatively nice passenger station in 1913 for Argenta, considering it was only a couple of miles down the track from the Little Rock station. (Clifton Hull Collection, courtesy of Bill Pollard.)

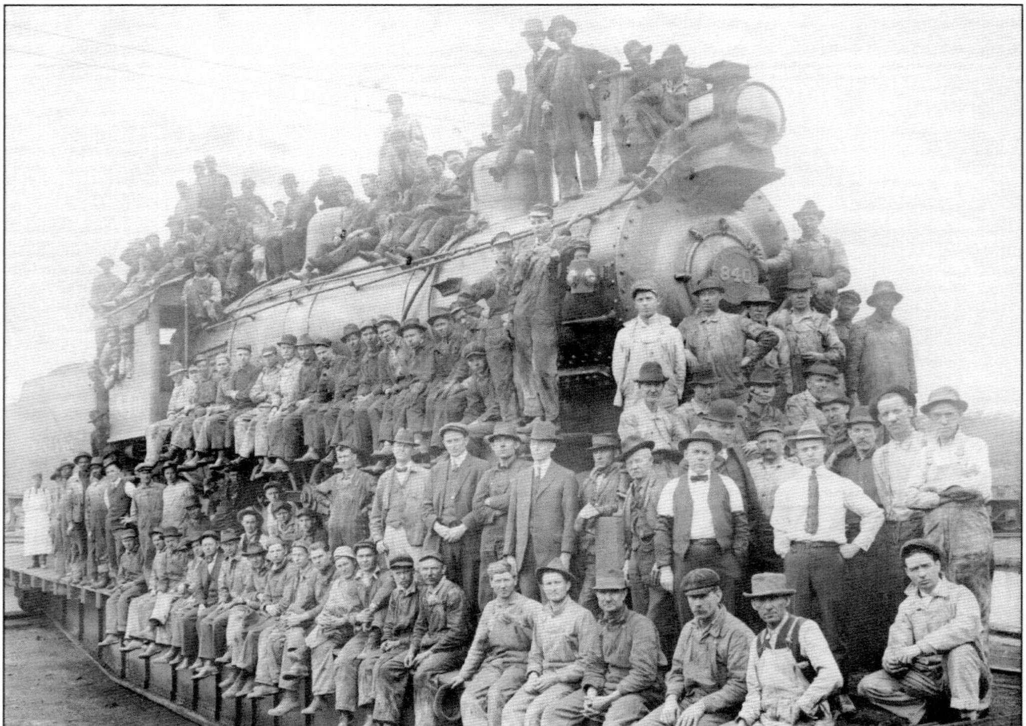

After moving to Biddle Yard, employees and managers were again brought together for a group photograph. Conditions look rather hazy on this day in June 1917, with those near the camera looking clear while those farther back are obscured. Again, well-dressed executives stand out compared to the soot-covered workers. (Clifton Hull Collection, courtesy of Bill Pollard.)

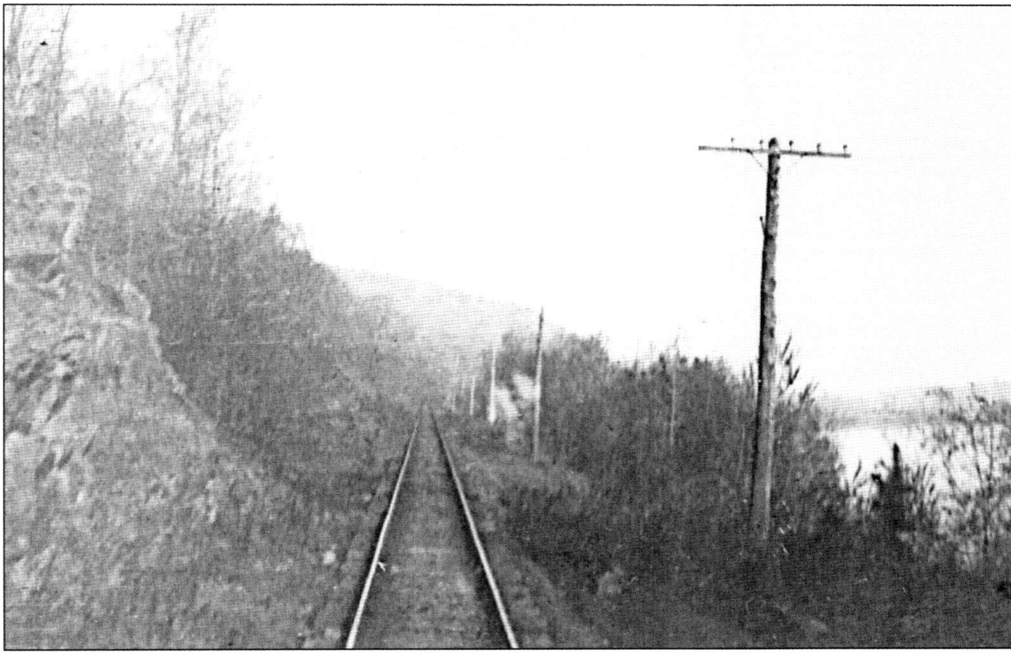

This postcard mailed in 1909 shows the Rock Island's main line heading west outside of Little Rock where the rails paralleled the Arkansas River before passing by Pinnacle Mountain. More than a century later, though now run by a different railroad, this stretch of track looks very similar. (Author's collection.)

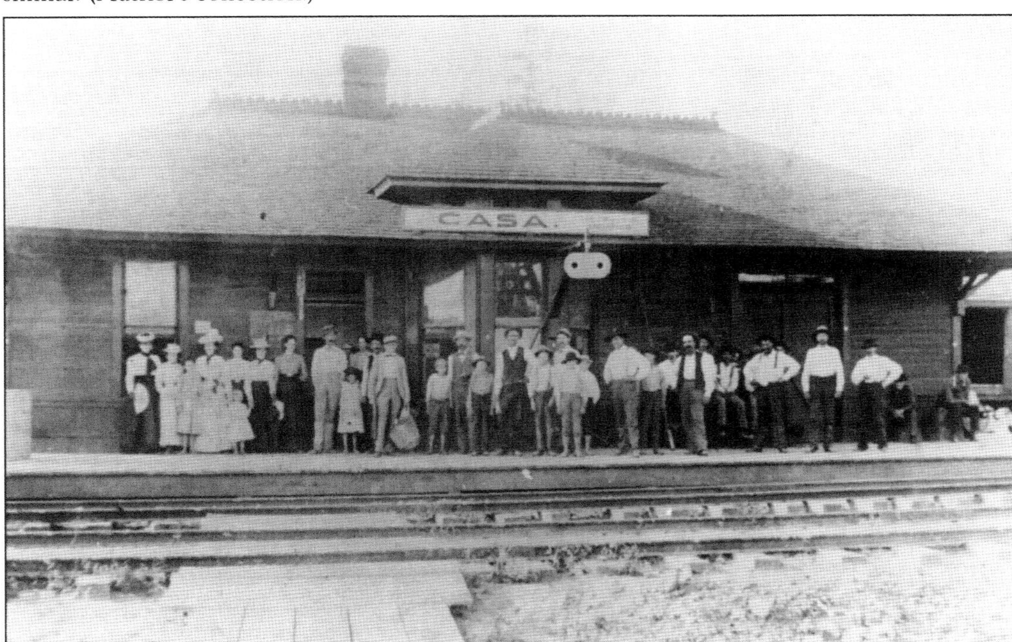

A well-dressed crowd, likely of residents, poses in front of the depot in Casa. It is believed this was the original depot built by the Choctaw, Oklahoma & Gulf. The town was impacted by the Great Depression, suffering a sharp drop in its population from which it never recovered. (Courtesy of the Butler Center for Arkansas Studies.)

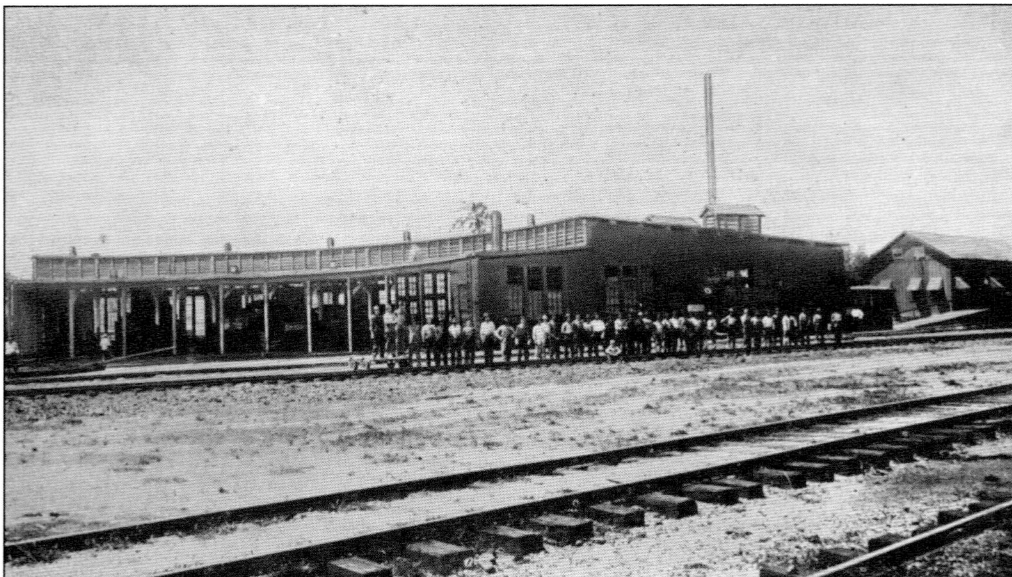

C. R. I. & P. Round House, El Dorado, Ark.

Being the largest city in this part of southern Arkansas near the Louisiana border, El Dorado was a key location for the Rock Island. Here, employees pose at the railroad's roundhouse. After drilling finally produced oil, the city experienced a sudden surge in population in the 1920s, with people coming from all over to work for oil companies and businesses that came to serve those people. (Courtesy of the Butler Center for Arkansas Studies.)

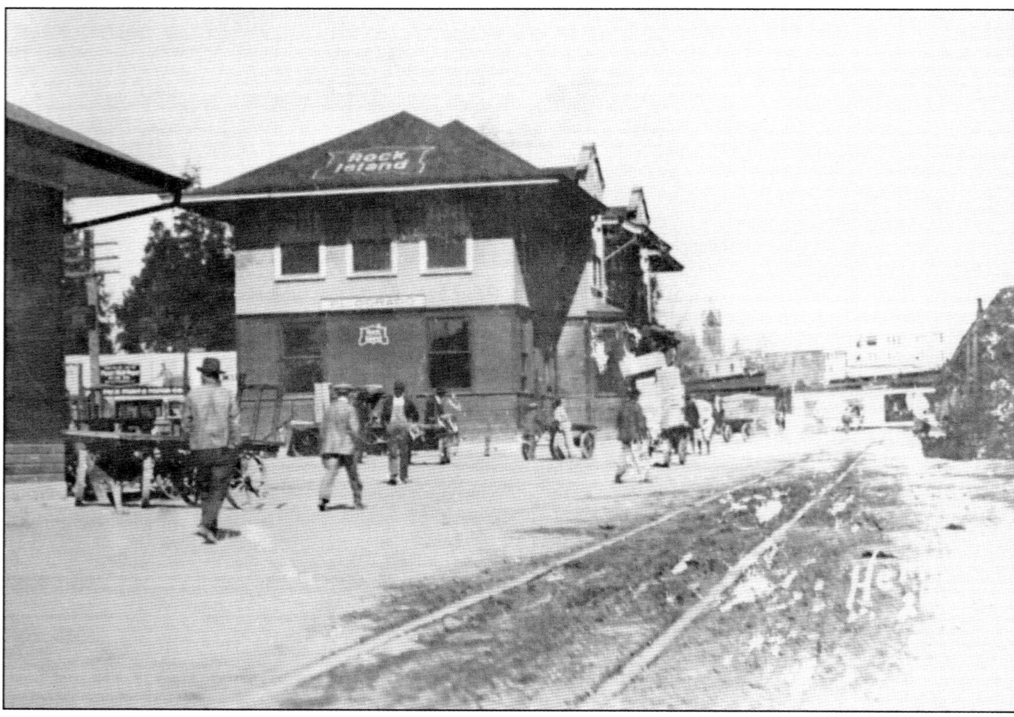

The Rock Island had a large two-story passenger station in El Dorado, which looks busy on this day. (Courtesy of the UALR Center for Arkansas History and Culture.)

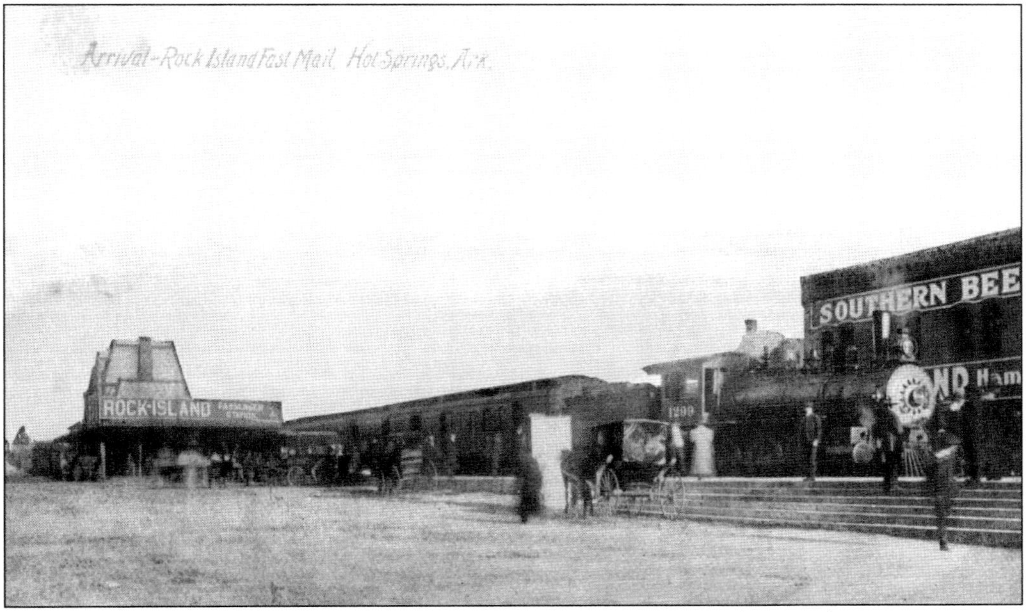

An early-1900s postcard shows a train at the Hot Springs station and horse-drawn carriages on the street. As the name suggests, springs of hot water flow out of the ground here, which many sought out for their healing properties. The area had been designated by Congress as a federal reservation in 1832. (Courtesy of the Butler Center for Arkansas Studies.)

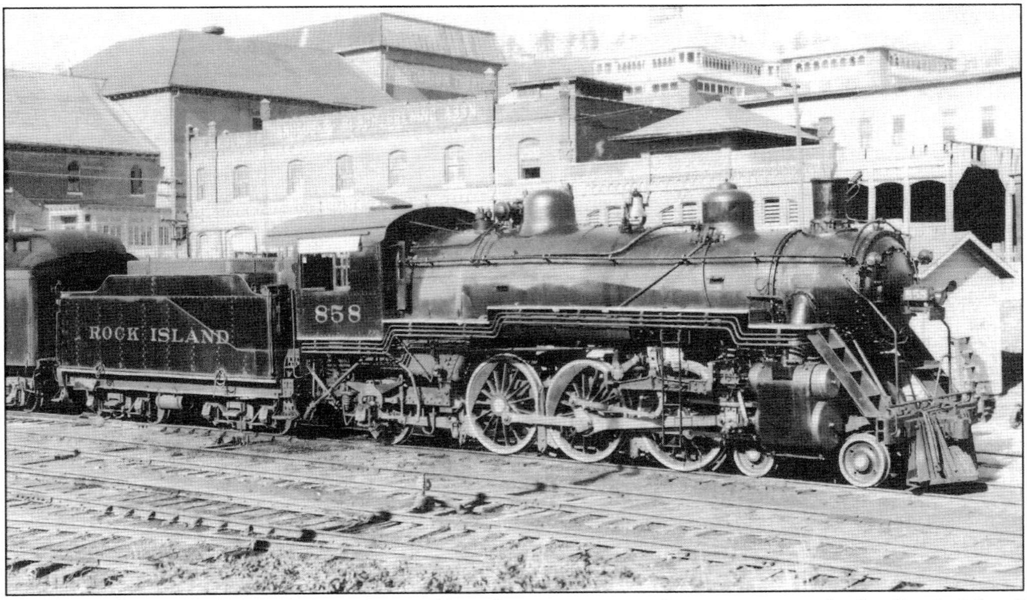

The city with its bathhouses and grand hotels was a major destination, with the Rock Island running Pullman cars from Chicago to Hot Springs via the Illinois Central Railroad at Memphis. This photograph from February 1926 shows Engine No. 858 leading a train in the city. Hot Springs was also notorious for illegal gambling and as a hangout for mobsters like Al Capone and others. (Courtesy of Bill Pollard.)

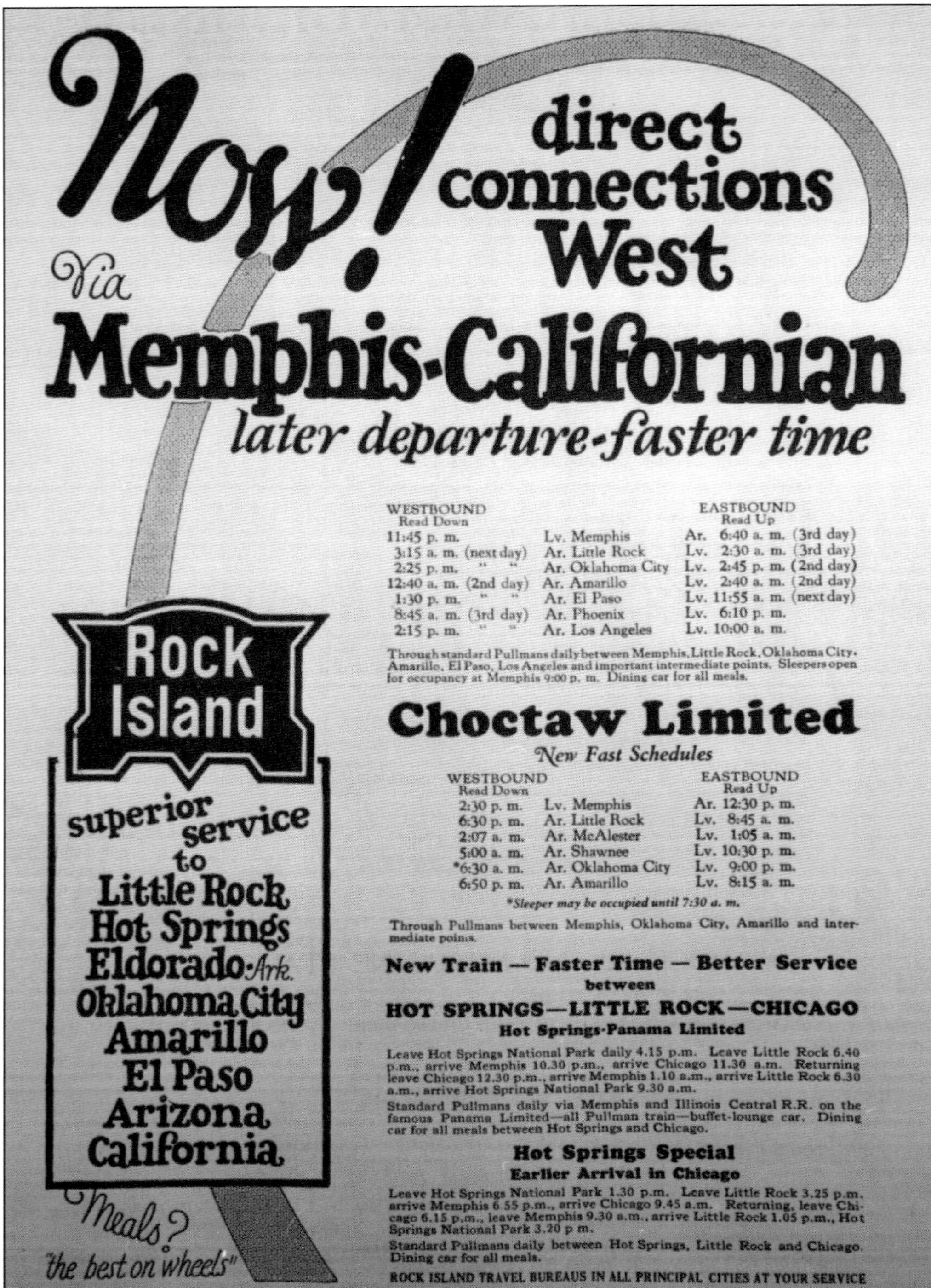

An ad in the August 1925 issue of the Rock Island's magazine, the *Rocket*, touts passenger service in Arkansas, highlighting the Memphis-Californian, a train that offered connecting service to Los Angeles via the Southern Pacific Railroad. Also included are the Choctaw Limited and Hot Springs Limited trains. (Clifton Hull Collection, courtesy of Bill Pollard.)

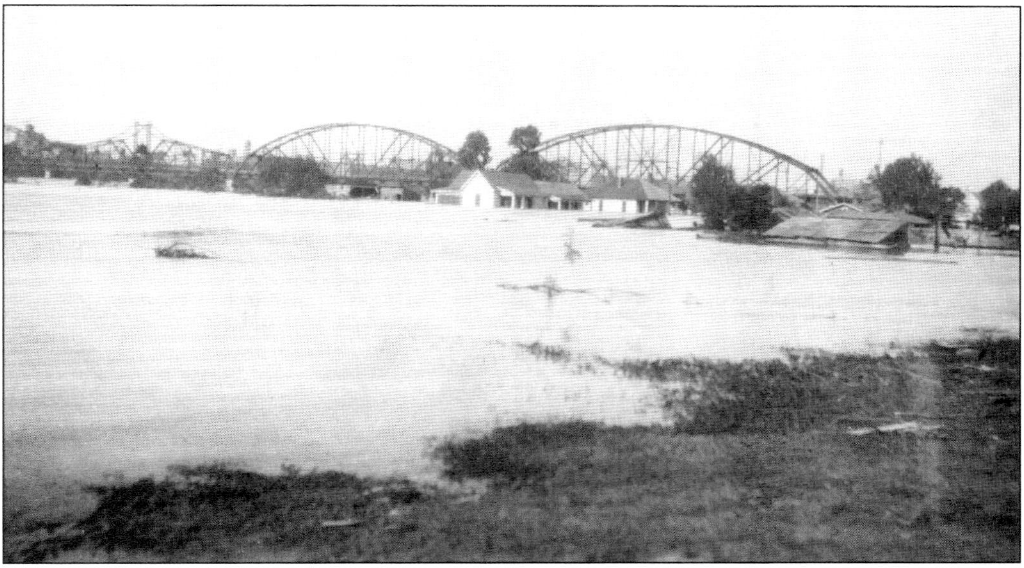

In 1927, Arkansas experienced the most destructive flooding in state history. Heavy rain in the spring caused rivers to swell beyond their banks. Already inundated because of melting snow from Canada, the Mississippi River backed up, leaving water nowhere to go. One of the Missouri Pacific's two bridges crossing the Arkansas River at Little Rock was washed out, but the Rock Island's bridge (seen here from the North Little Rock side) survived the flood. (Courtesy of the Butler Center for Arkansas Studies.)

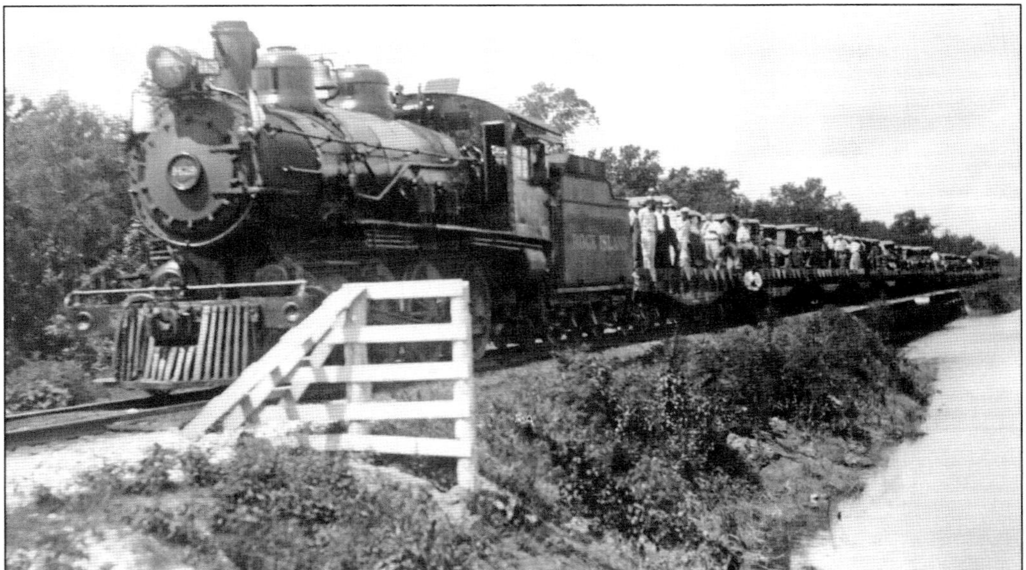

Flooding again occurred in 1928, with the White River and its tributaries in eastern Arkansas causing US Highway 70 to be closed. The Rock Island was able to continue operation thanks to constant work by track maintenance crews. Local leaders in Brinkley were concerned about the loss of money from tourists and worked with the railroad to arrange "shuttle trains." Ramps would be used for automobiles to drive onto railroad flatcars. Here, a train in the summer of 1928 slowly moves through a flooded area west of Brinkley with passengers looking on. (Courtesy of Bill Pollard.)

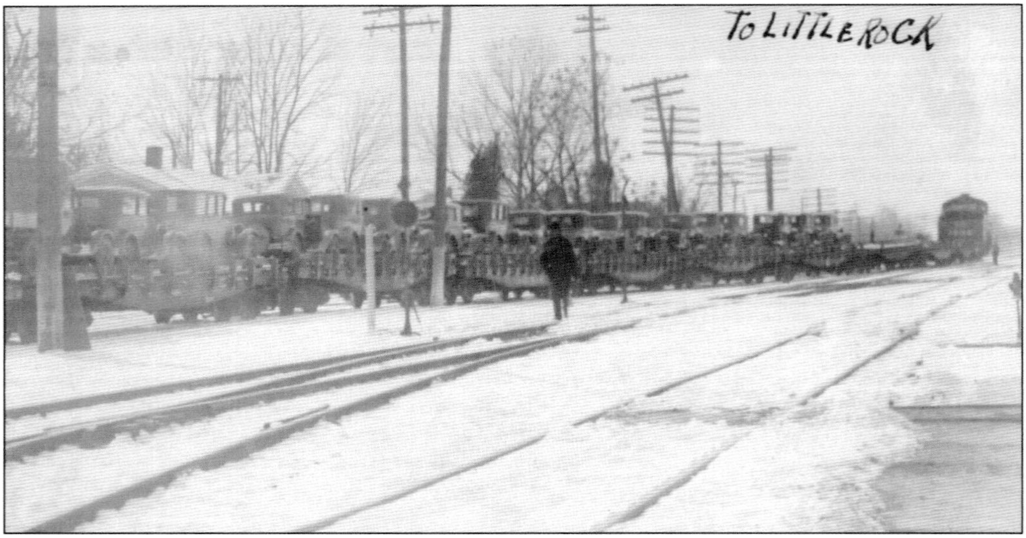

Despite highway improvements, shuttle trains were again operated in January 1930. During the initial days of operation, the ground was covered with snow, looking like it would have been a cold ride for drivers who took the option to remain in their vehicles. Passenger coaches were also included for each train. While a toll was paid for each vehicle and person, the shuttle trains were viewed by the railroad as a public service. (Courtesy of Bill Pollard.)

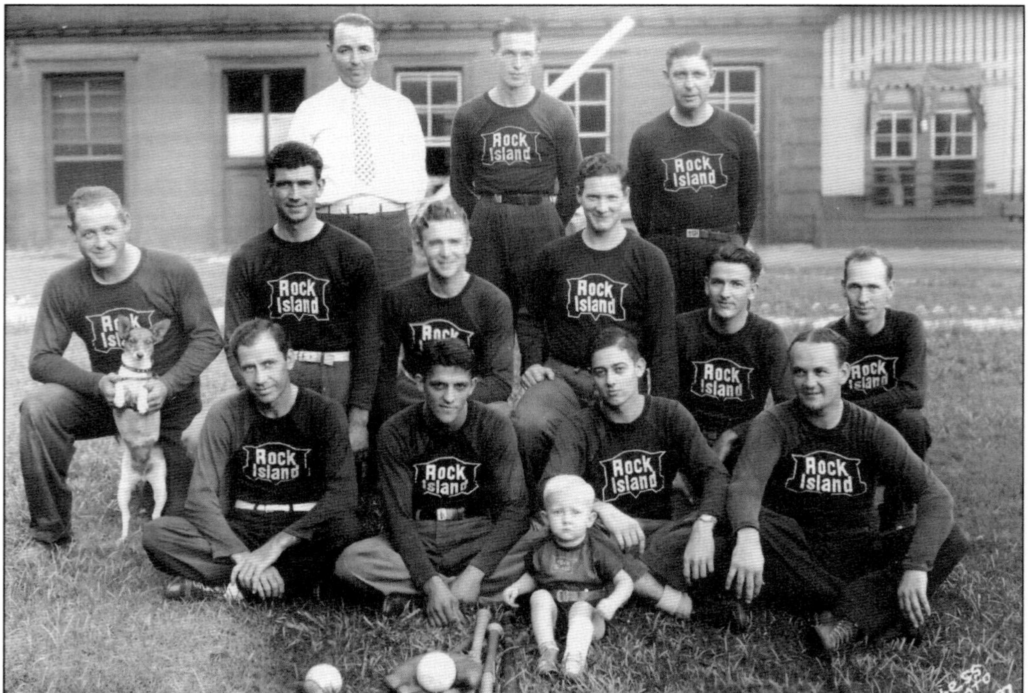

There are more questions than answers about this photograph from September 1937 showing a group in Little Rock wearing Rock Island uniforms with bats, a glove, and a couple of softballs. Are they Rock Island employees who play against other businesses? That was not uncommon at that time. Or could this simply be a team sponsored by the railroad? The photograph was taken by a Little Rock photography studio. (Courtesy of the Clinton School of Public Service.)

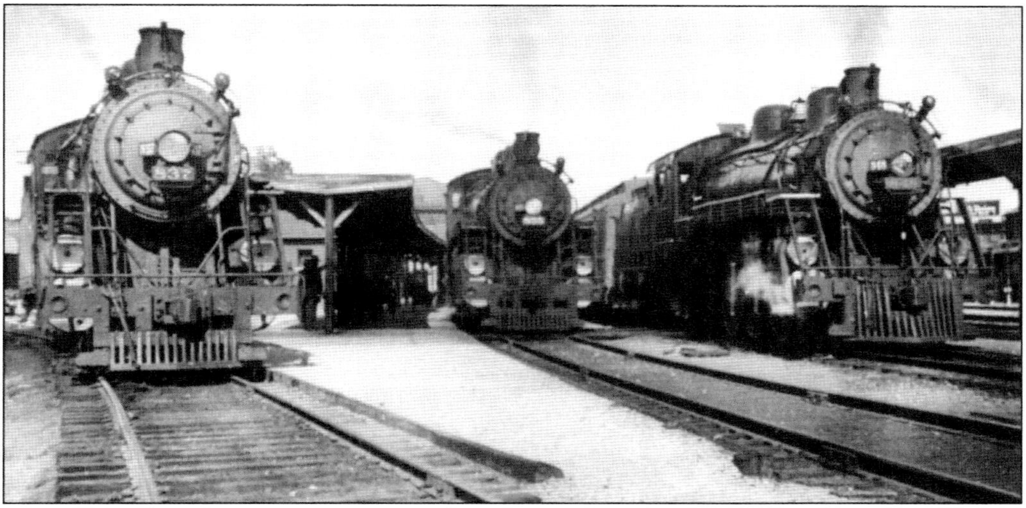

This is an impressive scene at the Little Rock station in the 1930s with an engine change for the Hot Springs Limited and a local waiting to head west for Booneville. (Clifton Hull Collection, courtesy of Bill Pollard.)

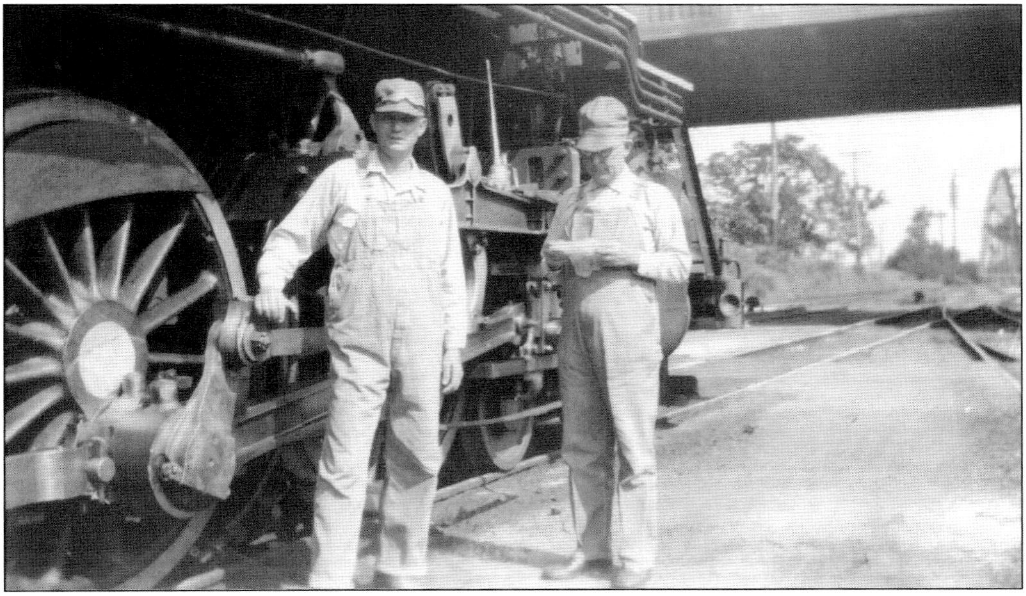

Working for the railroad in the time before automatic blocks signals were in widespread use by the Rock Island could be dangerous. Engineer David R. Smith (left), pictured here with another employee outside the Little Rock station, would later be killed in a head-on collision between two passenger trains on April 4, 1943. It occurred just three miles down the track from this spot, near what was known as Tie Plant outside North Little Rock. Smith was running a military train carrying troops from Little Rock to Memphis, which crashed into a fast-moving passenger train traveling from Memphis to Hot Springs. The engineer of the other train was also killed, while 71 people were injured. The daylight accident happened in a curve with limited visibility. Coordination of trains on that stretch of track was handled by timetable, and train orders and the Interstate Commerce Commission noted there was confusion in this case. In its report, the ICC recommends the Rock Island install a block signal system, noting that would have prevented this accident. (Courtesy of David W. Smith.)

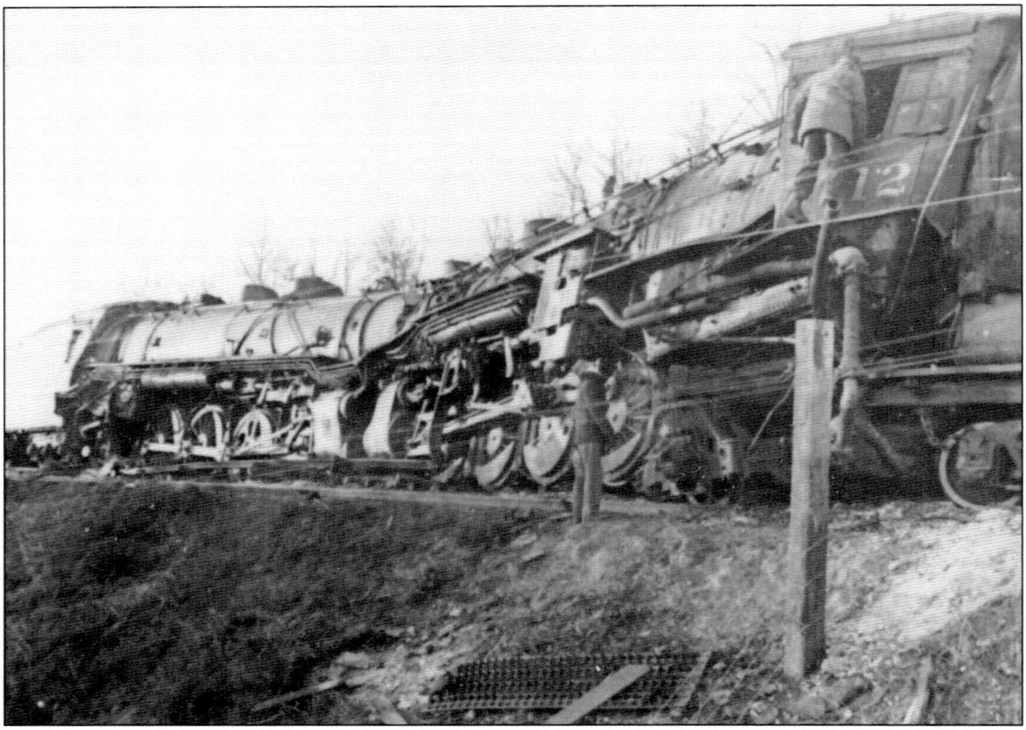

There was another head-on crash, involving westbound passenger train No. 111 and an eastbound local freight, but this one occurred west of Little Rock on January 15, 1948, killing two people and injuring 17. The federal investigation report concludes this accident, like the one that killed Smith, could have been avoided had block signals been in use. (Courtesy of the Earl Saunders Collection, UALR Center for Arkansas History and Culture.)

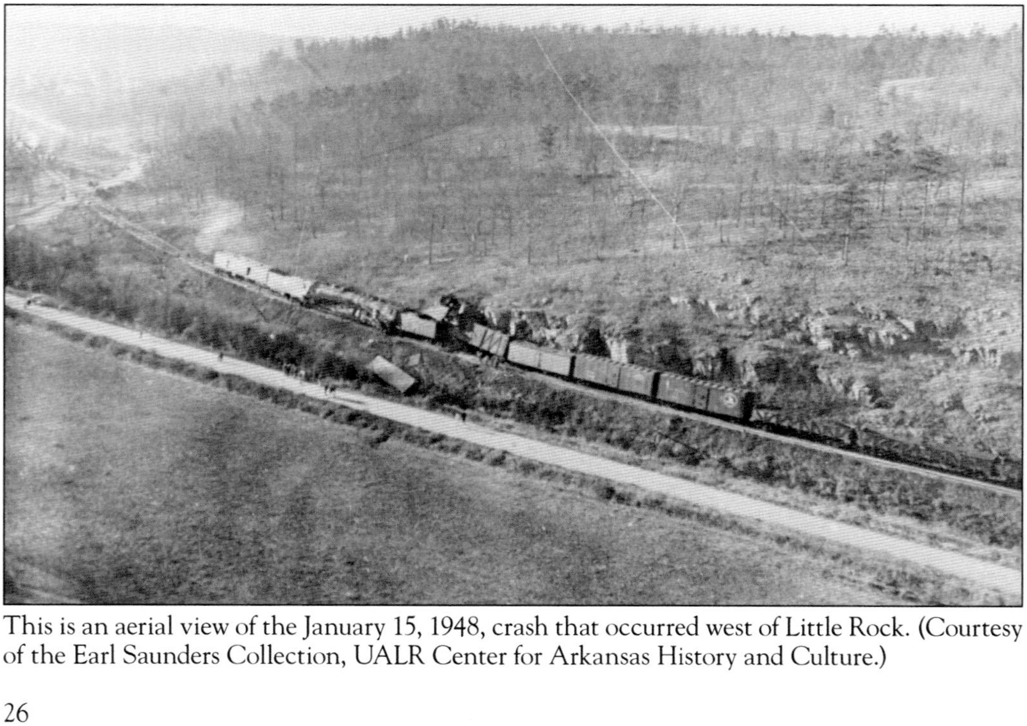

This is an aerial view of the January 15, 1948, crash that occurred west of Little Rock. (Courtesy of the Earl Saunders Collection, UALR Center for Arkansas History and Culture.)

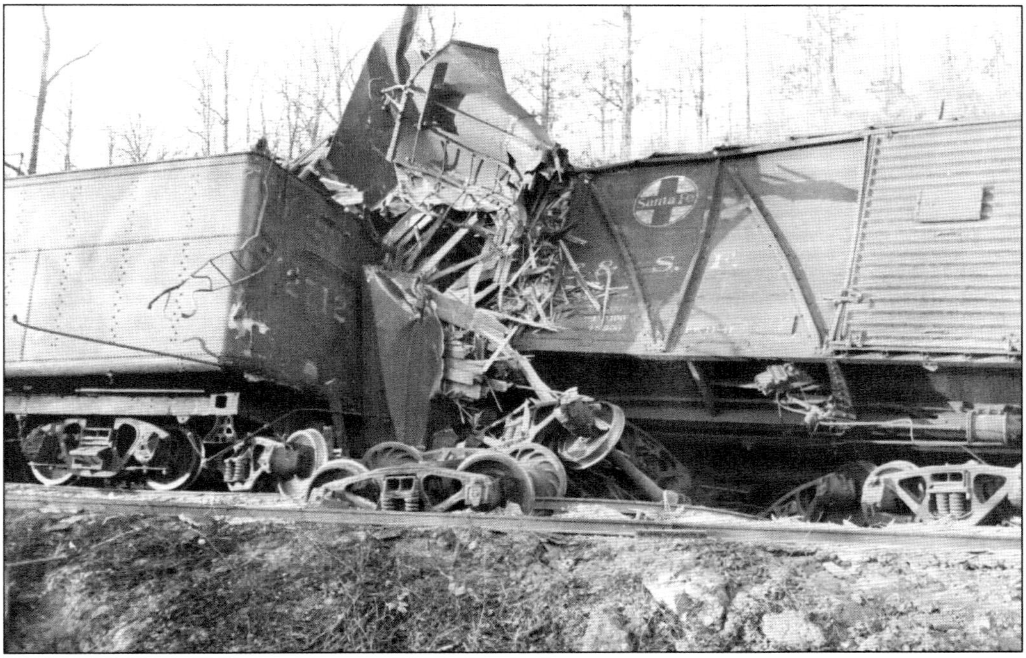

The force of the impact visible is clear from this wooden boxcar that shattered against the steel tender. (Courtesy of the Earl Saunders Collection, UALR Center for Arkansas History and Culture.)

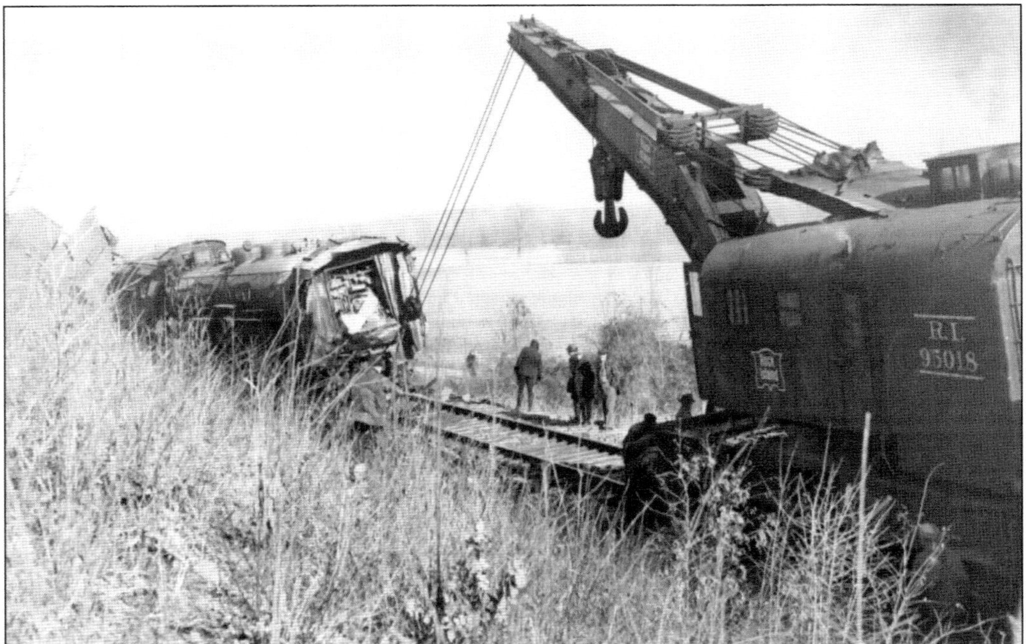

It must have been grim work for people who had to come out and clean up accidents like this, possibly knowing employees who were killed. Here, the Rock Island's wrecker that was kept in Little Rock is being used to rerail one of the damaged locomotives. It would not be until after a few more accidents that the Rock Island installed block signals on its main lines. (Courtesy of the Earl Saunders Collection, UALR Center for Arkansas History and Culture.)

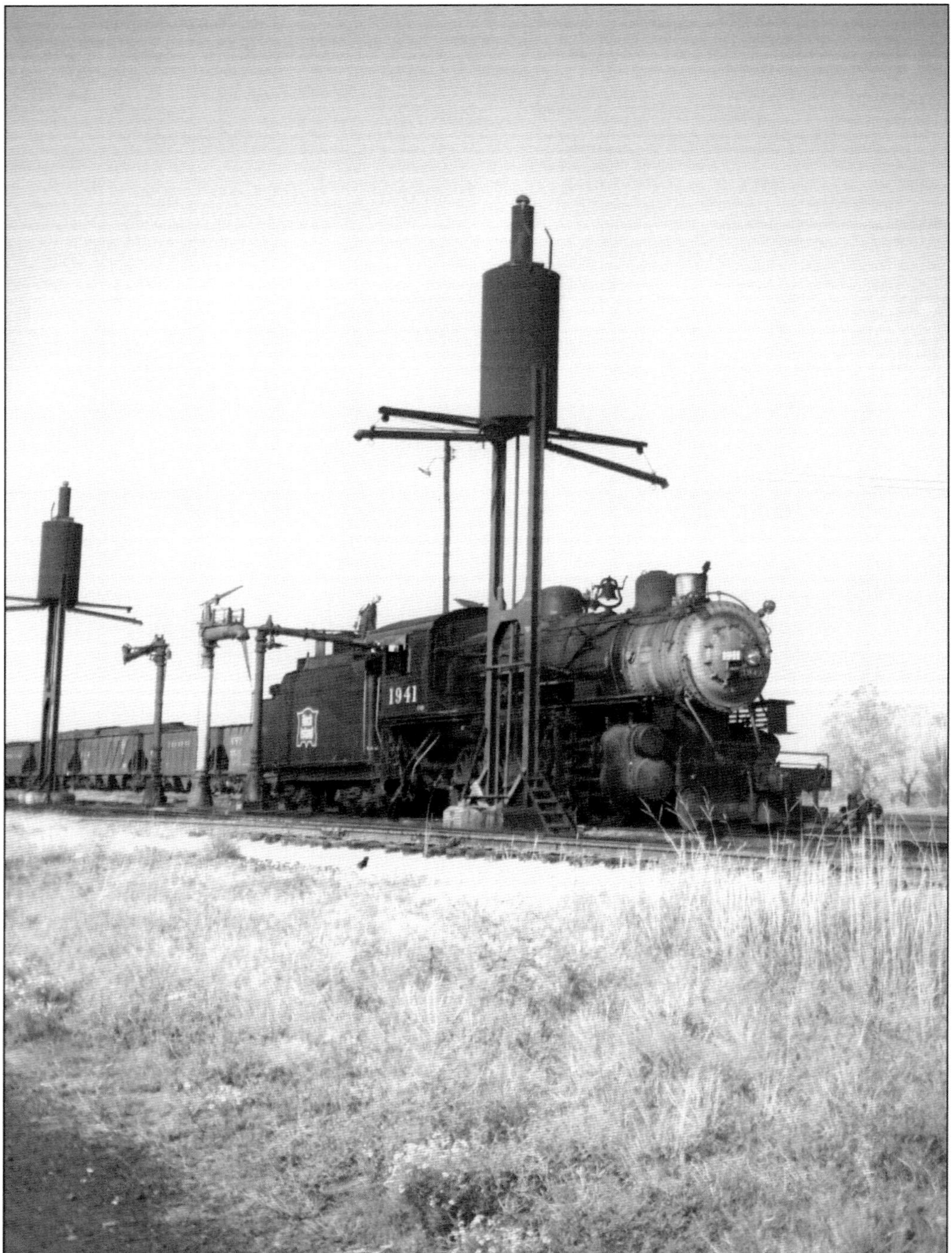

Steam-powered Locomotive No. 1941, which features a 2-8-0-wheel arrangement, is pictured taking fuel at Booneville, Arkansas, in 1945. Within a few years, steam was phased out for diesel engines. (Clifton Hull Collection, courtesy of Bill Pollard.)

Two

A New Era of Passenger Service

In the late 1920s, the Rock Island began utilizing gas-electric motor cars to replace steam engines on branch line passenger trains. These locomotives were an early effort at internal combustion power for railroads, but what turned heads was the introduction of streamlined diesel trains.

L.T. Walker started working for the Rock Island out of Little Rock as a brakeman in August 1942, witnessing the transition. In a 1988 interview, he said that "the steam engine was fascinating, but we burned oil and it was hard to keep clean. Most people wore overalls and by the time you got to Memphis or Booneville or El Dorado, climbing up and down the engine, you'd have grease all over you."

Not only were diesels cleaner and cheaper to operate, but it was also easier to pull heavier trains by simply adding more engines. With steam locomotives, if there was the need to double-head, meaning the use of two locomotives, an additional engine crew was needed.

The Rock Island, like other railroads, touted the new streamlined trains as a more comfortable form of long-distance travel, with diner, lounge, and sleeper cars as part of an effort to lure back a growing number of people who were opting to drive or fly. The Little Rock passenger station was remodeled during this time, with an invitation to a chamber of commerce event there on July 17, 1942, noting the station "has been improved and modernized throughout to make it of maximum service and convenience to patrons."

But times were changing, and fewer people were traveling by rail. In August 1953, the Choctaw Rocket had been replaced with the Budd Company's Rail Diesel Car, or RDC. This model was a self-propelled, one-car stainless-steel train that, if needed during a busy travel period, could also pull a regular coach car. Typically, there were few passengers, and the railroad primarily made money carrying US mail and packages for the Railway Express Agency. When mail contracts ended, so too did passenger service on the Rock Island in Arkansas.

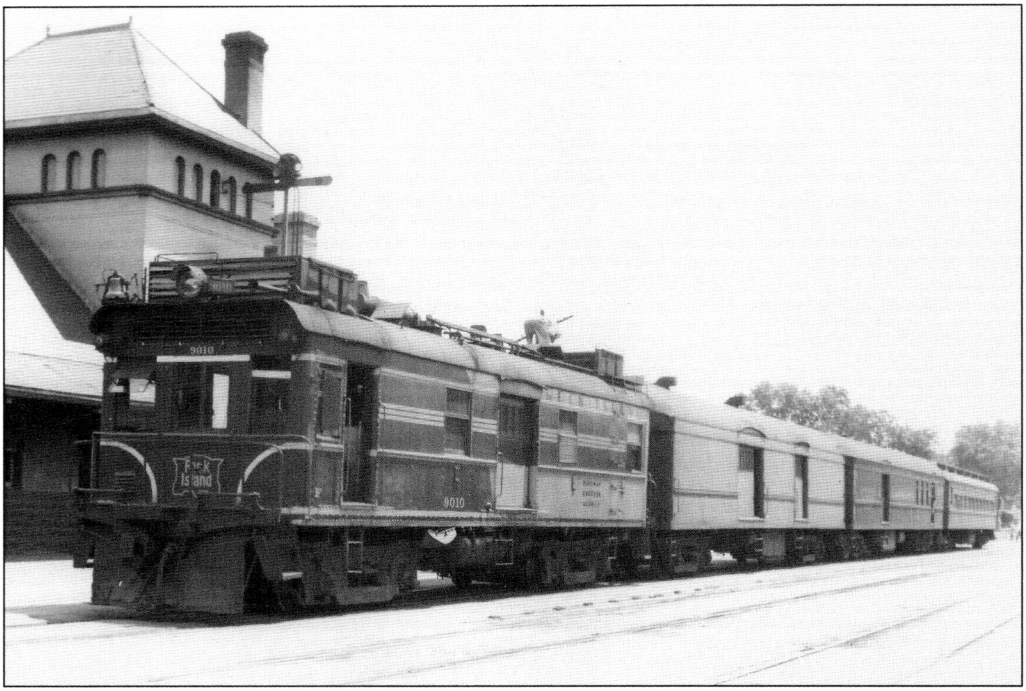

Motor Car No. 9010 leads a passenger train at Hot Springs in 1944. This locomotive had been built as a gas-electric, but was later converted to a more efficient diesel-electric in 1941. The gas or diesel engine drove electric generators that powered traction motors on each axle. (Courtesy of the UALR Center for Arkansas History and Culture.)

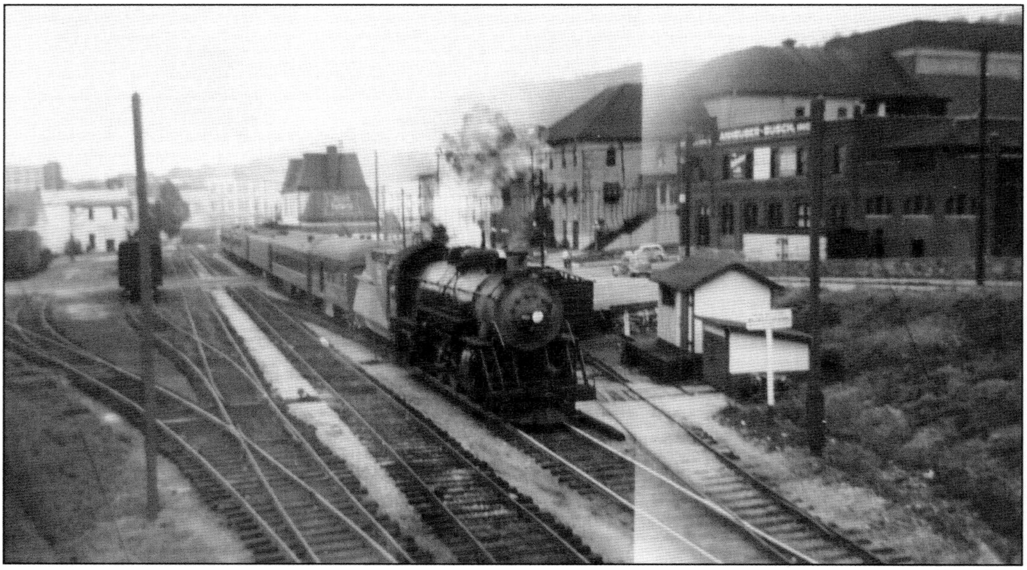

Steam was not completely gone by 1949; here, one is leading the Hot Springs Limited at its namesake city. The station in the background had been the original one for the Hot Springs Railroad, built in 1876. Also known as the "Diamond Jo" Line, the railroad was built by Joseph Reynolds, a wealthy businessman. It is said that he constructed the line between Malvern and Hot Springs because he did not like riding stagecoaches. (Courtesy of Bill Pollard; photograph by Randy Tardy.)

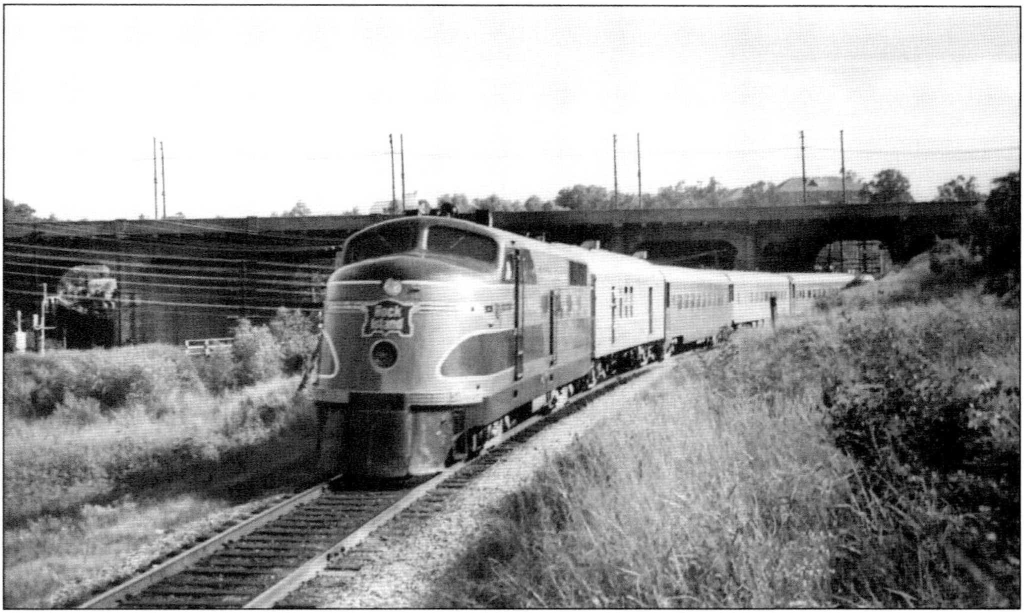

The Rock Island unveiled its streamlined Choctaw Rocket with great fanfare on November 17, 1940. Here, an eastbound train passes under the Third Street overpass in Little Rock in 1949. The train ran between Memphis and Amarillo, Texas, where a connection could be made with the Santa Fe. The first run of the Choctaw Rocket featured the governor of Arkansas, Little Rock's mayor, and several members of the Choctaw tribe. (Courtesy of Bill Pollard; photograph by John Mills.)

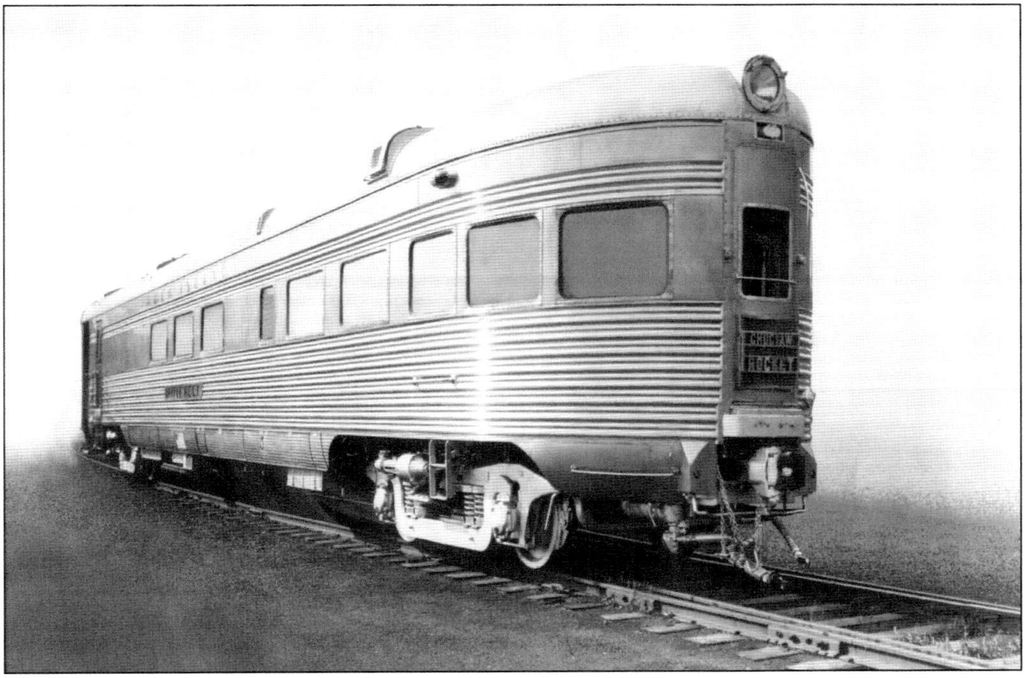

Built in 1940 by Pullman-Standard for the debut of the Choctaw Rocket, Car No. 431 was named after the city of Little Rock. It served as a parlor-diner-observation car. Similar cars used on the Choctaw Rocket were named after other cities served by the train. (Courtesy of Bill Pollard.)

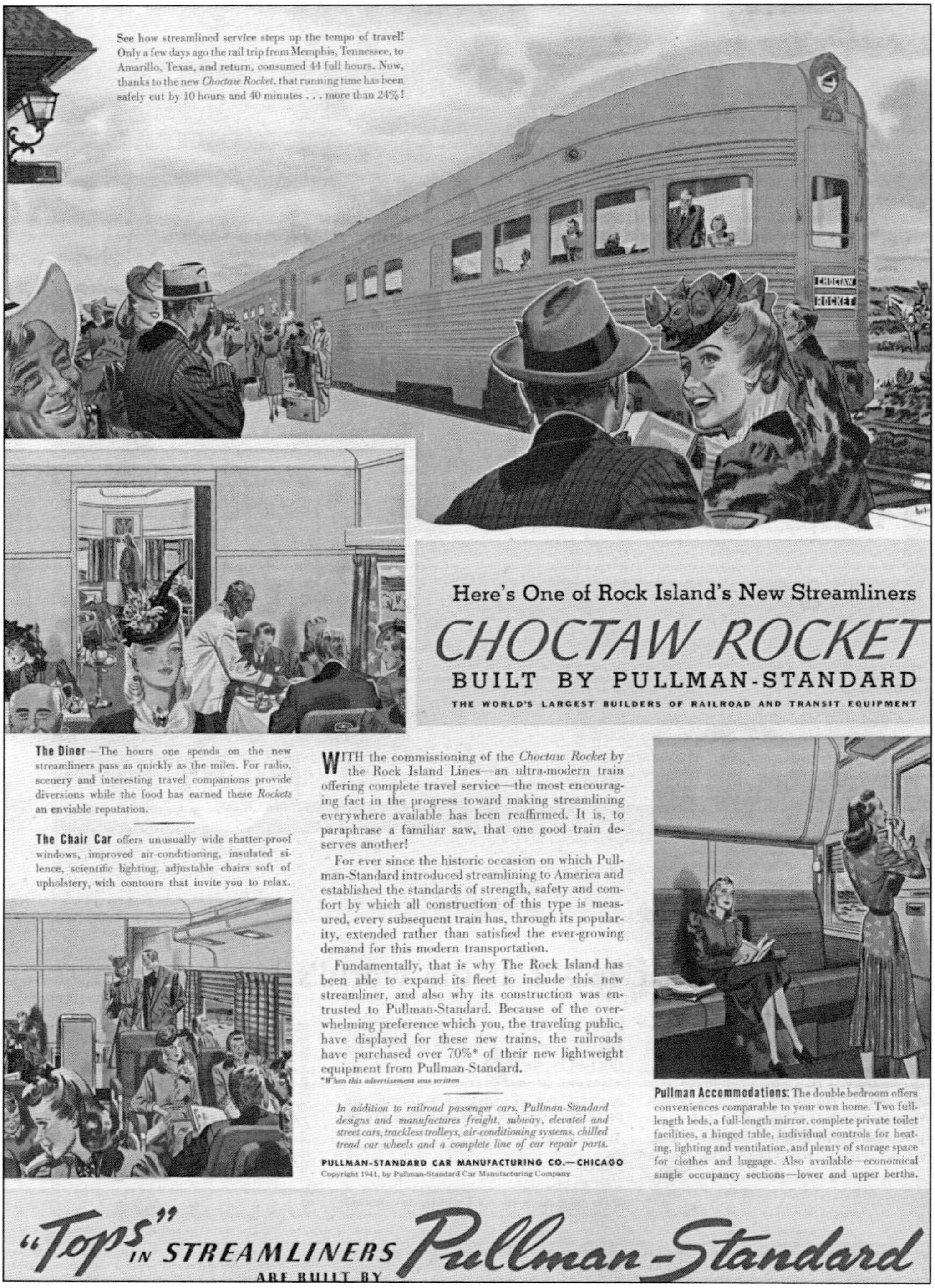

This advertisement touts the new Choctaw Rocket as "an ultra-modern train offering complete travel service." The double bedroom, it says, "offers conveniences comparable to your own home." The ad presents a carefully crafted image of glamour and luxury. (Courtesy of Bill Pollard.)

Choctaw Rocket

Dinner a la Carte

RELISHES

Sliced Tomatoes, 25 — Ripe or Green Olives, 20 — Sliced Cucumbers, 25
Prune Juice, 20 — Tomato Juice, 20 — Pineapple Juice, 20
Green Onions, 15 — Chow Chow, 20 — Radishes, 15

FISH, STEAKS AND CHOPS

Fresh Fish Saute, 70
Grilled Sirloin Steak, 1.50 — Lamb Chops with Bacon, 90
Fried Spring Chicken, Country Style, 95
Ham with Eggs, 75 — Bacon with Eggs, 75
Broiled or Fried Ham, 75 — Broiled or Fried Bacon, 75

EGGS, ETC.

Eggs: Boiled, Fried, Scrambled, 35 — Poached on Toast, 50
Omelettes: Plain, 30; with Ham or Bacon, 60; a la Creole, 60

VEGETABLES

Potatoes: Hashed Browned, 20 — German Fried, 20 — French Fried, 20
Stewed Tomatoes, 20 — Peas, 20 — Stewed Corn, 20

COLD MEATS AND SALADS

Cold Roast Ham, 80 — Cold Ox Tongue, 80 — Cold Assorted Meats, 80
(Served with Potato Salad)
Head Lettuce, 25 — Combination Salad, 35
(Served with French Dressing or Mayonnaise)
Imported Sardines, 50 — Special Dressing, 15 — Baked Beans, 40
Deviled Ham Sandwich toasted, with Potato Salad and Sliced Tomato, 50

BREAD

Assorted Bread, 10 — Toast, 15 — Milk Toast, 30
Dry Cereals with Cream, 30

DESSERTS

Ice Cream, 20 — Sundae, 25 — Pie, 20; a la Mode, 35 — Preserves, 25
Prunes, 30 — Melon, 25 — Marmalade, 25
Cheese: Imported 35; Domestic, 25

BEVERAGES

Coffee per Pot, 25; Cup 15 — Cocoa, Whipped Cream, 25 — Tea per Pot, 20
Malted Milk, 25 — Postum, 25
Bottle Milk, 15 — Sanka Coffee per Pot, 25 — Butter Milk, 15

Rock Island

J-10-300

This dinner menu for passengers of the Choctaw Rocket shows the same offerings one would find at a fine restaurant. As passenger service declined in the 1950s, dinners were replaced by meal stops at station lunchrooms at Little Rock and elsewhere. (Courtesy of the Clinton School of Public Service.)

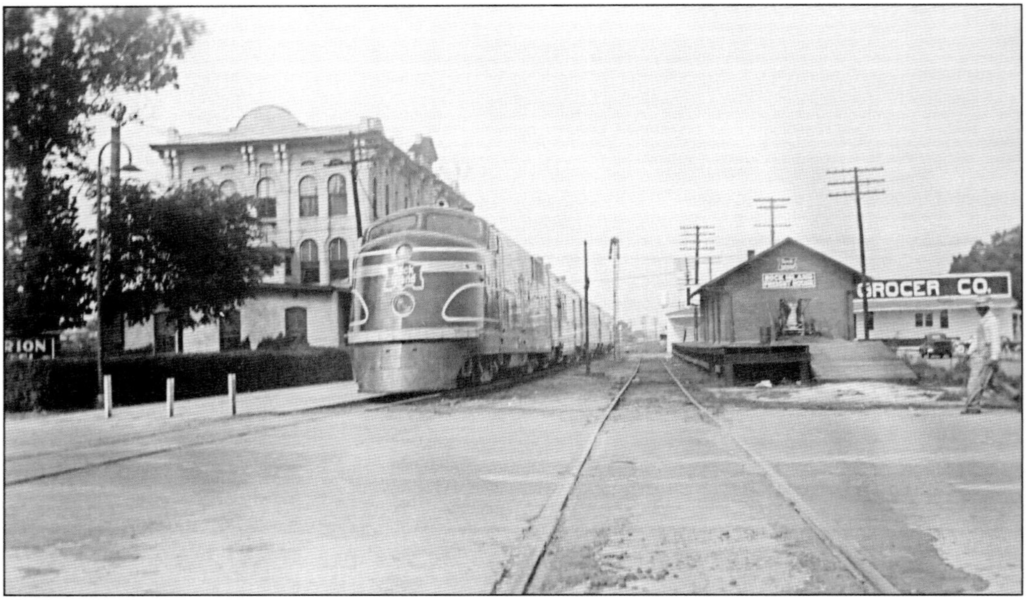

Here is an eastbound Choctaw Rocket in Forrest City, possibly around 1941. The large building to the left is the Hotel Marion, which, at this time, had the ground floor being jointly used as a passenger station by the Rock Island and Missouri Pacific. Construction on it began in 1885 along what was the Memphis & Little Rock Railroad. It also featured a restaurant for passengers. (Courtesy of Bill Pollard.)

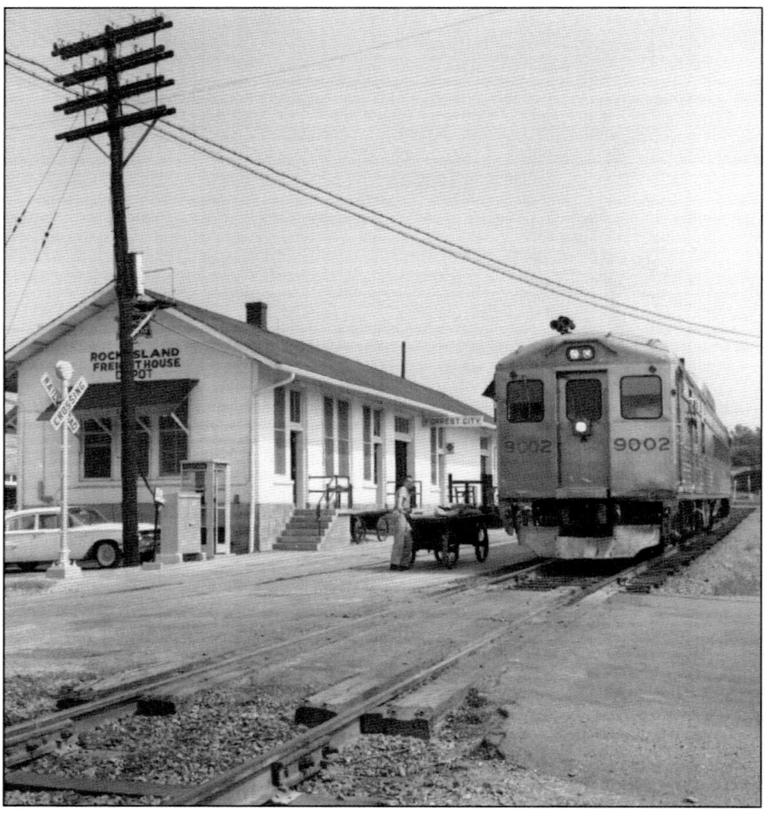

In 1953, the Rock Island replaced the Choctaw Rocket with a one-car, self-propelled train called the Choctaw Rockette. In late 1958, the Hotel Marion in Forrest City was torn down and passenger the waiting room and ticket office were moved across the track into what had been the railroad's freight depot. This photograph is from 1960. (Photograph by Edward Wojtas, Rock Island Railroad.)

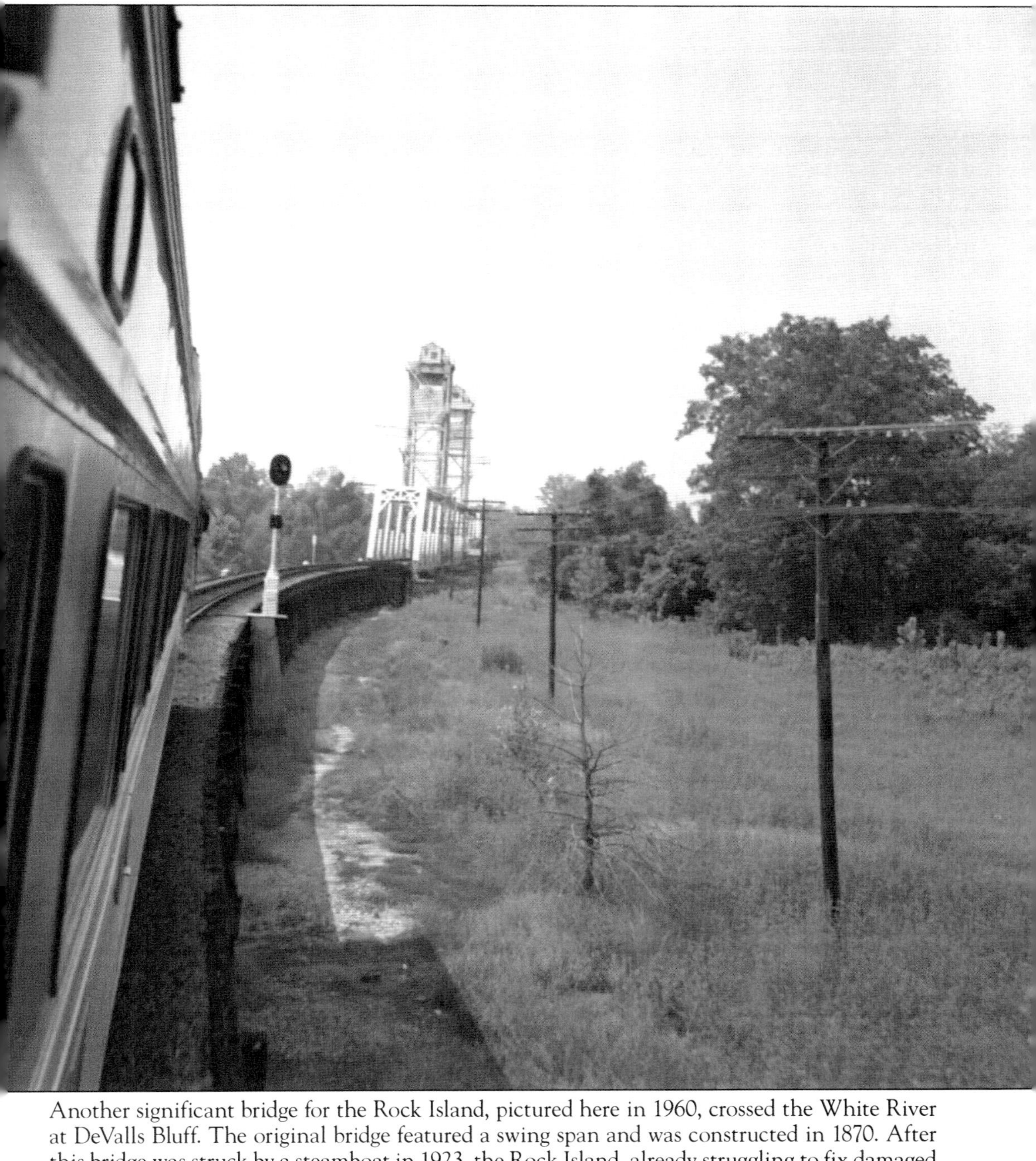

Another significant bridge for the Rock Island, pictured here in 1960, crossed the White River at DeValls Bluff. The original bridge featured a swing span and was constructed in 1870. After this bridge was struck by a steamboat in 1923, the Rock Island, already struggling to fix damaged and leaning piers, opted to build a new bridge. The Baltimore through-truss bridge featured a 55-foot vertical-lift span. In the years after the railroad was shut down, the bridge was essentially abandoned and the lift span was locked in the up position. A new bridge for US Highway 70 was built alongside it and uses the grade where the track once ran as the highway approach on each side. (Photograph by Edward Wojtas, Rock Island Railroad.)

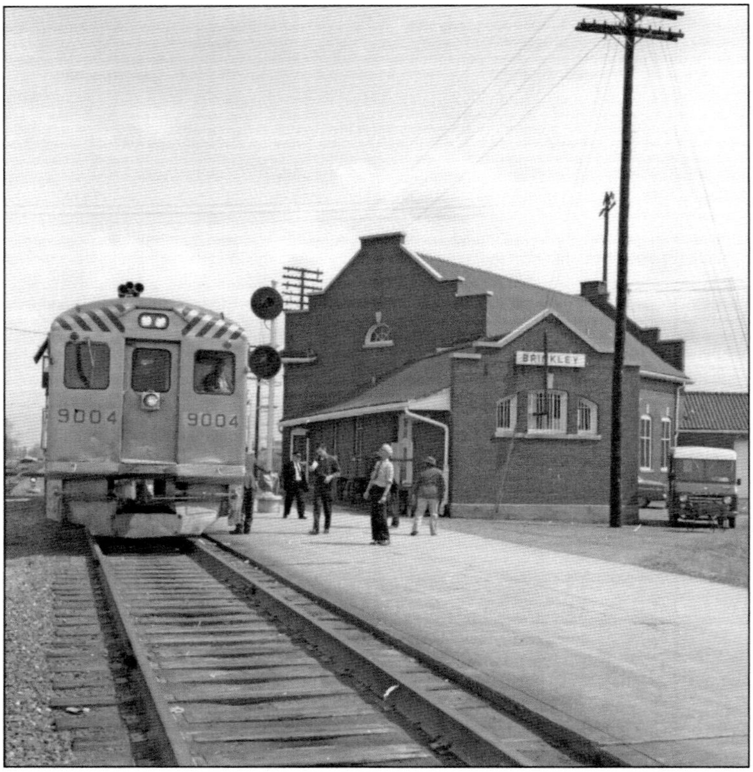

In 1960, the RDC stops to pick up passengers at Brinkley's Union Station, where the Rock Island track crossed with the Cotton Belt. It was a major transfer point for passengers. The building was opened on September 16, 1912, replacing a previous station that was destroyed by a devastating tornado that hit the town on March 8, 1909. The Cotton Belt, which ran north-south, had trackage rights on the Rock Island from here east to Memphis. (Photograph by Edward Wojtas, Rock Island Railroad.)

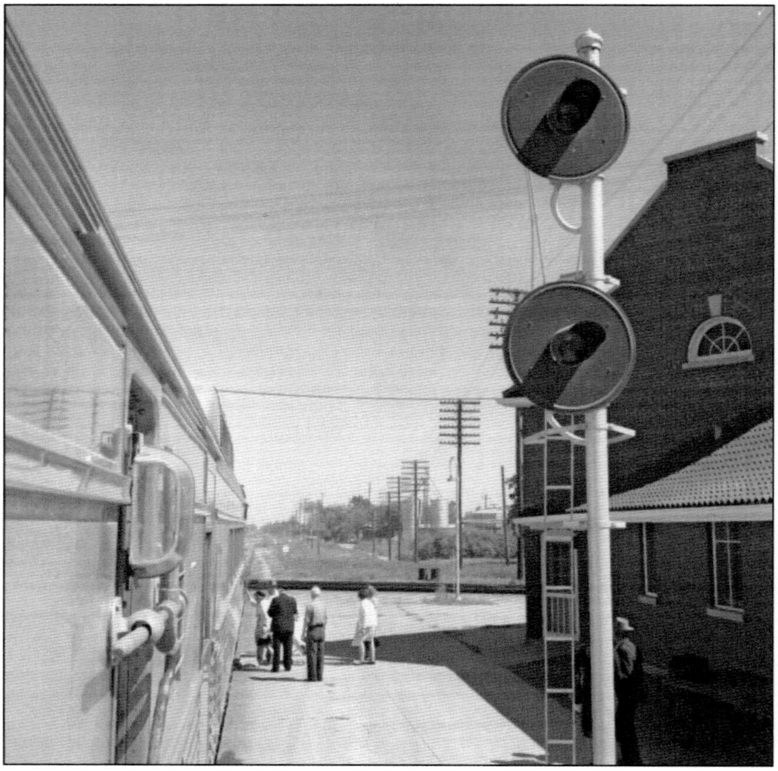

Passengers file onto the train at Brinkley. After the 1980 shutdown of the Rock Island, Union Station was abandoned and had been slated for demolition until the late 1990s, when a campaign to save it was launched. Union Pacific, which had acquired the building, eventually deeded it to the city, which restored it, making it the Central Delta Museum. The museum celebrates its railroad heritage. (Photograph by Edward Wojtas, Rock Island Railroad.)

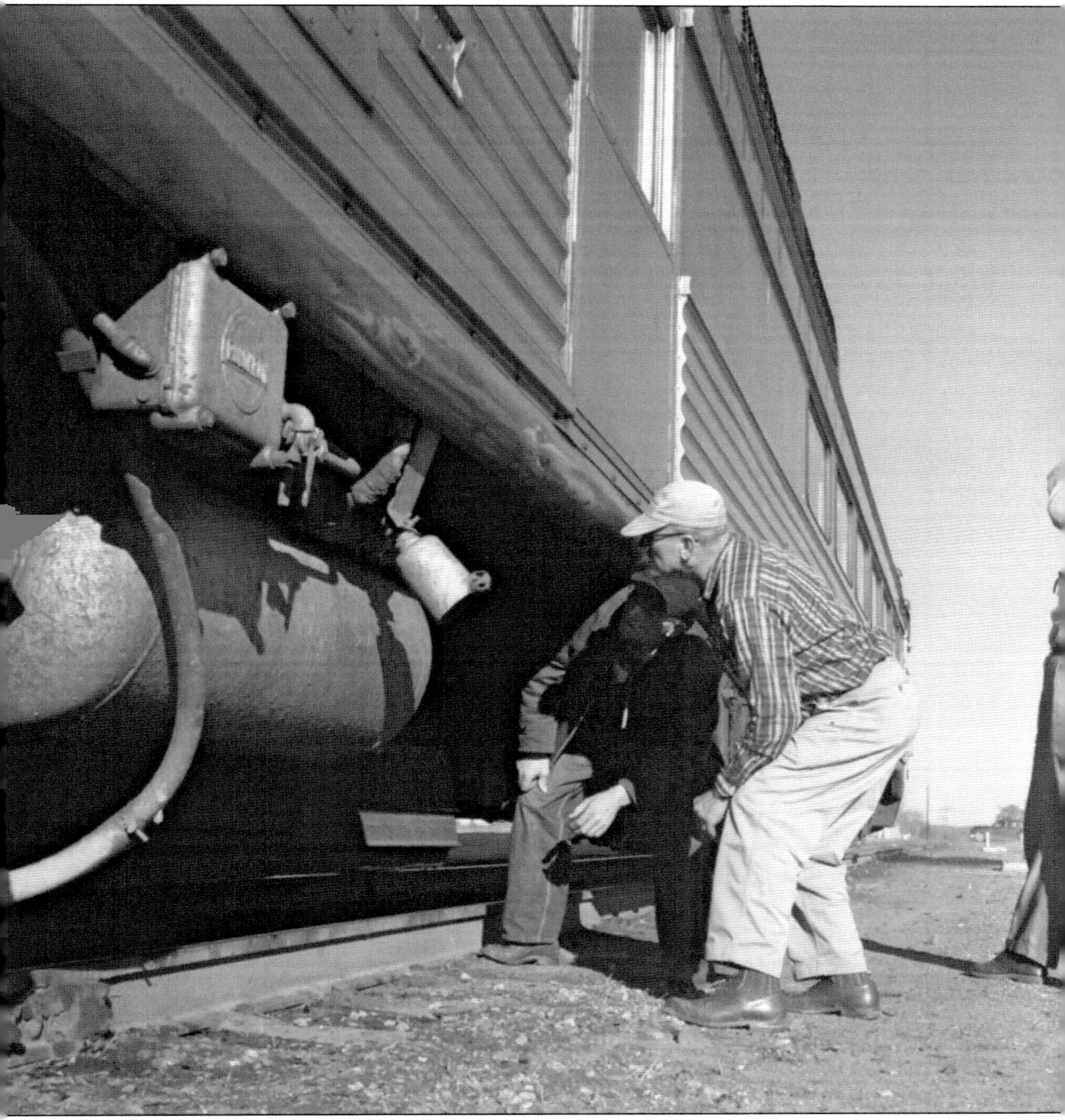

Here, employees check underneath an RDC during a stop. Many of these images were taken by Rock Island company photographer Edward Wojtas, who was also editor of the employee magazine. In 1960, he extensively traveled through Arkansas and Oklahoma, capturing candid shots of crews and locations that were significant in the history of the Rock Island. (Photograph by Edward Wojtas, Rock Island Railroad.)

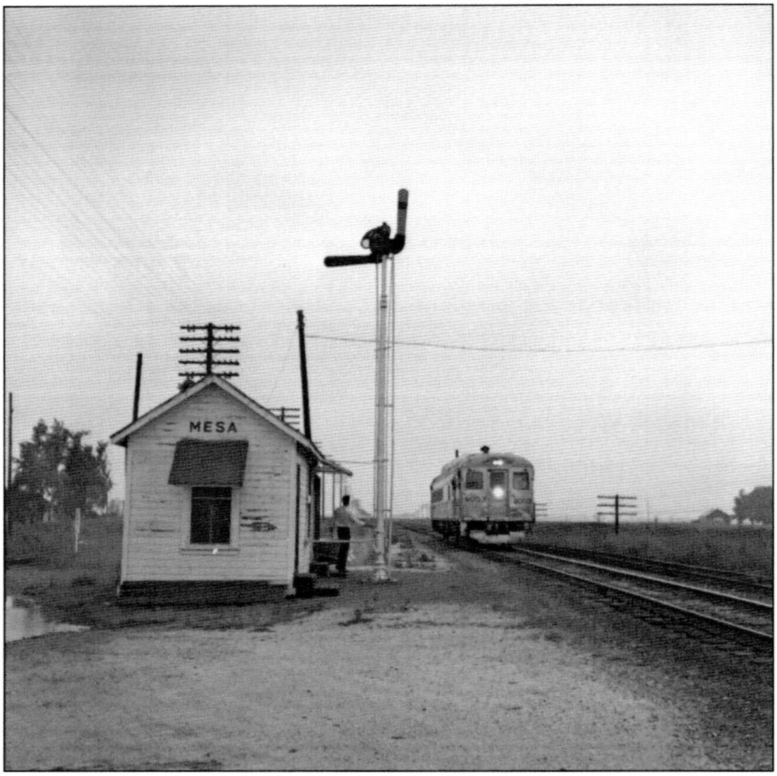

The semaphore train order signal is pictured at the small depot at Mesa in 1960. This location was an important junction point where branch lines ran south to Stuttgart and north to Searcy; however, by this time, the branch had been abandoned north of Des Arc. (Photograph by Edward Wojtas, Rock Island Railroad.)

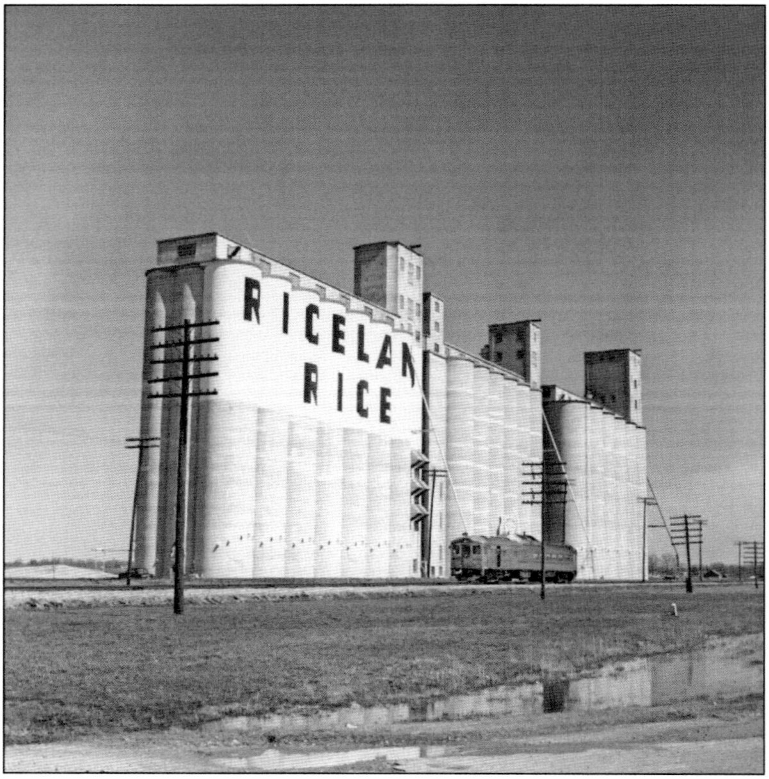

An RDC passes a large Riceland Rice facility in Hazen in 1960. Built directly along the tracks, this is the kind of industrial client that faced challenges moving its product after the railroad was later shut down. (Photograph by Edward Wojtas, Rock Island Railroad.)

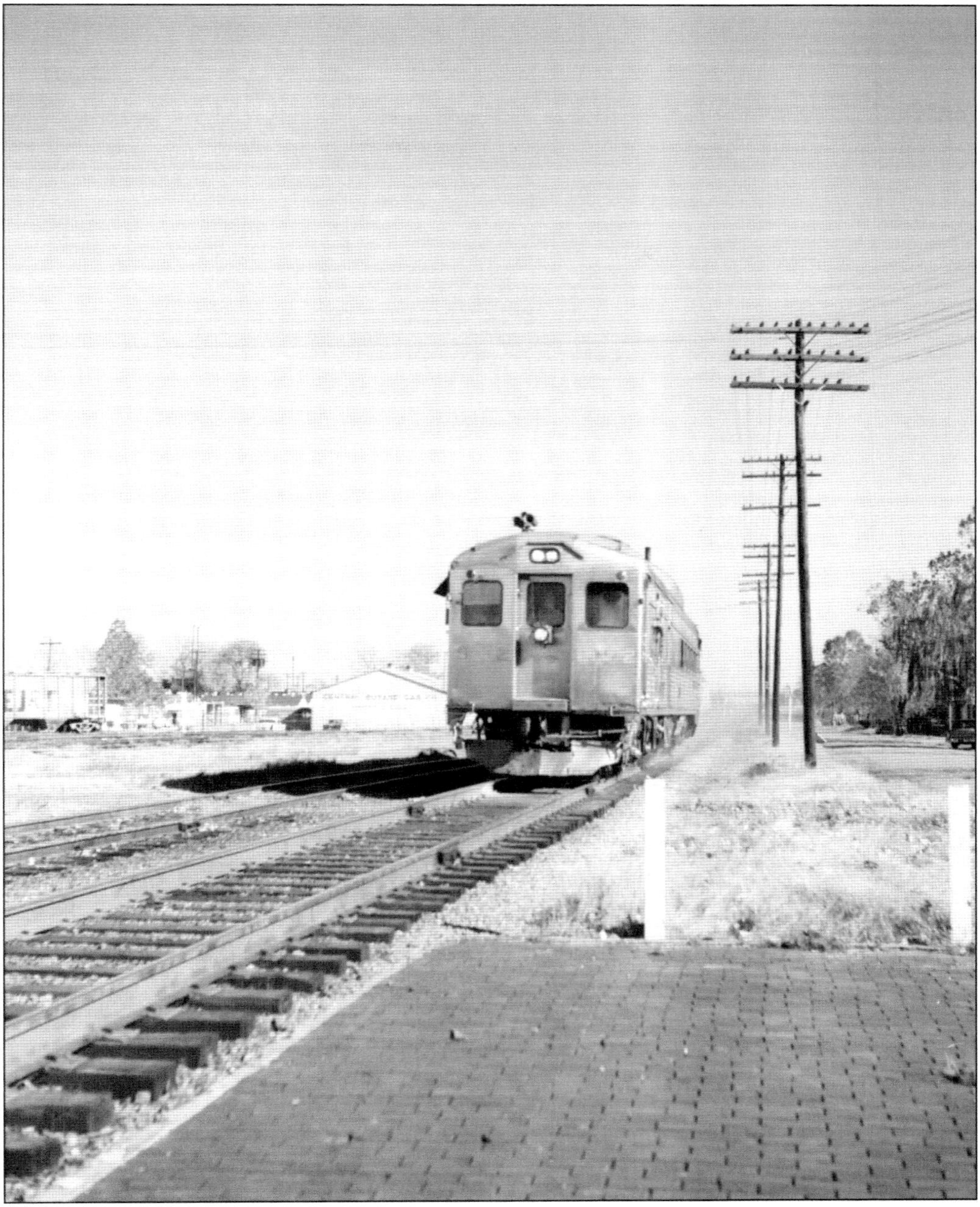

Heading west in 1960, RDC No. 9002 is approaching the North Little Rock depot. When the number of passengers was larger, the railroad could easily attach an additional coach to be pulled by the RDC, which had 550 horsepower. One negative compared to traditional trains was that the lightweight railcars were more susceptible to damage when they struck vehicles at grade crossings. (Courtesy of Bill Pollard; photograph by Clifton Hull.)

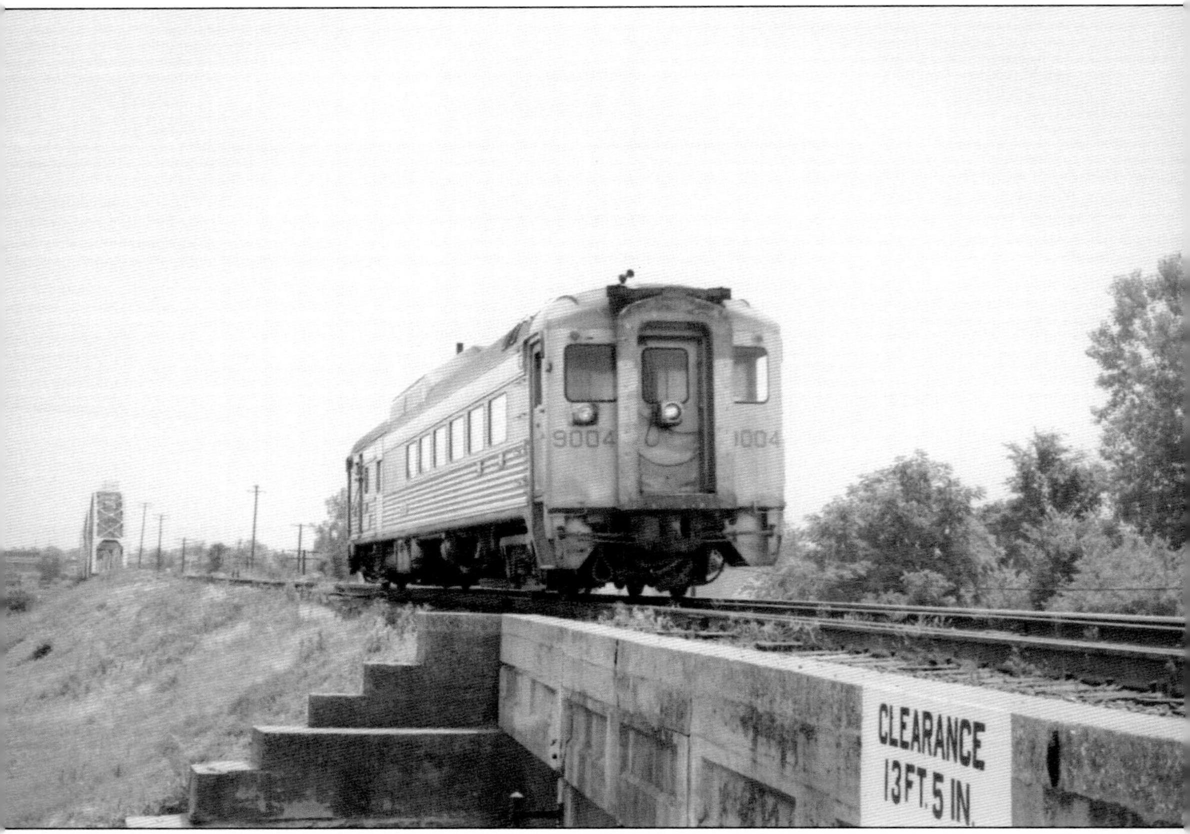

The Rock Island's track made a 90-degree curve in North Little Rock, pictured here in 1963 approaching the Arkansas River bridge. Note how high the track bed had been built so that it would be level with the river crossing. Before the bridge was built in 1899, this neighborhood was known as Huntersville Ferry Station. (Courtesy of Bill Pollard; photograph by Clifton Hull.)

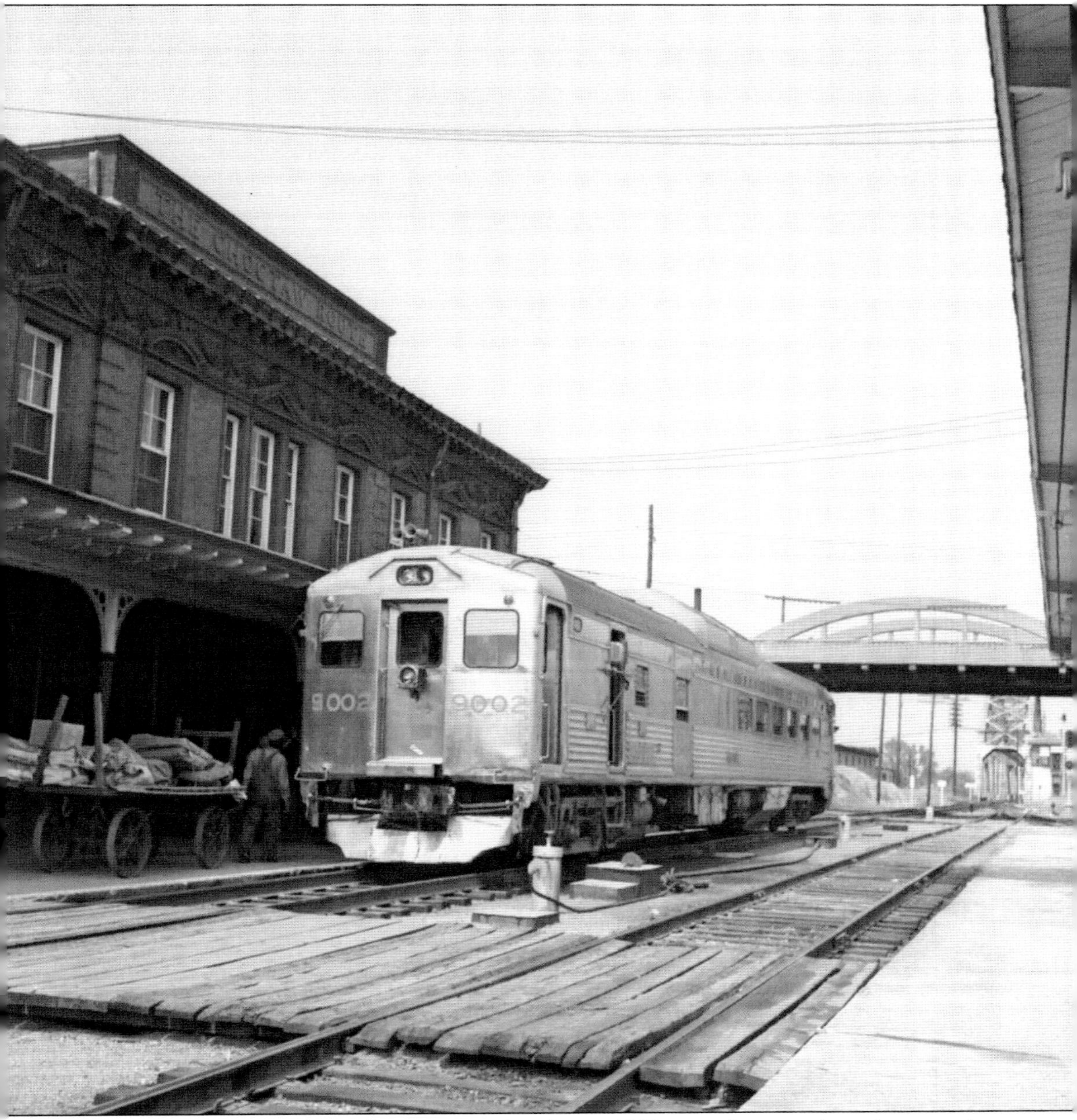

After arriving at the Little Rock station on this day in 1960, a mail cart with packages and mailbags to be exchanged is pulled out. The RDCs were also called doodlebugs. (Photograph by Edward Wojtas, Rock Island Railroad.)

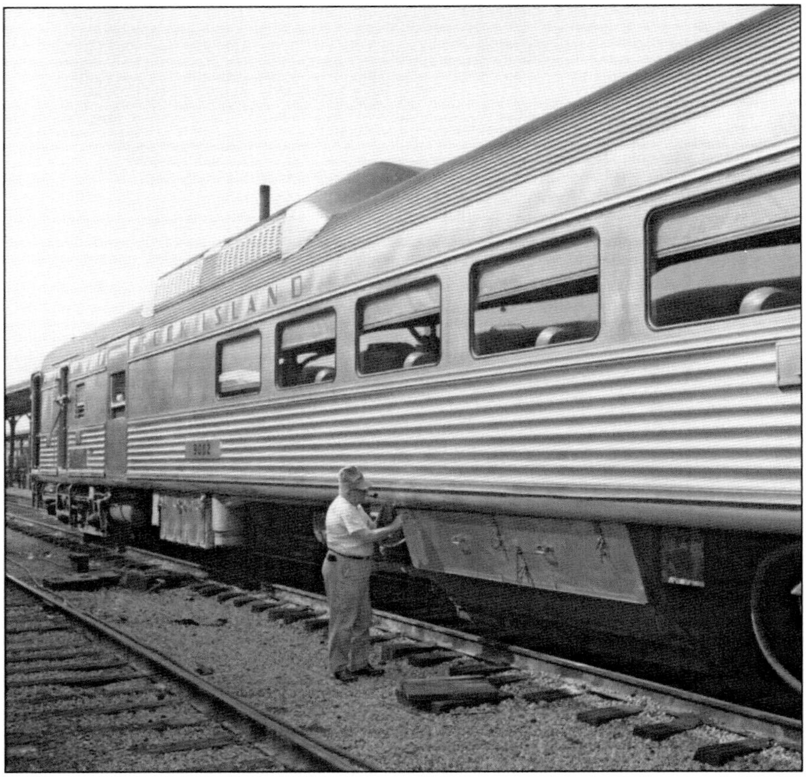

Employee Hugh Wilbank accesses a storage compartment underneath the RDC while parked at the Little Rock station in 1960. (Photograph by Edward Wojtas, Rock Island Railroad.)

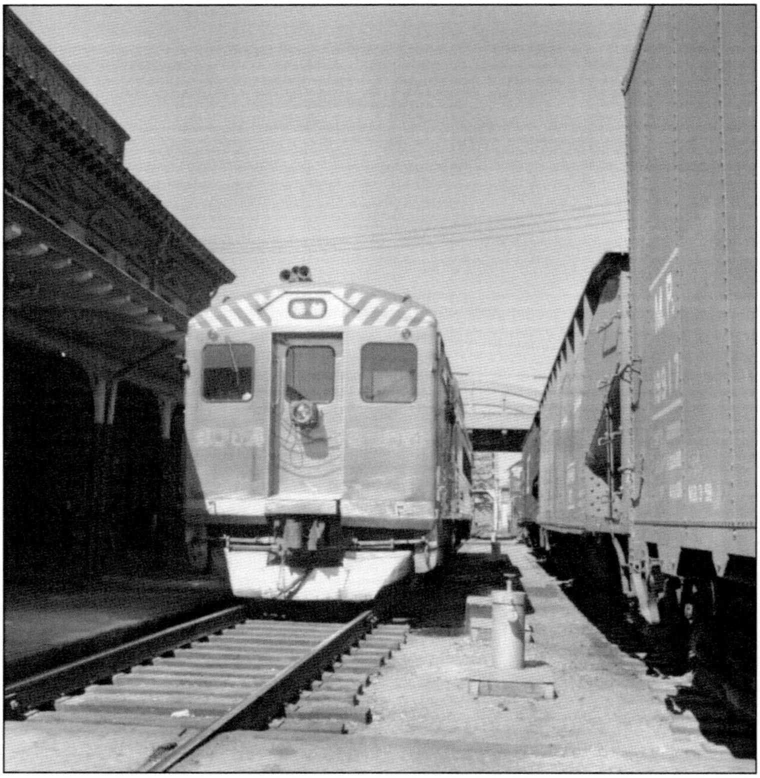

A freight train passes on the right approaching the Arkansas River Bridge while the RDC is parked at the Little Rock station in 1960. (Photograph by Edward Wojtas, Rock Island Railroad.)

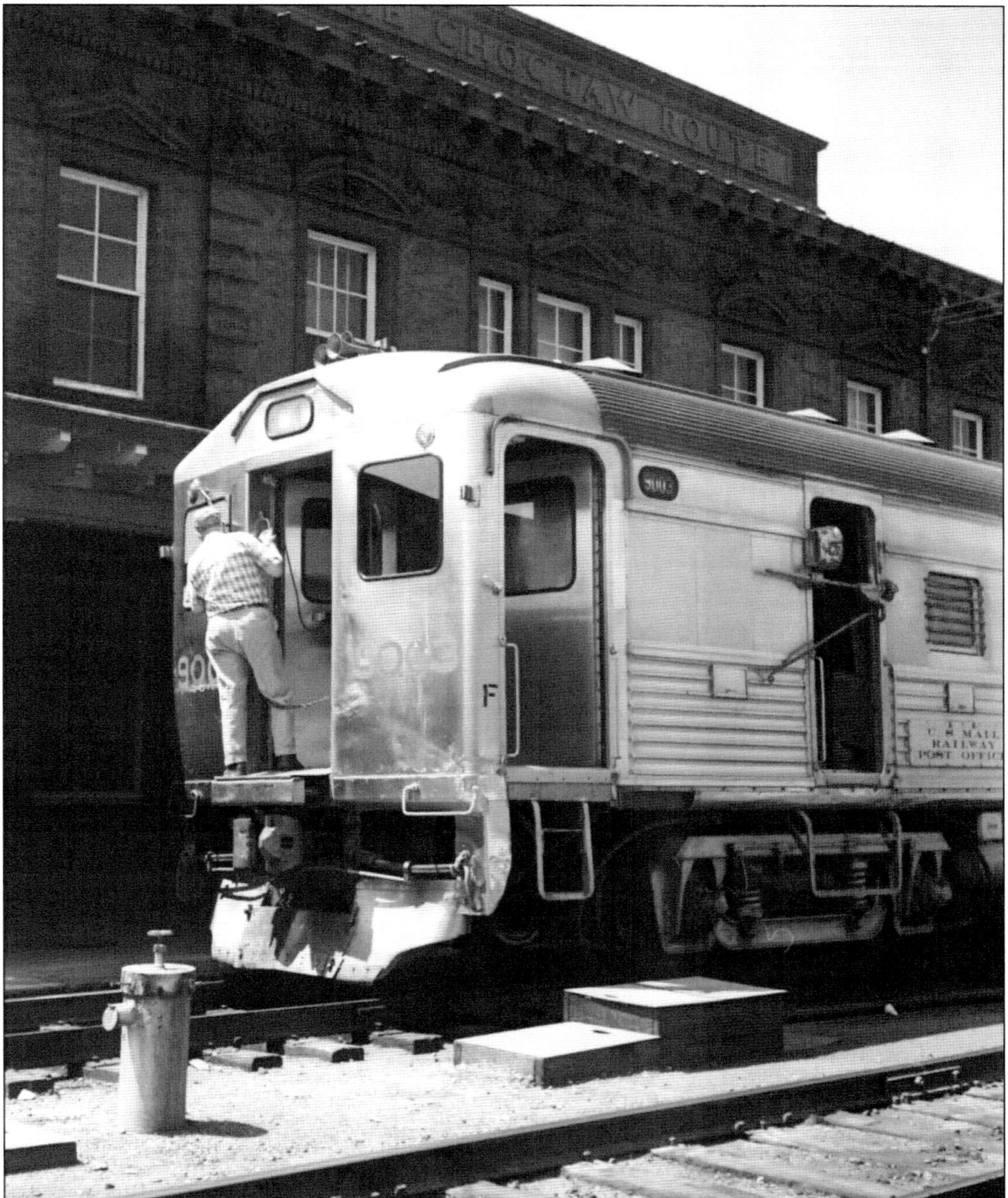

A carman cleans the windshield of an RDC at the Little Rock station in 1961. This station once housed a full restaurant, but in later years, a smaller café provided lunch for passengers on the westbound Choctaw Rockette. (Courtesy of Bill Pollard; photograph by Clifton Hull.)

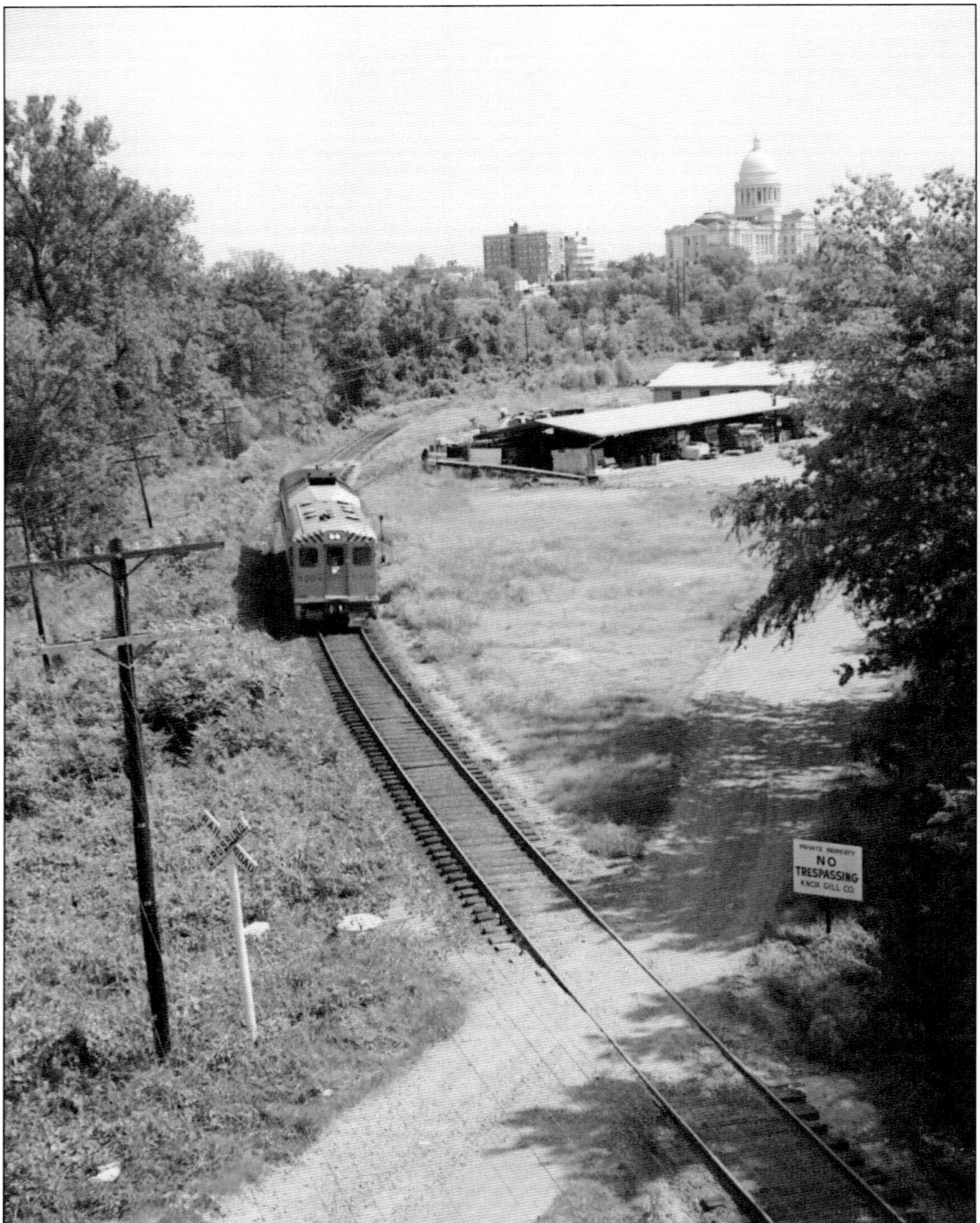

Having just departed the Little Rock station and passing through Biddle Yard, RDC No. 9004 is heading west and approaching a grade crossing in September 1963. This photograph was taken from the Cantrell Road overpass with the Arkansas State Capitol in the background. (Courtesy of Bill Pollard; photograph by Clifton Hull.)

This 1960 photograph shows the meeting of two trains heading in different directions, with one pulled off on a siding at Houston, Arkansas. (Photograph by Edward Wojtas, Rock Island Railroad.)

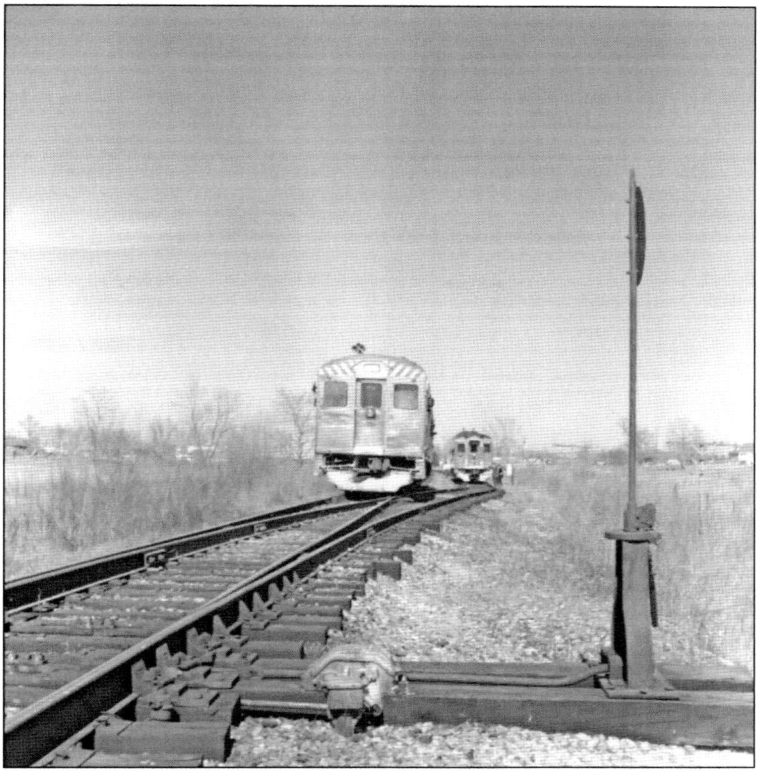

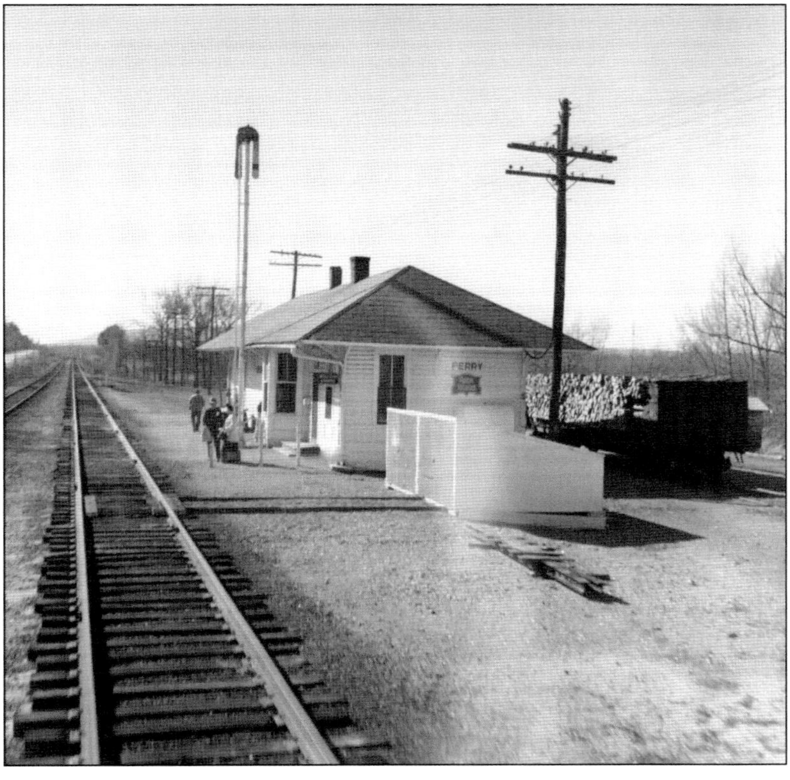

An RDC heading west in 1960 approaches the depot at Perry; note the passengers waiting to get on board. (Photograph by Edward Wojtas, Rock Island Railroad.)

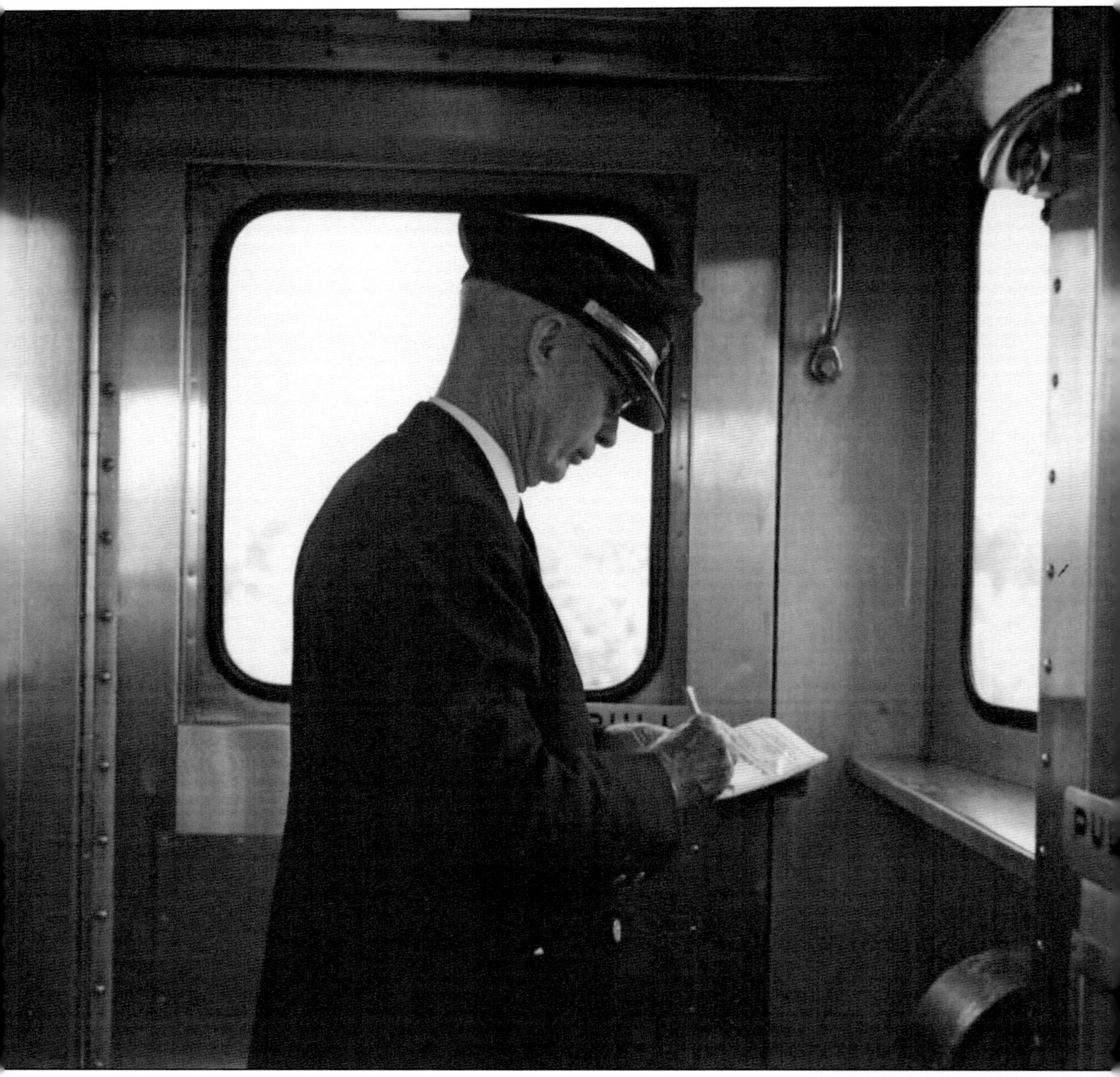

Conductor Jessie James is pictured on board an RDC in Arkansas in 1960. (Photograph by Edward Wojtas, Rock Island Railroad.)

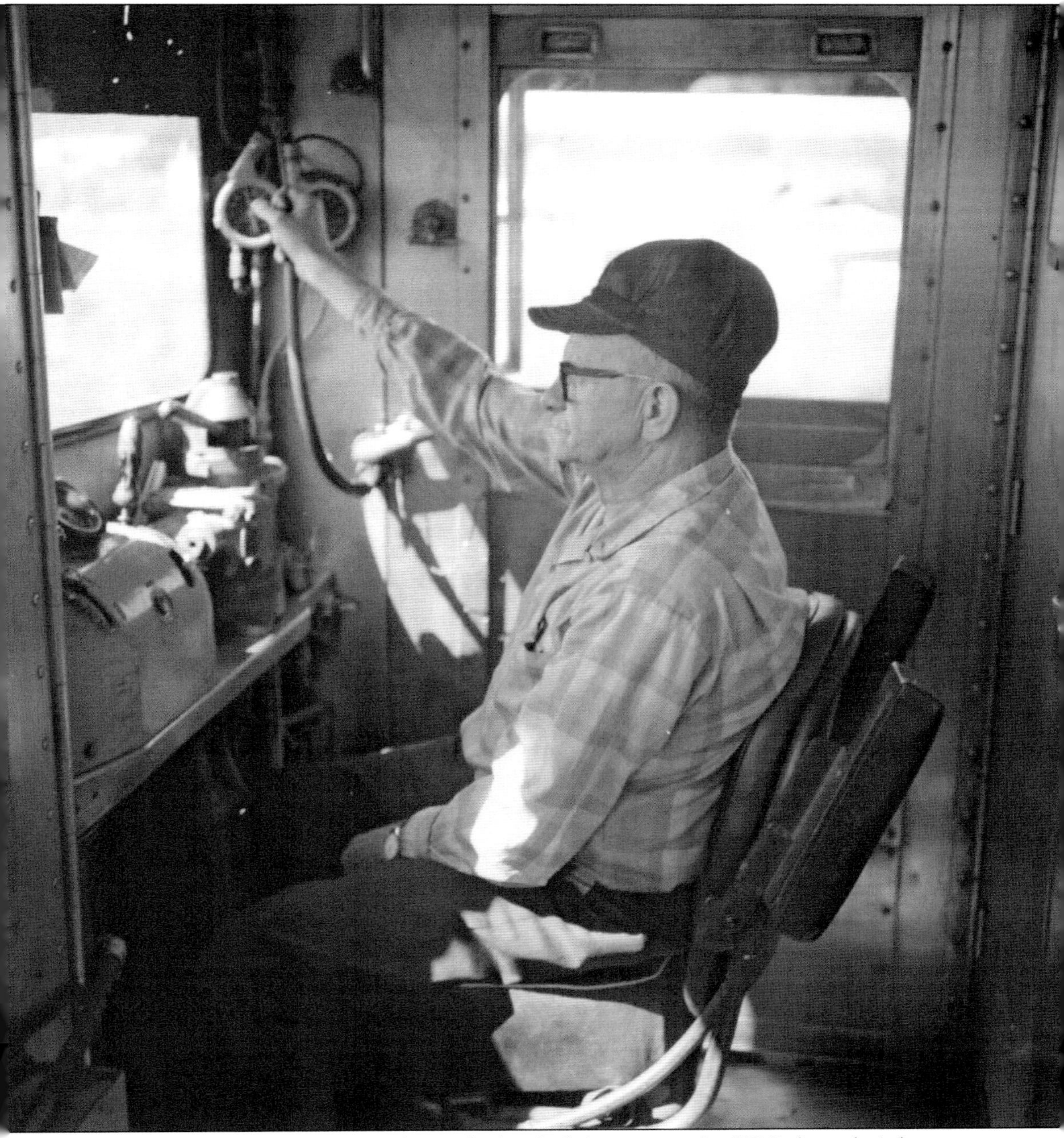

Engineer Pye Holiman is watching the track ahead while running the RDC through Arkansas in 1960. (Photograph by Edward Wojtas, Rock Island Railroad.)

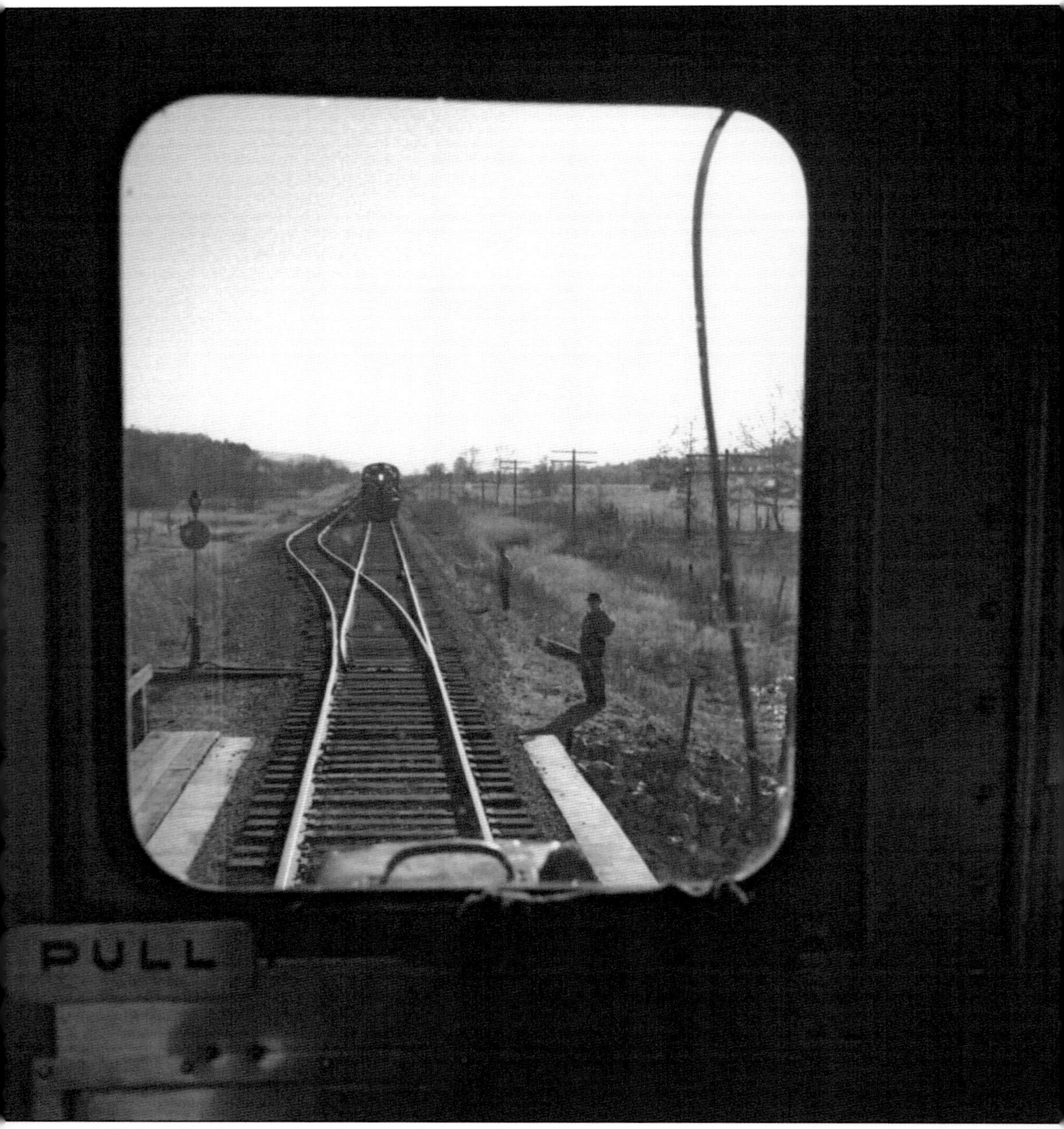

With a freight train on the main line on this day in 1960, an employee at the switch to the right has lined up the track for the RDC to move onto a siding. (Photograph by Edward Wojtas, Rock Island Railroad.)

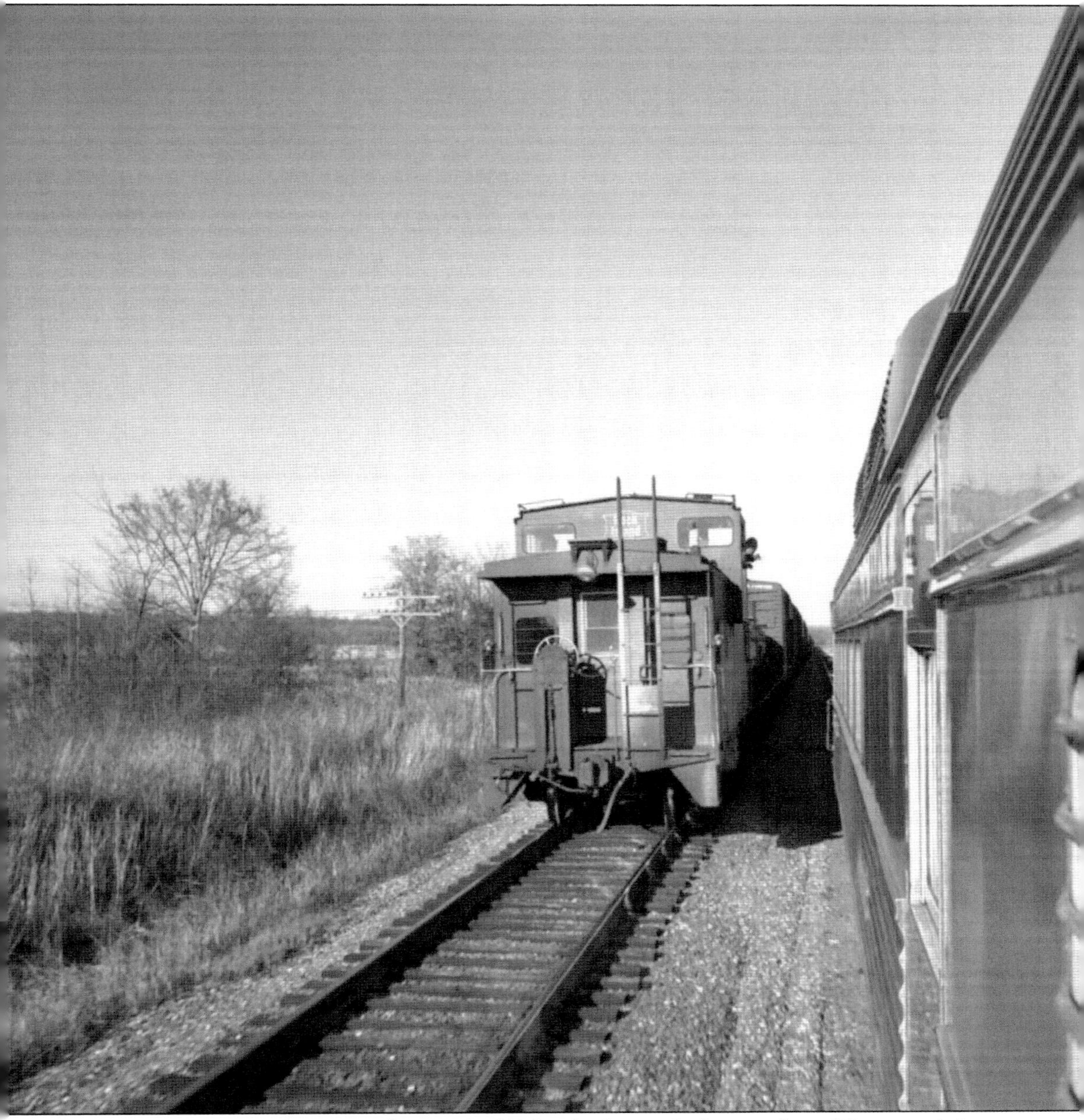

The caboose of the freight train rolls past the RDC, which is parked on a siding. (Photograph by Edward Wojtas, Rock Island Railroad.)

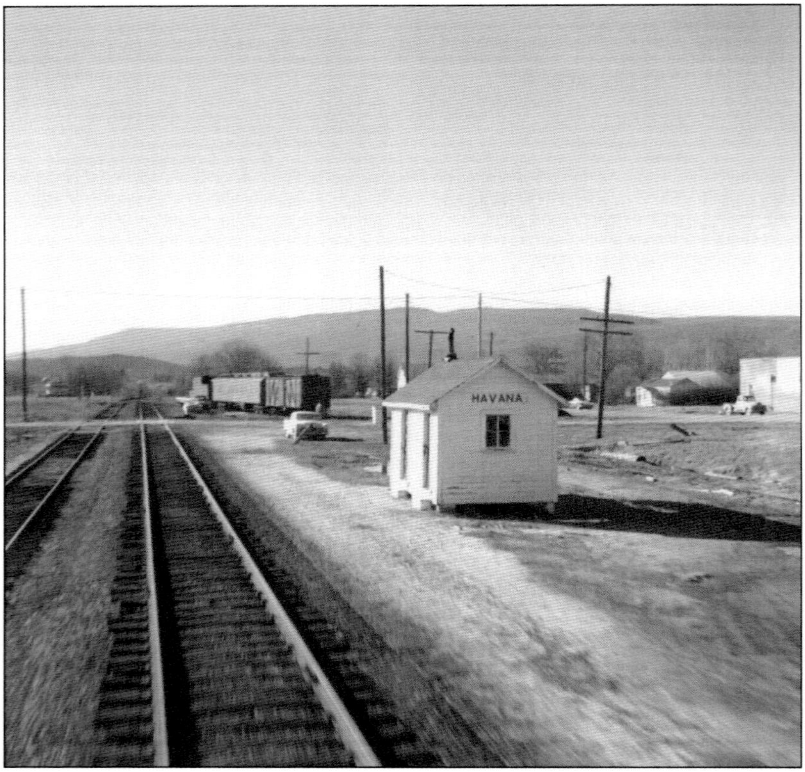

The mountains in the distance grow taller as the RDC speeds past the Rock Island's small building in Havana in 1960. (Photograph by Edward Wojtas, Rock Island Railroad.)

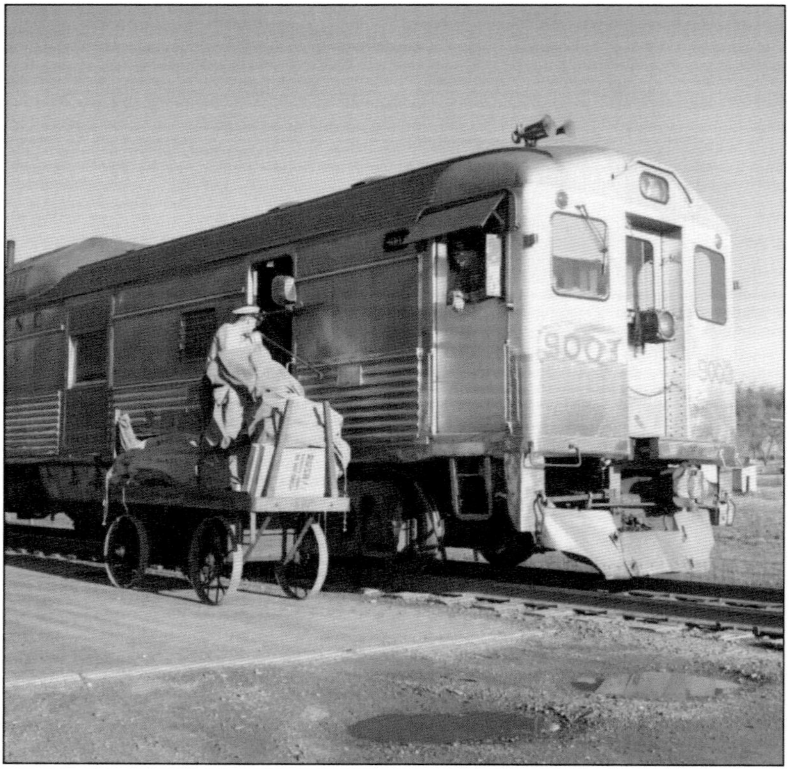

While the number of passengers was declining, mail service still provided important revenue for the Rock Island in 1960. At each stop, baggage wagons were brought out with packages and mailbags to be loaded and unloaded. (Photograph by Edward Wojtas, Rock Island Railroad.)

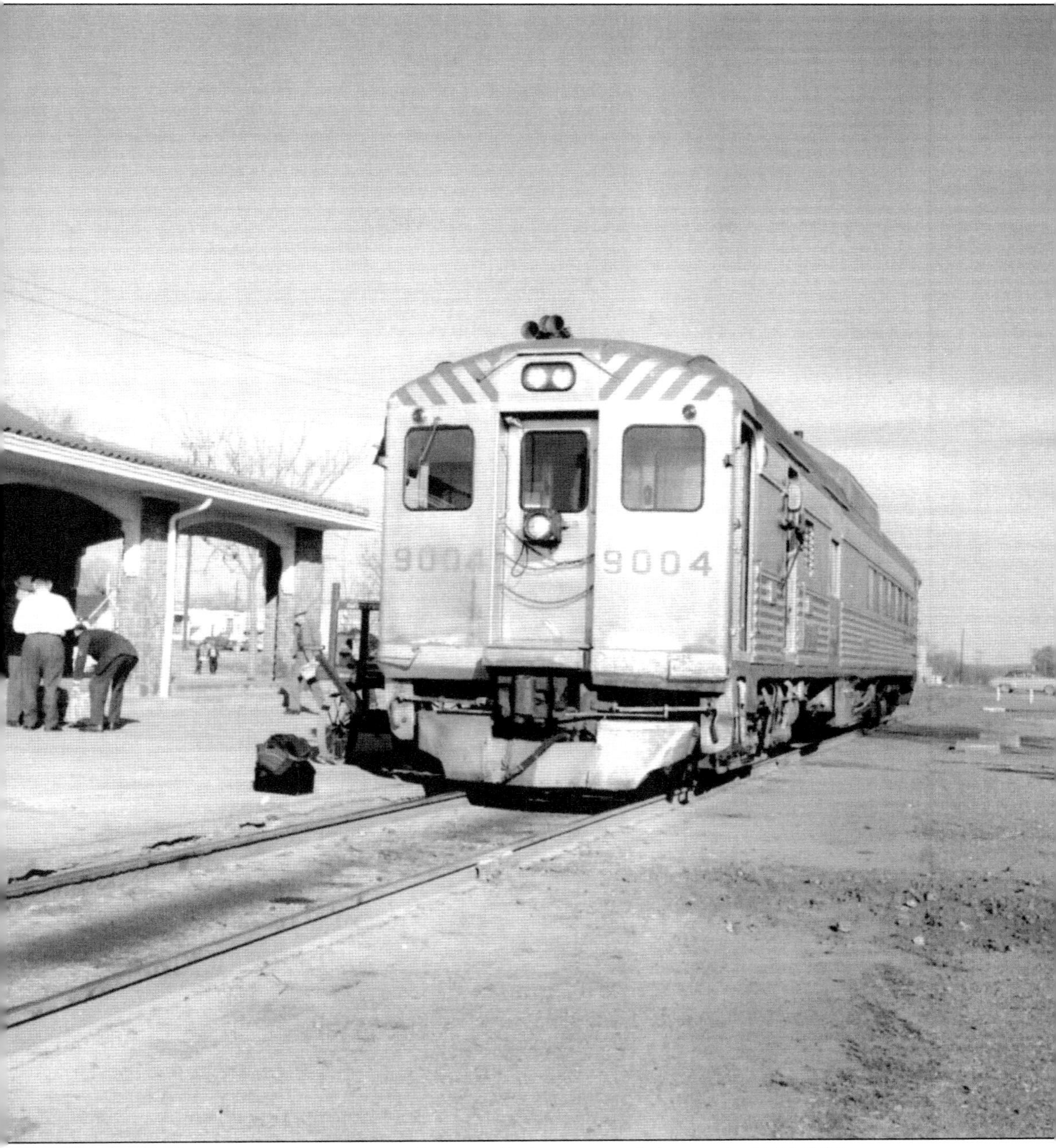

Here, an RDC arrives at the station in Booneville in western Arkansas in 1960. This was a crew change point; the crew out of Little Rock would eventually take another train east to Memphis and then finally back to Little Rock. That is likely a crew member's bag to the left of the RDC. (Photograph by Edward Wojtas, Rock Island Railroad.)

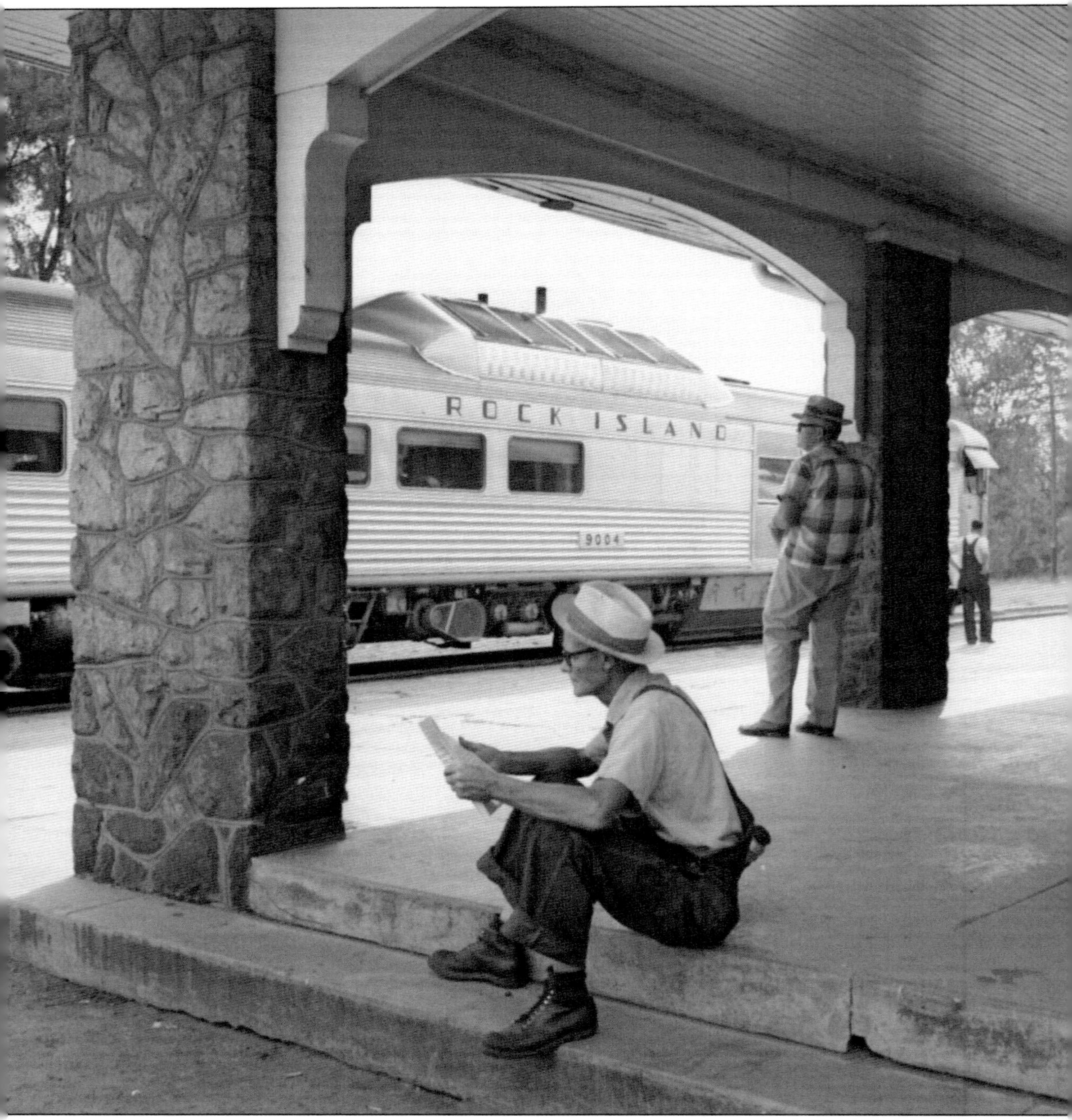

Rock Island freight conductor Harvey Ray sits outside the Booneville station waiting to take an eastbound freight to Little Rock once it arrives from Oklahoma. This station had originally been a restaurant for passengers and was remodeled into a station in the mid-1940s. (Photograph by Edward Wojtas, Rock Island Railroad.)

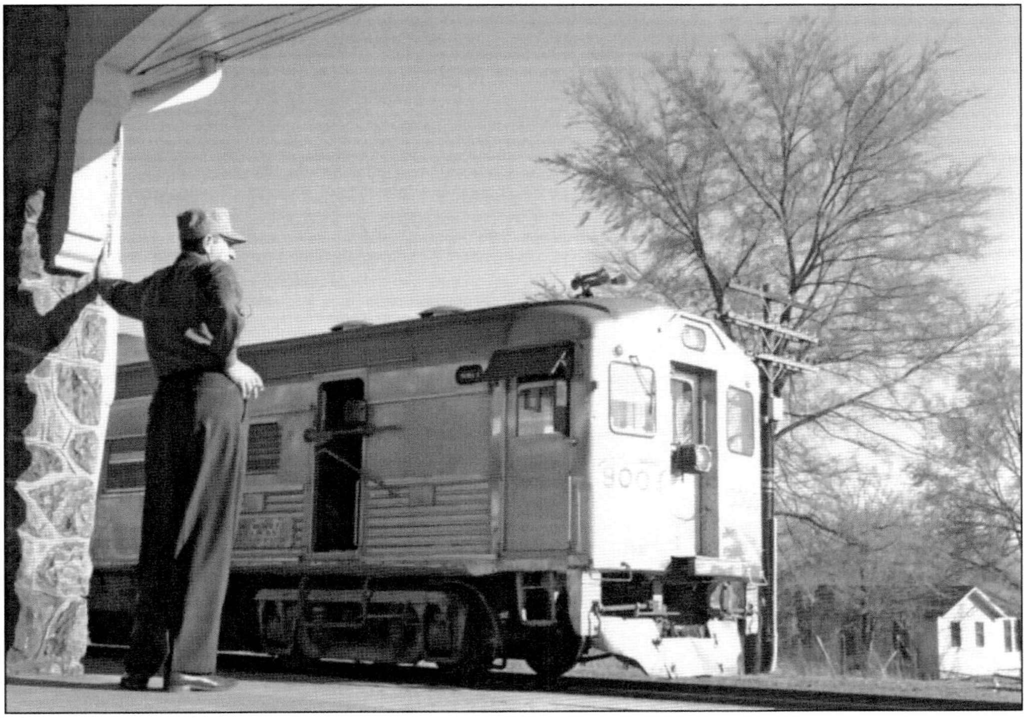

Pictured in 1960, this train will continue heading west and cross into Oklahoma. (Photograph by Edward Wojtas, Rock Island Railroad.)

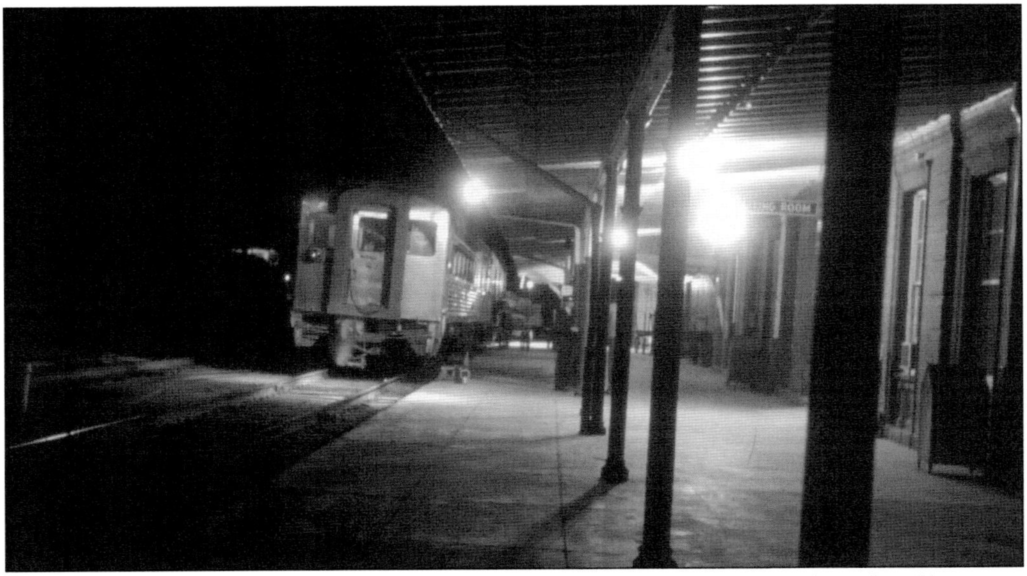

The end of passenger rail service on the Rock Island in Arkansas came with the railroad losing an important mail contract. Shortly after midnight on November 10, 1967, the last westbound train stopped at the Little Rock station, where it was photographed by railroad historian Bill Pollard, who spoke about the occasion in a 2015 interview. He said, "There were not many passengers riding that train, it was primarily a mail and express train. But in the year before the railway post office was removed, it was one of the more lucrative passenger runs on the Rock Island because it did have so much mail and express." (Photograph by Bill Pollard.)

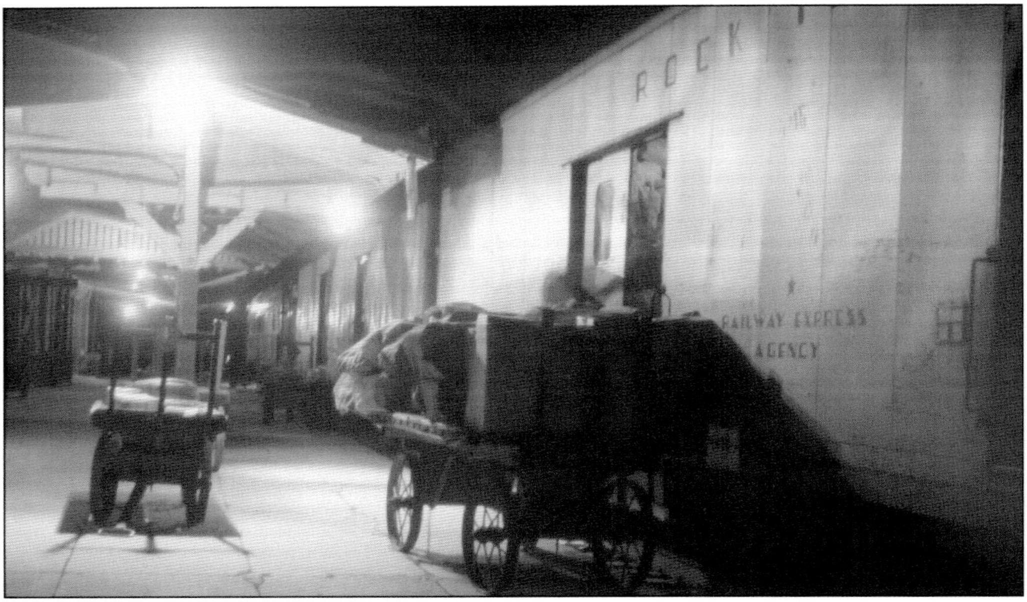

Pollard described the atmosphere in the darkness for that last westbound run as somber, with everyone realizing it was the end of an era. The conductors and engine crew would be losing their positions, but because of seniority, they would not be losing their jobs. They would revert to freight service. "There was a little bit of dismay with that and the ticket office was going to close and there was a lot of turmoil that was going on, but I've looked at those pictures since then and thought not a soul on that platform, me or anybody else, had any inkling that 13 years later the railroad itself was going to be gone. I mean, 13 years sounds like a long time and in a flash it was gone." (Photograph by Bill Pollard.)

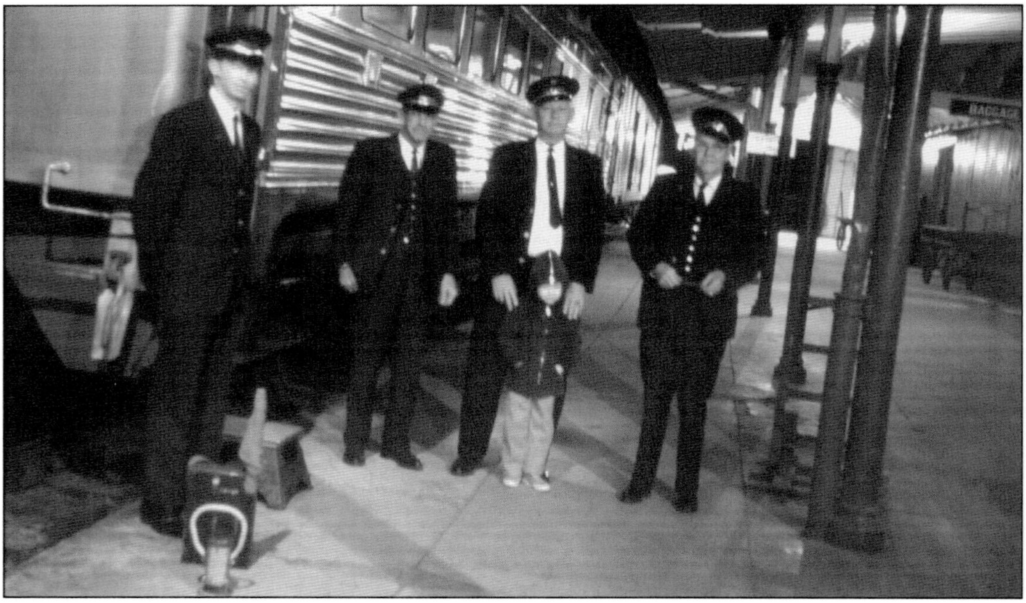

Pollard asked the inbound and outbound train crews to pose for a photograph. From left to right are Doyle Johnson, brakeman; Milas Cauthron, brakeman; John Fay McCauley, conductor; and J.G. "Guy" Bailey, conductor; the young boy is Alan Pollard, the youngest brother of the photographer. (Photograph by Bill Pollard.)

Three

Quiet Stations and Depots

Even before passenger service came to a complete end on the Rock Island, the depots, which had once been the center of action in many communities, began to look very lonely. Downtown areas were typically built around the railroad lines, but as traffic on highways increased, that is where many of the businesses gravitated. Mom-and-pop businesses were disappearing, and larger chain stores were built in undeveloped areas, expanding the sizes of towns.

The end of passenger service sealed the fate for several depots. The handling of freight operations continued in some, but many depots were closed as diesel locomotives did not need to stop as frequently for servicing as the steam locomotives had. The old buildings that were still used took on responsibilities for freight going to larger areas.

In some cases, the unused depots were sold to businesses, which set up shop inside. Others were sold or donated to towns. Many just sat abandoned, sometimes with old railroad papers and supplies inside, waiting for a new use. Some would survive to see a new life, but many did not.

One of the most striking examples of an abandonment was the once grand Little Rock station. In 1968, the year after passenger service ended, the Rock Island completed work on an office building at Biddle Yard to consolidate operations there.

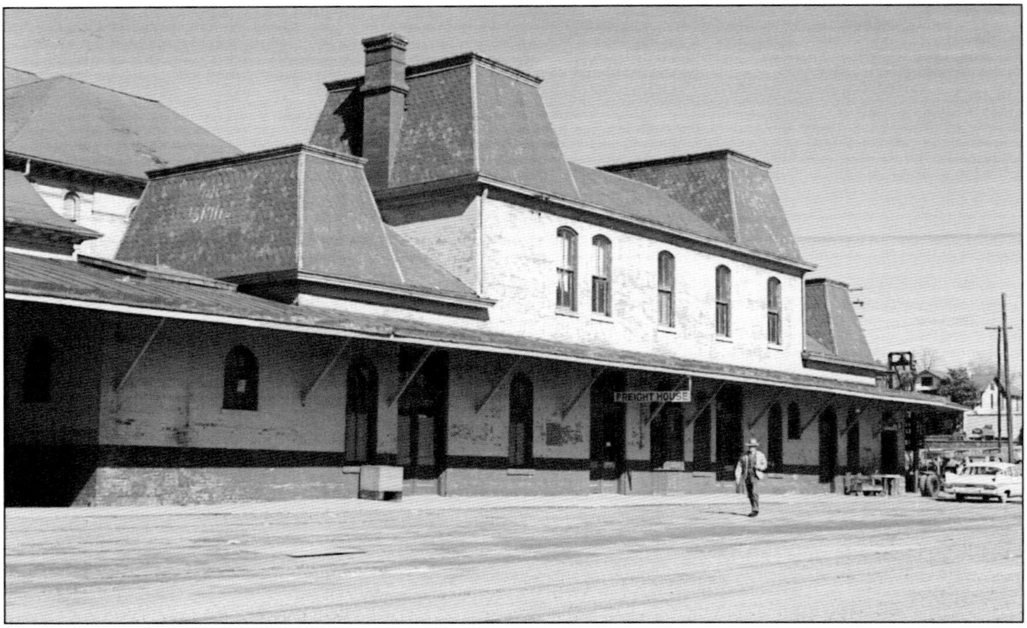

The Hot Springs station is pictured just before it was torn down in November 1961. Note the barely visible Rock Island logo on the roof. The Hot Springs Convention Center would be built in its place. The branch line to Hot Springs still had several key industries that kept it active, but obviously, the large passenger station was no longer needed. (Courtesy of Bill Pollard; photograph by Clifton Hull.)

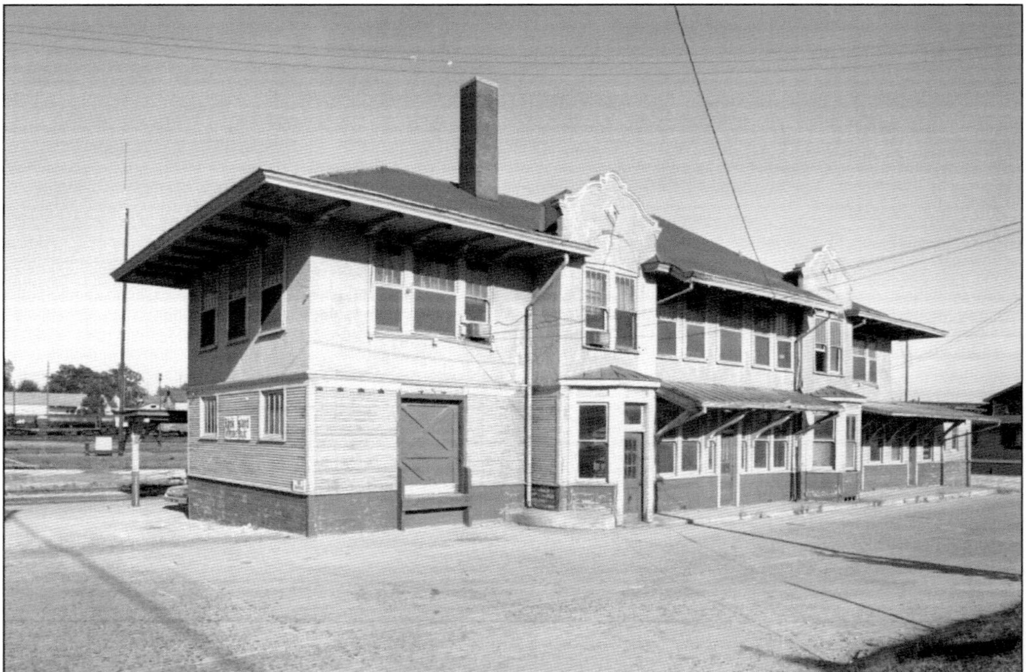

The large El Dorado station was looking rather desolate by the time this photograph was taken, likely in the 1960s. (Courtesy of the UALR Center for Arkansas History and Culture; photograph by Earl Saunders.)

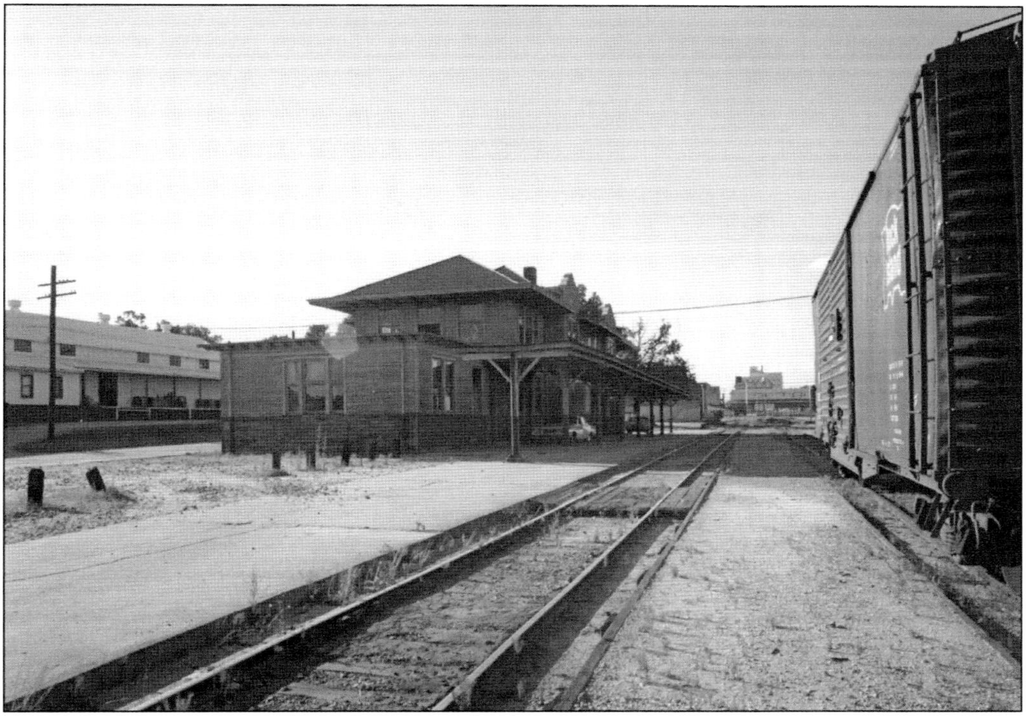

A Rock Island boxcar is seen outside the El Dorado station in the 1960s. (Courtesy of the UALR Center for Arkansas History and Culture; photograph by Earl Saunders.)

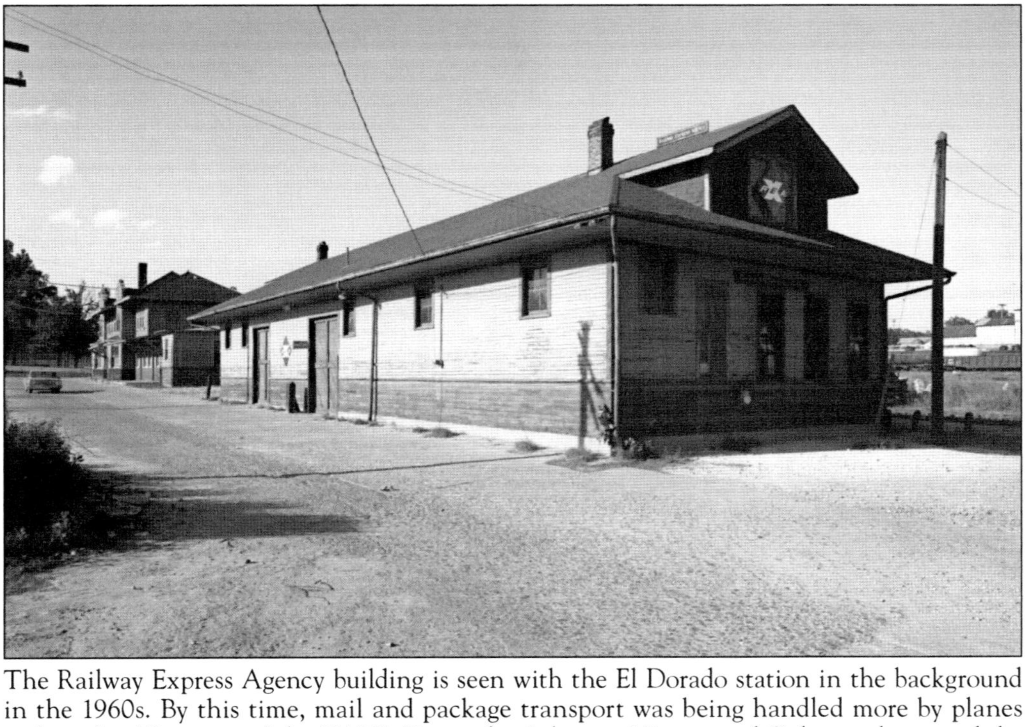

The Railway Express Agency building is seen with the El Dorado station in the background in the 1960s. By this time, mail and package transport was being handled more by planes and trucks. (Courtesy of the UALR Center for Arkansas History and Culture; photograph by Earl Saunders.)

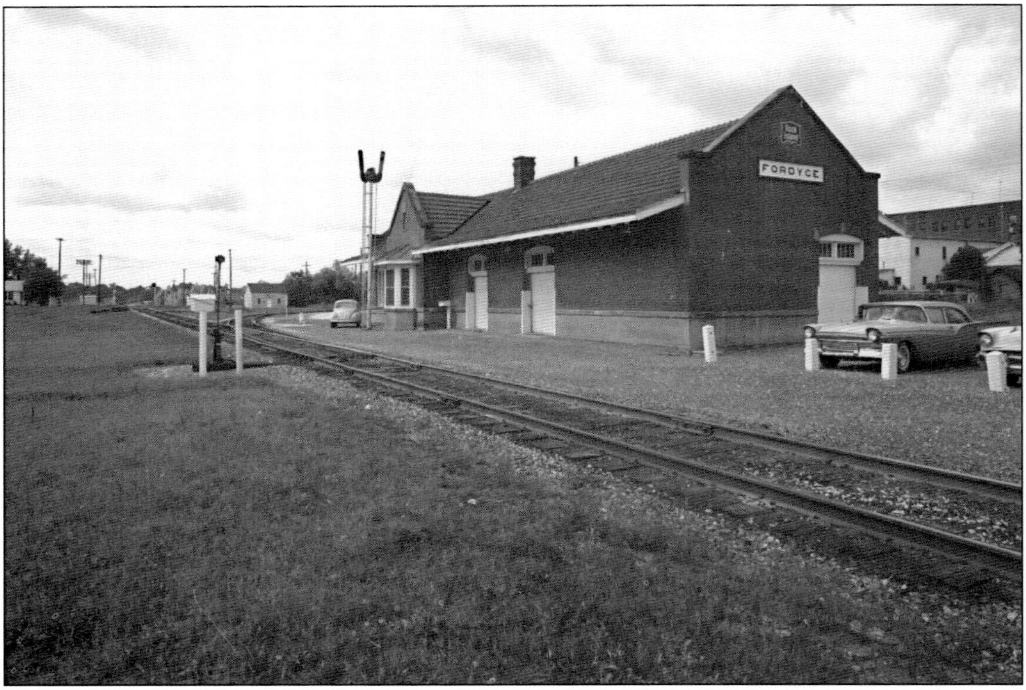

Fordyce continued to be busy as an interchange with the Cotton Belt Railroad, captured here in the 1960s. (Courtesy of the UALR Center for Arkansas History and Culture; photograph by Earl Saunders.)

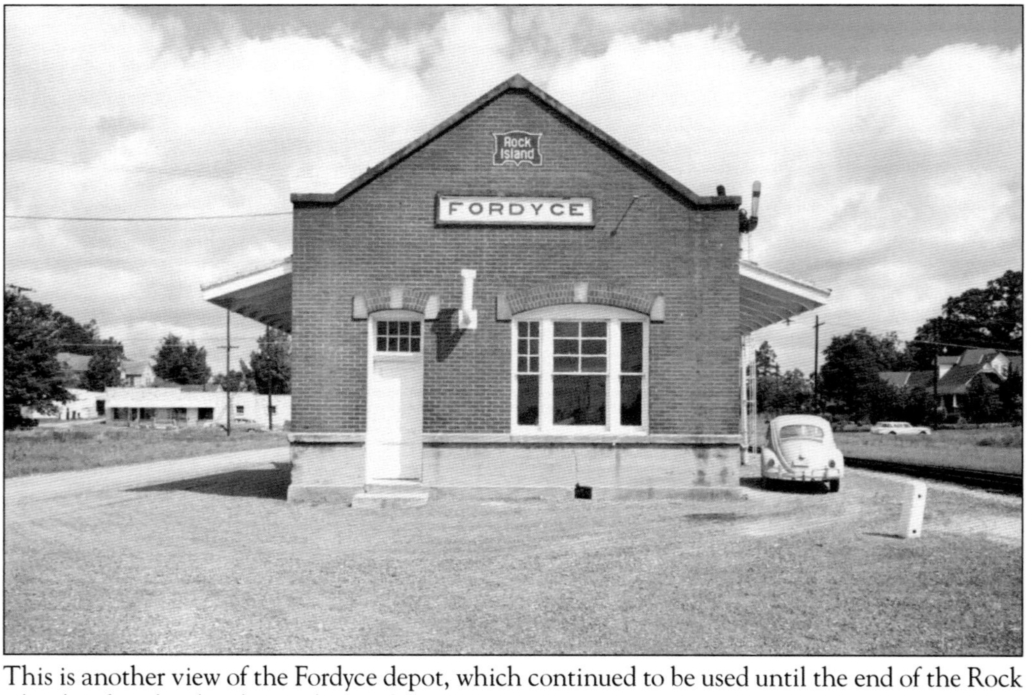

This is another view of the Fordyce depot, which continued to be used until the end of the Rock Island. After the shutdown, the Fordyce & Princeton Railroad took over this piece of track. So, fortunately, it never fell into disrepair. (Courtesy of the UALR Center for Arkansas History and Culture; photograph by Earl Saunders.)

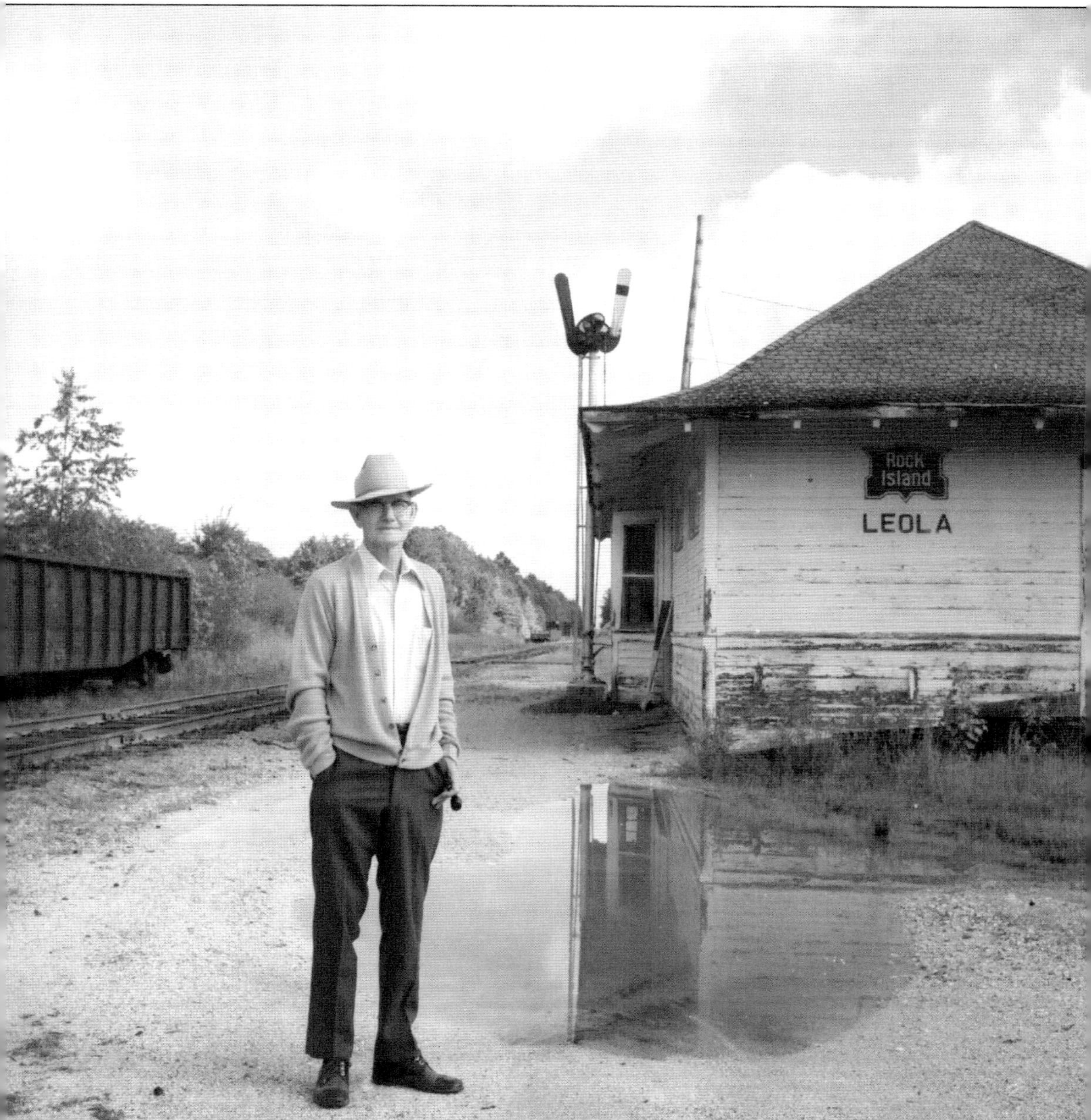

This is a May 15, 1976, portrait of longtime Leola station agent D.J. Lamb. The depot was closed the following month, with the station agent in Fordyce then handling Leola business as needed. (Courtesy of Bill Pollard; photograph by Clifton Hull.)

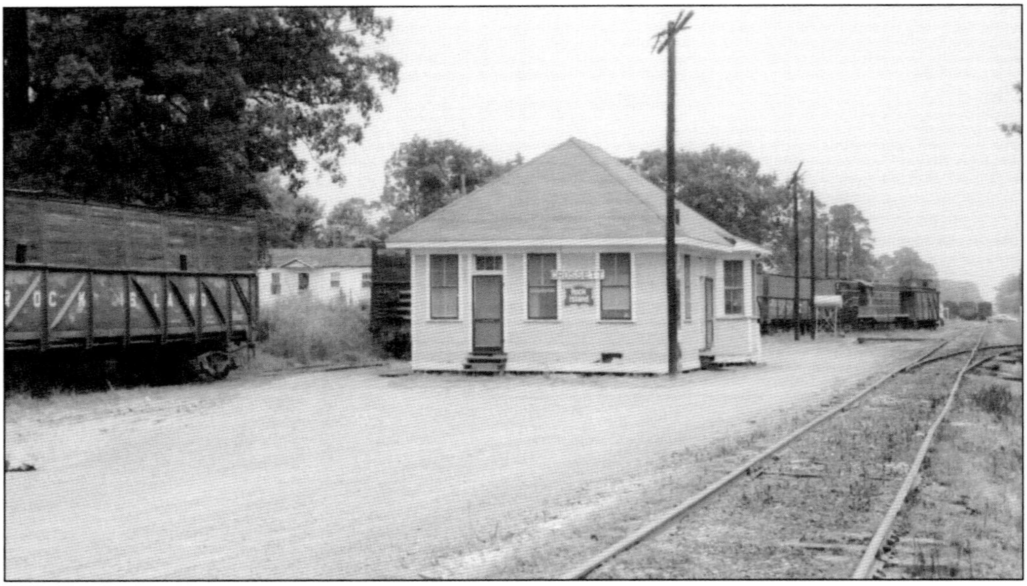

Crossett was at the end of a branch line near the southern border of Arkansas. It split off from the main line that extended into Louisiana via El Dorado. The branch line began at Tinsman, ending with the Crossett depot, pictured here in 1966. Note the engine and caboose in the background. (Courtesy of Bill Pollard; photograph by Clifton Hull.)

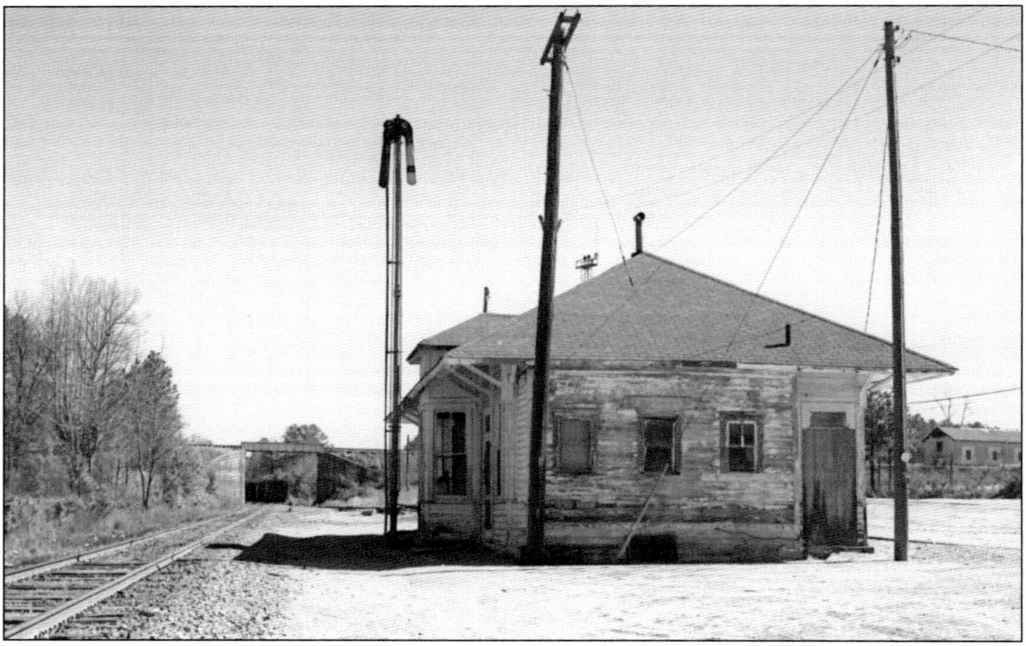

The depot at Bauxite is looking fairly ravaged on February 20, 1977. The town was named for the bauxite that was mined there and used in the production of aluminum. Many passengers arriving and departing here worked for mining companies, which saw a major spike in business serving the military during World War II. The overhead track crossing in the distance belonged to the Bauxite & Northern Railway Company, which linked industries with the Rock Island and Missouri Pacific. The Rock Island's track here was taken up in the years after its shutdown. (Courtesy of Bill Pollard; photograph by Clifton Hull.)

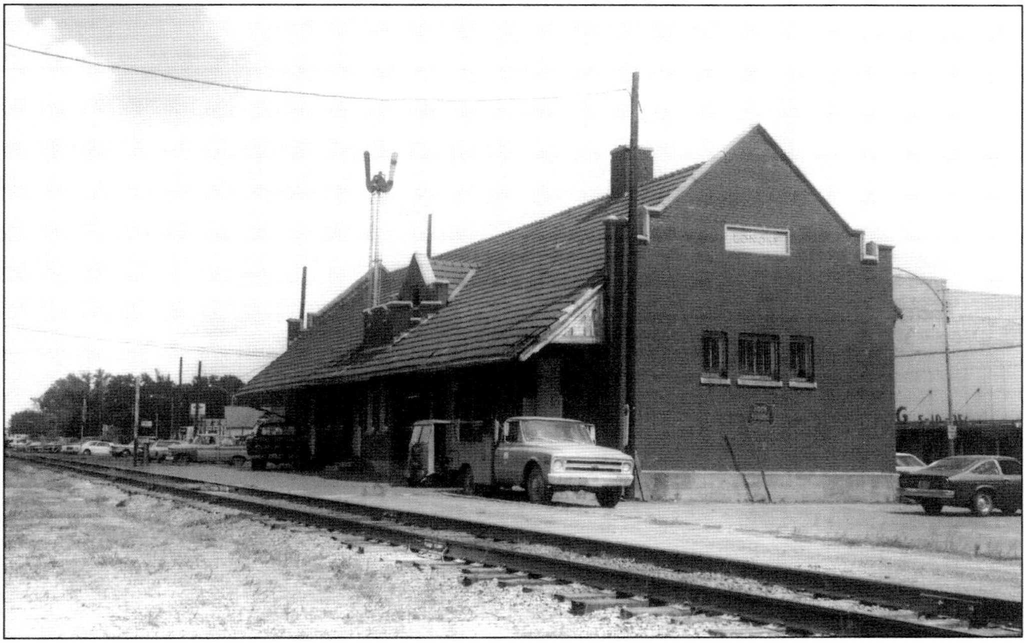

In the final years of the Rock Island and following its shutdown, photographer H.D. Conner produced a series of postcards showing many of the passenger depots. The Lonoke depot (pictured) was built in 1914. While passenger service had been gone more than a decade when this was taken, it was still in use by the railroad. This depot was well maintained, with the Lonoke Chamber of Commerce eventually taking over the building. (Author's collection.)

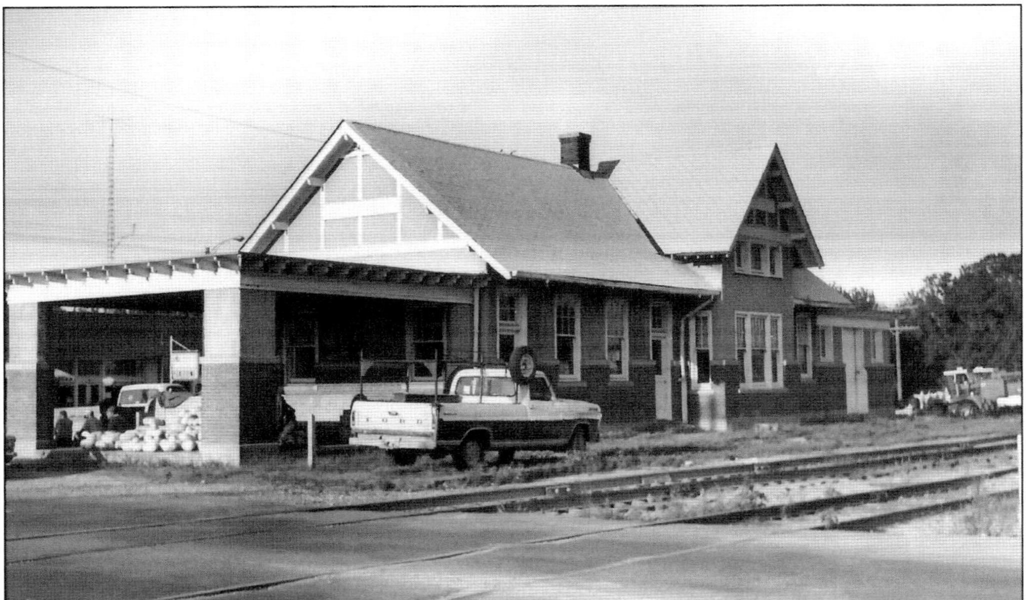

The next stop on the line heading east was the depot at Carlisle, photographed here in 1966. It appears that watermelons are being sold along the side of the building. This depot remained in good condition and later housed an insurance company. (Author's collection.)

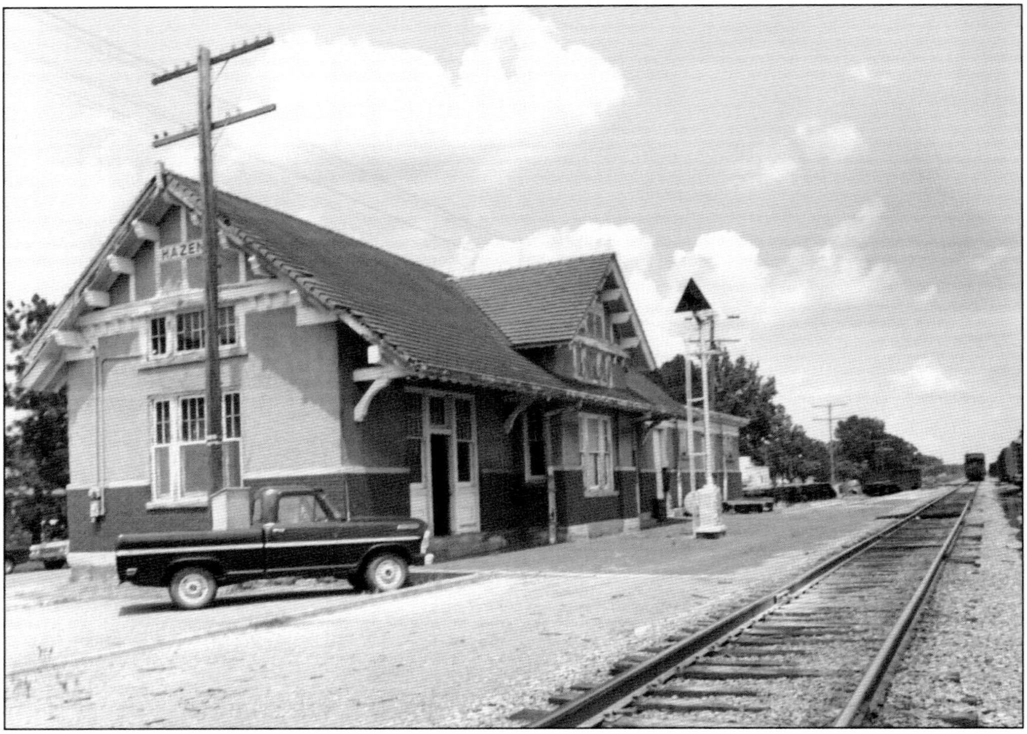

This 1960s or 1970s photograph shows the Hazen depot with a caboose visible in the distance. The town eventually acquired this stucco-and-brick building. (Courtesy of the UALR Center for Arkansas History and Culture; photograph by Earl Saunders.)

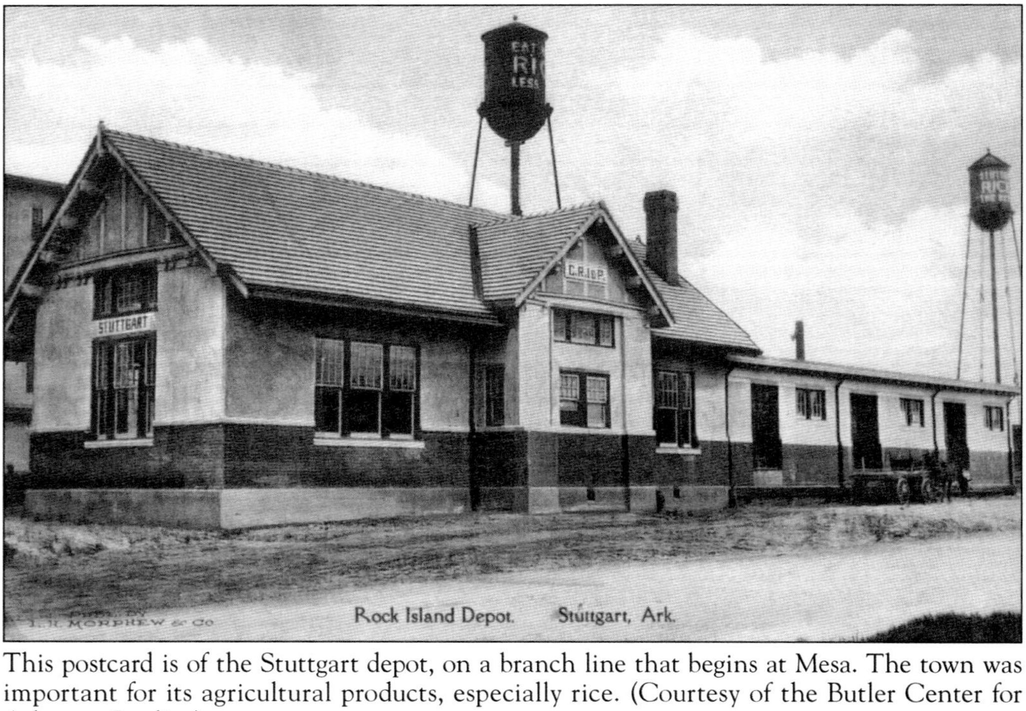

This postcard is of the Stuttgart depot, on a branch line that begins at Mesa. The town was important for its agricultural products, especially rice. (Courtesy of the Butler Center for Arkansas Studies.)

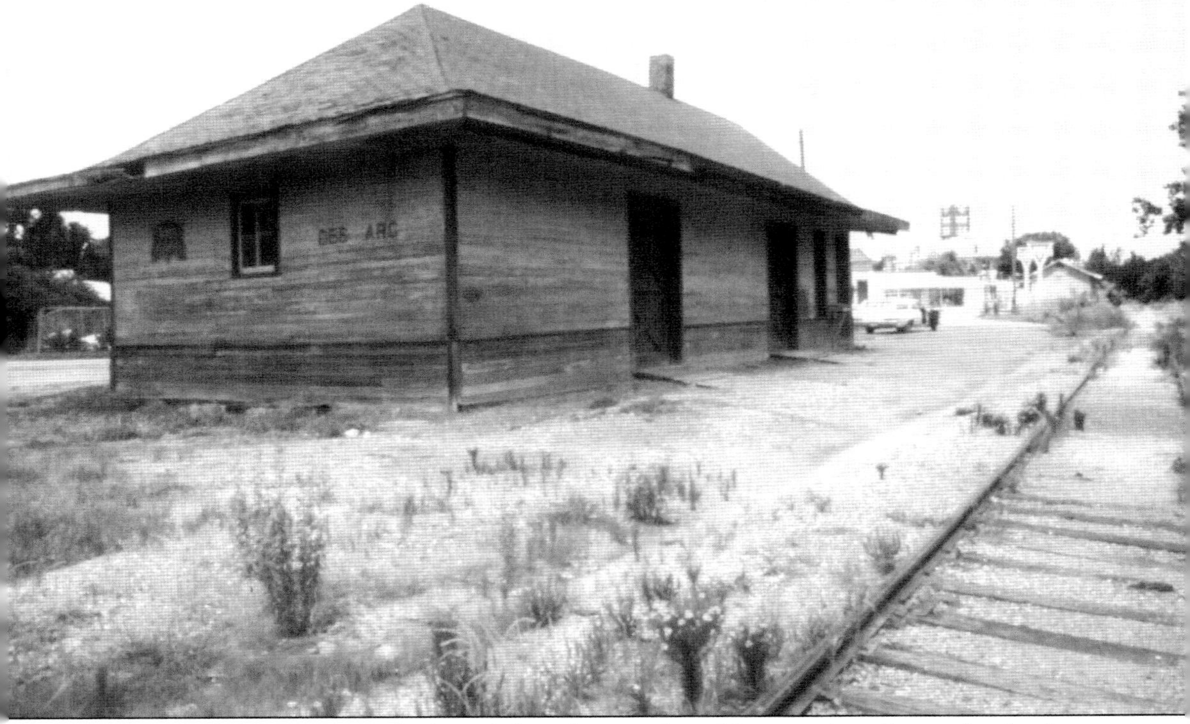

The Des Arc depot was along the branch line that ran from Mesa north to Searcy, but by the time this photograph was taken in the 1960s, the track north of here had been removed and this was the end of the line. (Courtesy of the UALR Center for Arkansas History and Culture; photograph by Earl Saunders.)

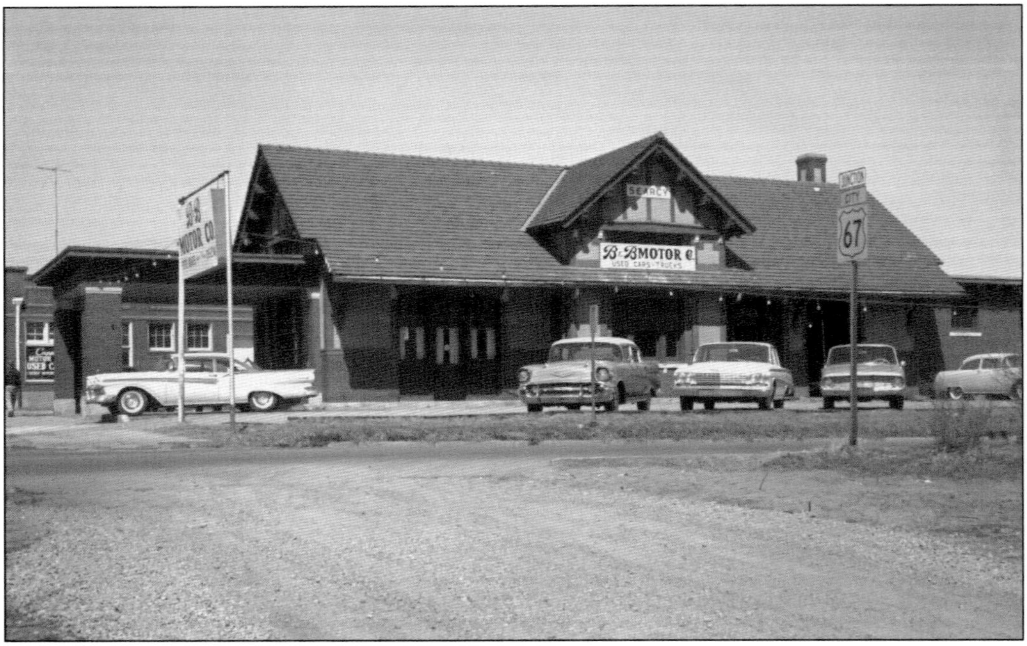

Here is the north end of the branch line to Searcy; however, by the time of this early-1960s photograph, the depot was no longer used by the railroad and housed a used car dealership called B&B Motor Company. (Courtesy of the UALR Center for Arkansas History and Culture; photograph by Earl Saunders.)

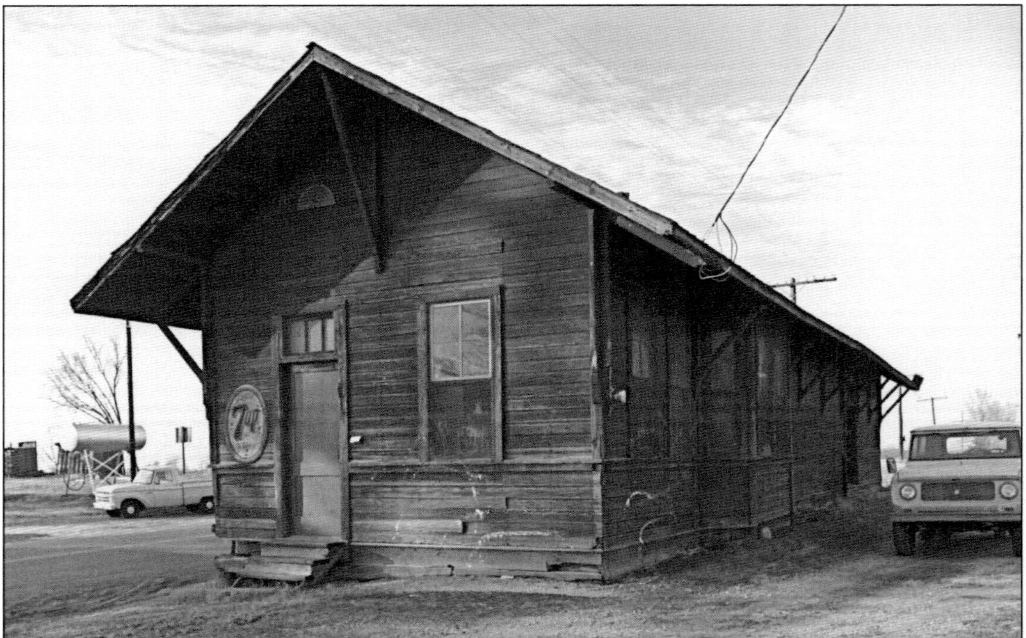

Here are the remains of what had been the depot at Weldon, which was part of the White and Black River branch line that ran up to Newport; but by this time, the rails had long since been removed. (Courtesy of the UALR Center for Arkansas History and Culture; photograph by Earl Saunders.)

Four

Arkansas River Bridge

The steel bridge over the Arkansas River was completed in 1899 for the Choctaw & Memphis Railroad, a subsidiary of the Choctaw, Oklahoma & Gulf, which was taken over a couple of years later by the Rock Island. With four spans, it was just over 1,600 feet long, not including the wooden approach on the North Little Rock side.

A contract for construction was let on March 21, 1899, with the first regularly scheduled train crossing it during a big celebration on December 10. When the Memphis & Little Rock Railroad was first surveying a route in the 1850s and considering a bridge, this was where it was planned. But problems completing the line and financial difficulties kept construction of a bridge at that time from ever moving beyond the planning stages.

Transfer boats originally moved railcars from one side of the river to the other. In 1873, the Cairo & Fulton Railroad built the Baring Cross Bridge to the west of this site, and the Memphis & Little Rock Railroad was able to arrange use of that bridge and laid a track through the middle of the downtown area that is today North Little Rock. But toward the end of the 1800s, as the Choctaw & Memphis announced aggressive expansion plans to build west, the deal to use the Baring Cross Bridge was ended, necessitating construction of the bridge later acquired by the Rock Island.

It proved to be a very sturdy bridge that in 1970 was renovated with a lift span to replace the swing bridge as part of improvements to the navigation channel of the Arkansas River. Then, in the years after the Rock Island closed, it survived more than a quarter century of sitting unused before being renovated into a pedestrian and cycling bridge at the Clinton Presidential Library.

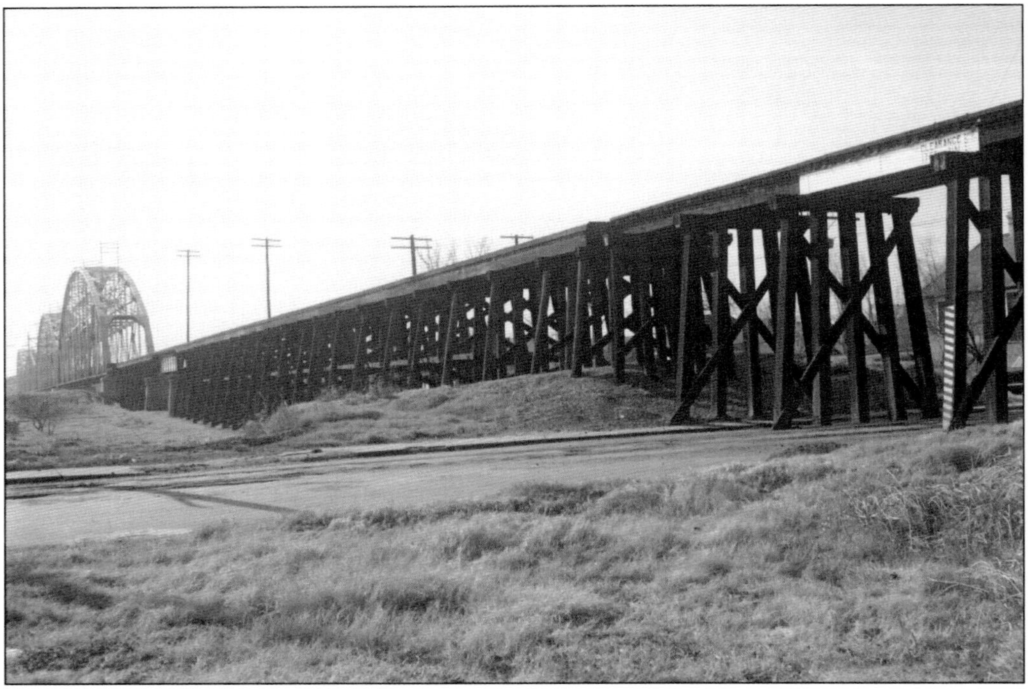

Pictured in the 1960s, wooden trestles were used for the northern approach to the Rock Island's Arkansas River Bridge in North Little Rock. The approach also included overpasses over several city streets. (Courtesy of the UALR Center for Arkansas History and Culture; photograph by Earl Saunders.)

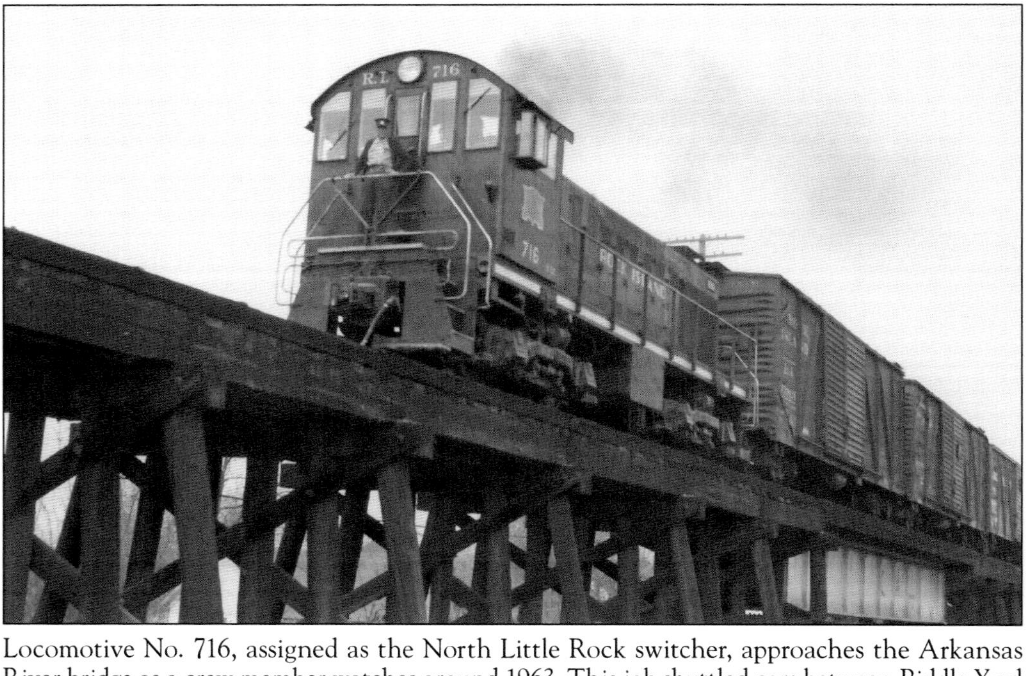

Locomotive No. 716, assigned as the North Little Rock switcher, approaches the Arkansas River bridge as a crew member watches around 1963. This job shuttled cars between Biddle Yard and North Little Rock and handled all switching north of the river. (Courtesy of Bill Pollard; photograph by Clifton Hull.)

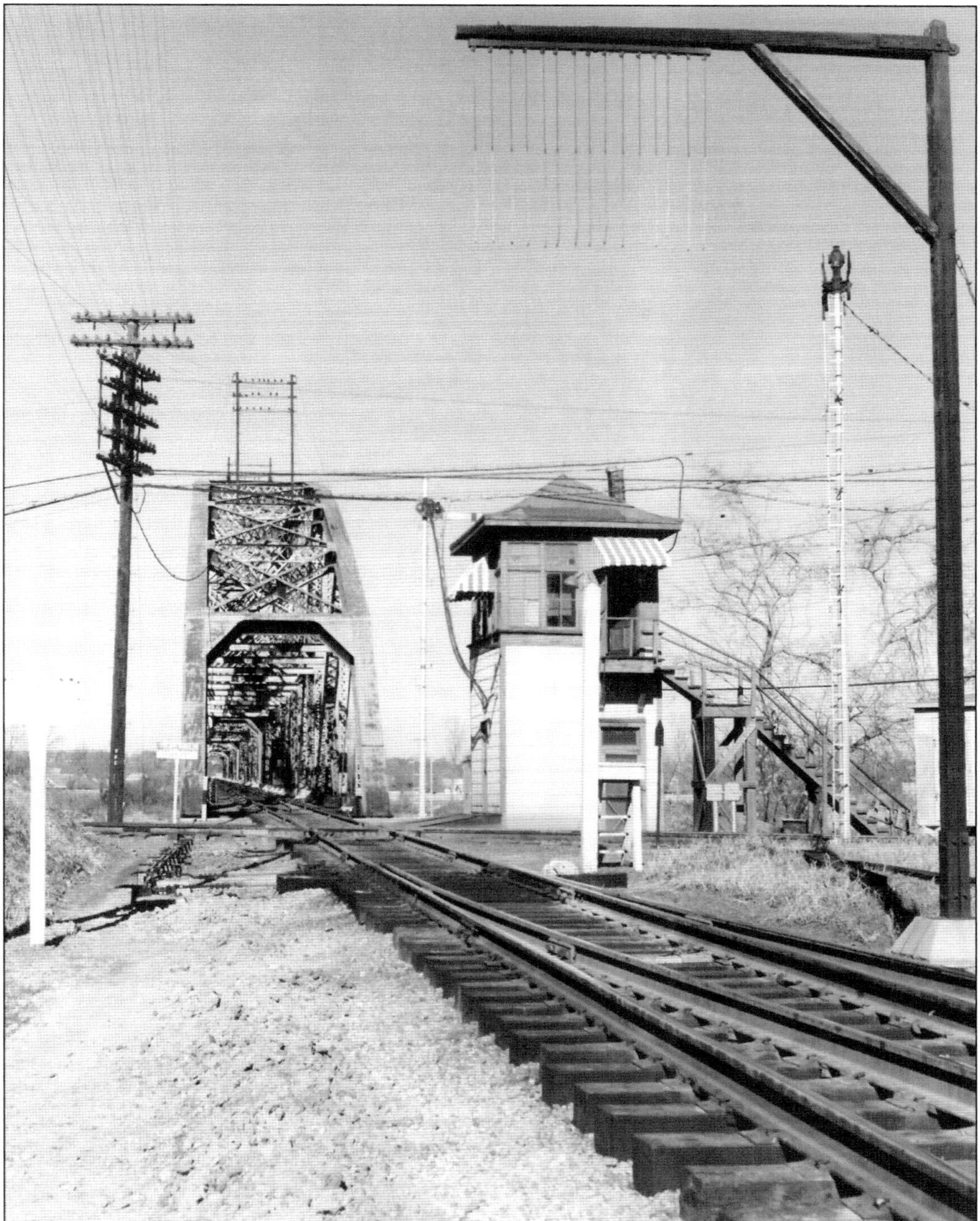

The two-story East Little Rock tower was a train order office for both Rock Island and Missouri Pacific to control traffic over the diamond where the two railroads crossed. Built in 1904, the tower is pictured here in 1961, two years before it was torn down and replaced with automatic signals. (Courtesy of Bill Pollard; photograph by Clifton Hull.)

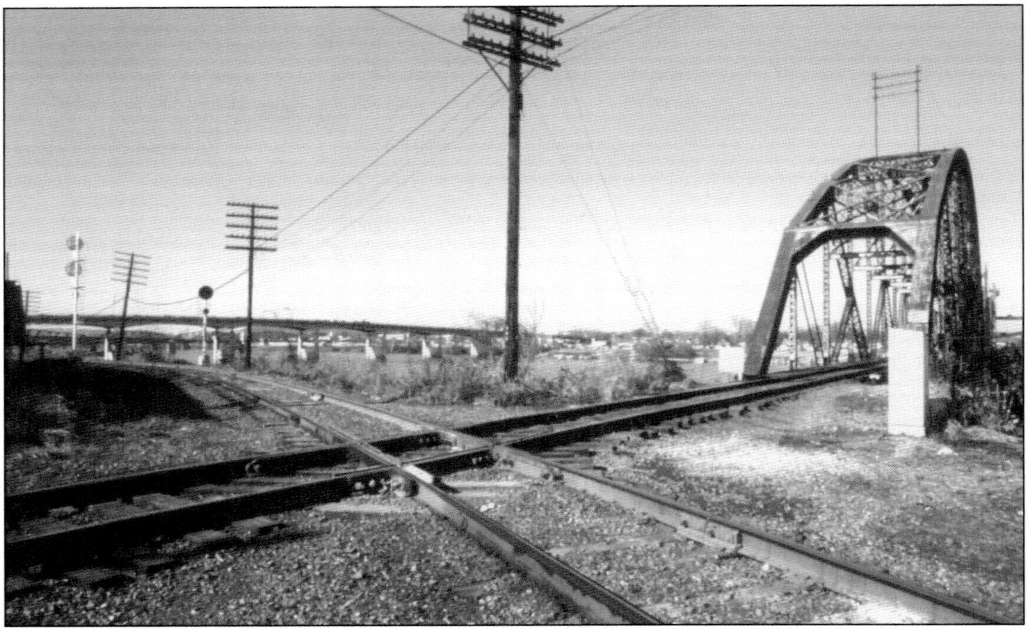

While taking a picture of the swing span being replaced with a lift span, photographer Earl Saunders made a point to also capture the diamond where the Rock Island and Missouri Pacific crossed directly in front of the south entrance to the Rock Island Bridge. (Courtesy of the UALR Center for Arkansas History and Culture; photograph by Earl Saunders.)

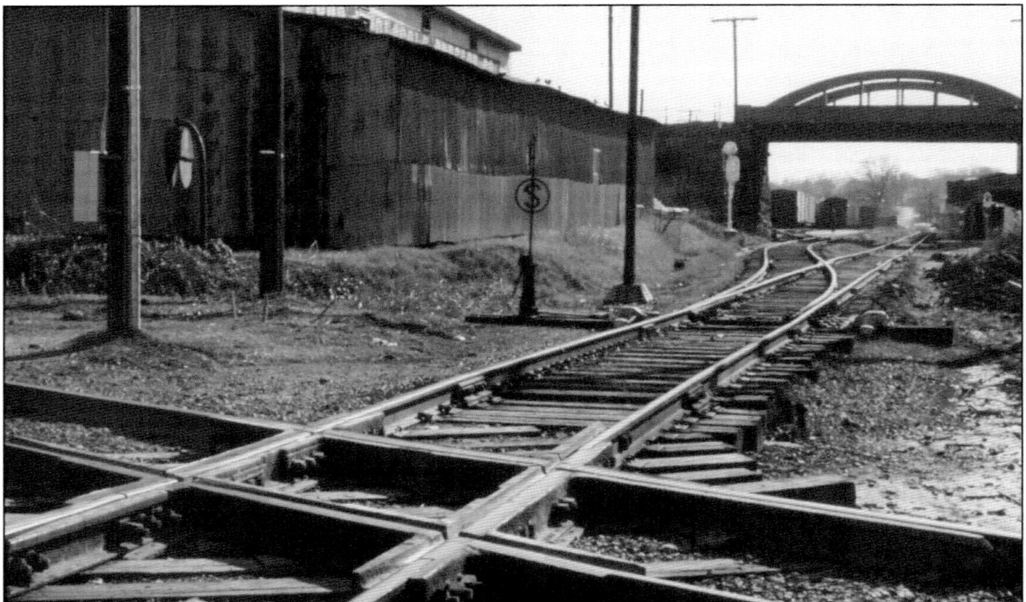

The Missouri Pacific Louisiana division track from Pine Bluff and McGehee passed through an industrial area near Little Rock's airport, across the Rock Island, and east to the Junction Bridge, which was that railroad's second crossing over the Arkansas River at Little Rock. Those rails would be removed with construction of the Clinton Presidential Library and visitors today would have no idea that spot was once where two busy rail lines intersected. (Courtesy of the UALR Center for Arkansas History and Culture; photograph by Earl Saunders.)

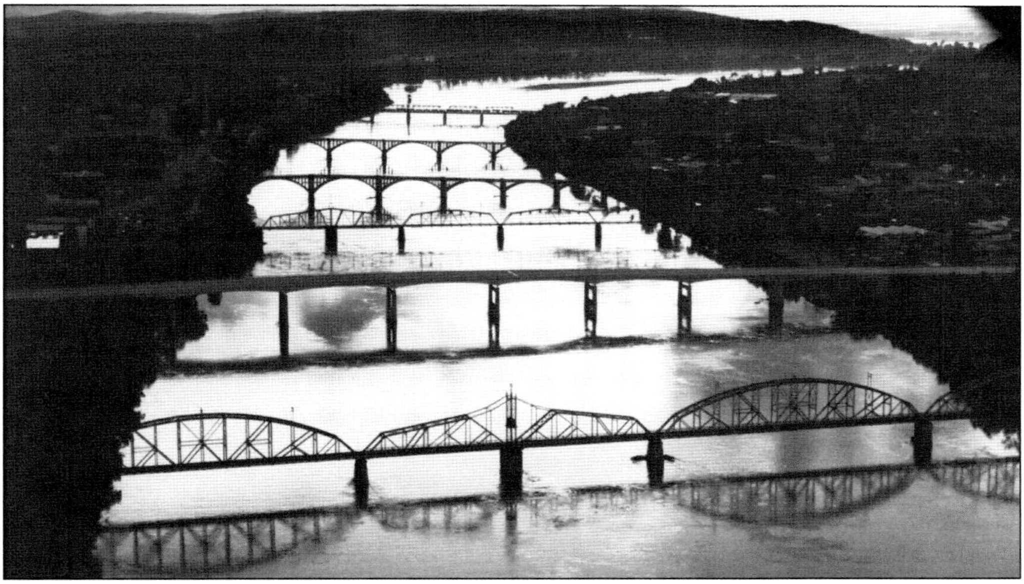

This aerial photograph shows the six bridges crossing the Arkansas River at Little Rock in 1965, with the Rock Island Bridge prominent in the foreground. This was just a few years before the swing span was replaced with a lift span. The photograph was taken to show the recently completed Interstate 30 bridge, which is the next bridge up after the Rock Island Bridge. (Courtesy of the Arkansas Highway and Transportation Department; photograph by Johnnie Gray.)

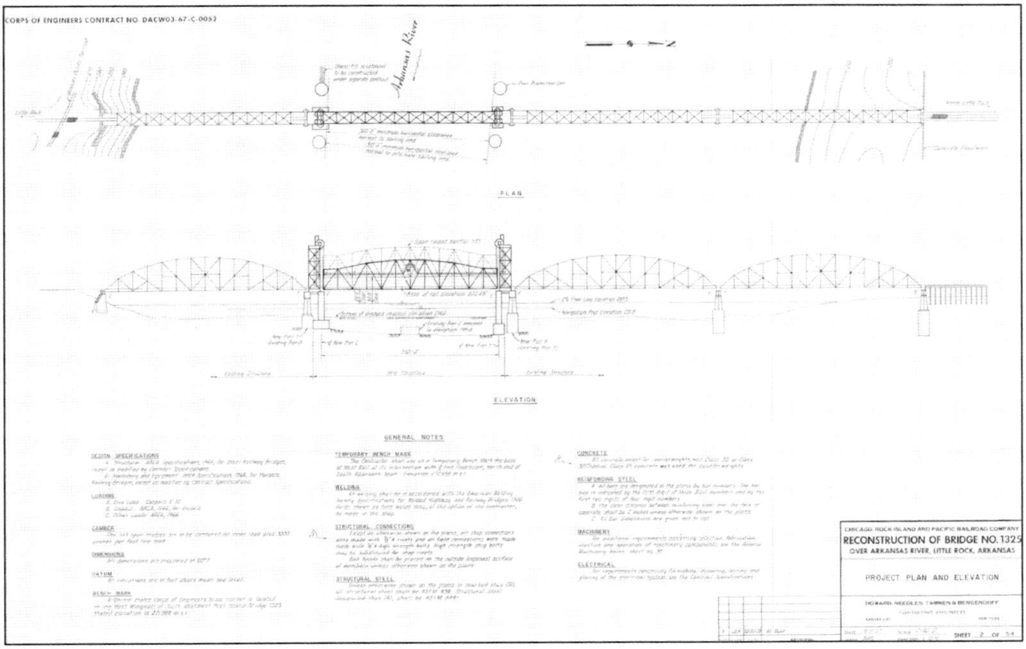

To make the Arkansas River suitable for commercial barge traffic year-round, the McClellan-Kerr Navigation System was devised. It used a series of locks and dams to artificially deepen and widen the river to allow river traffic to flow between the Mississippi River and Tulsa, Oklahoma. As part of this, older bridges over the Arkansas River had to have sections rebuilt or have lift spans installed. Here is a design plan from 1967 of the lift span to be installed on the Rock Island Bridge. (Courtesy of Union Pacific Railroad.)

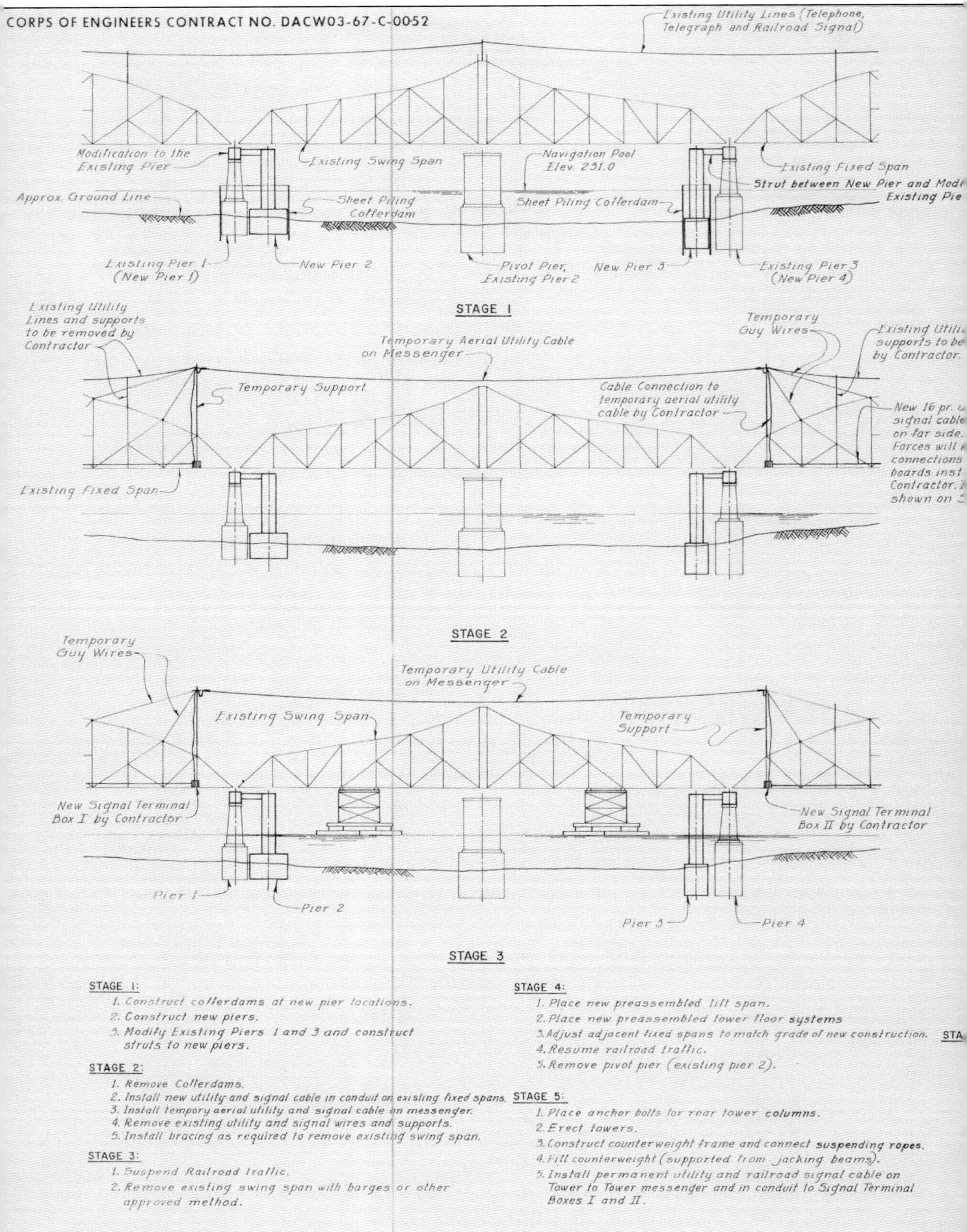

Pictured here is detailed breakdown of the construction sequence for removing the swing span

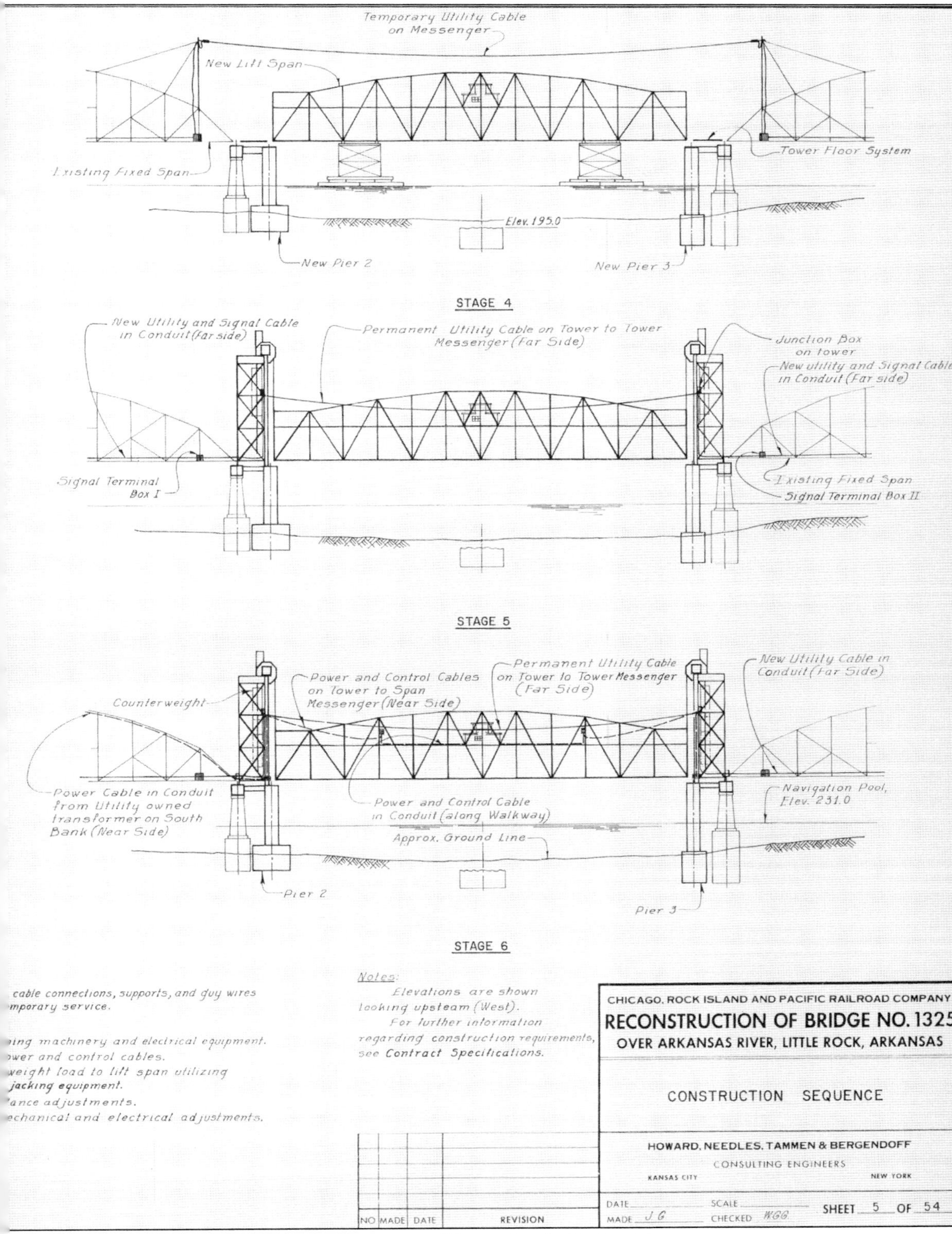

and then installing the lift span. (Courtesy of Union Pacific Railroad.)

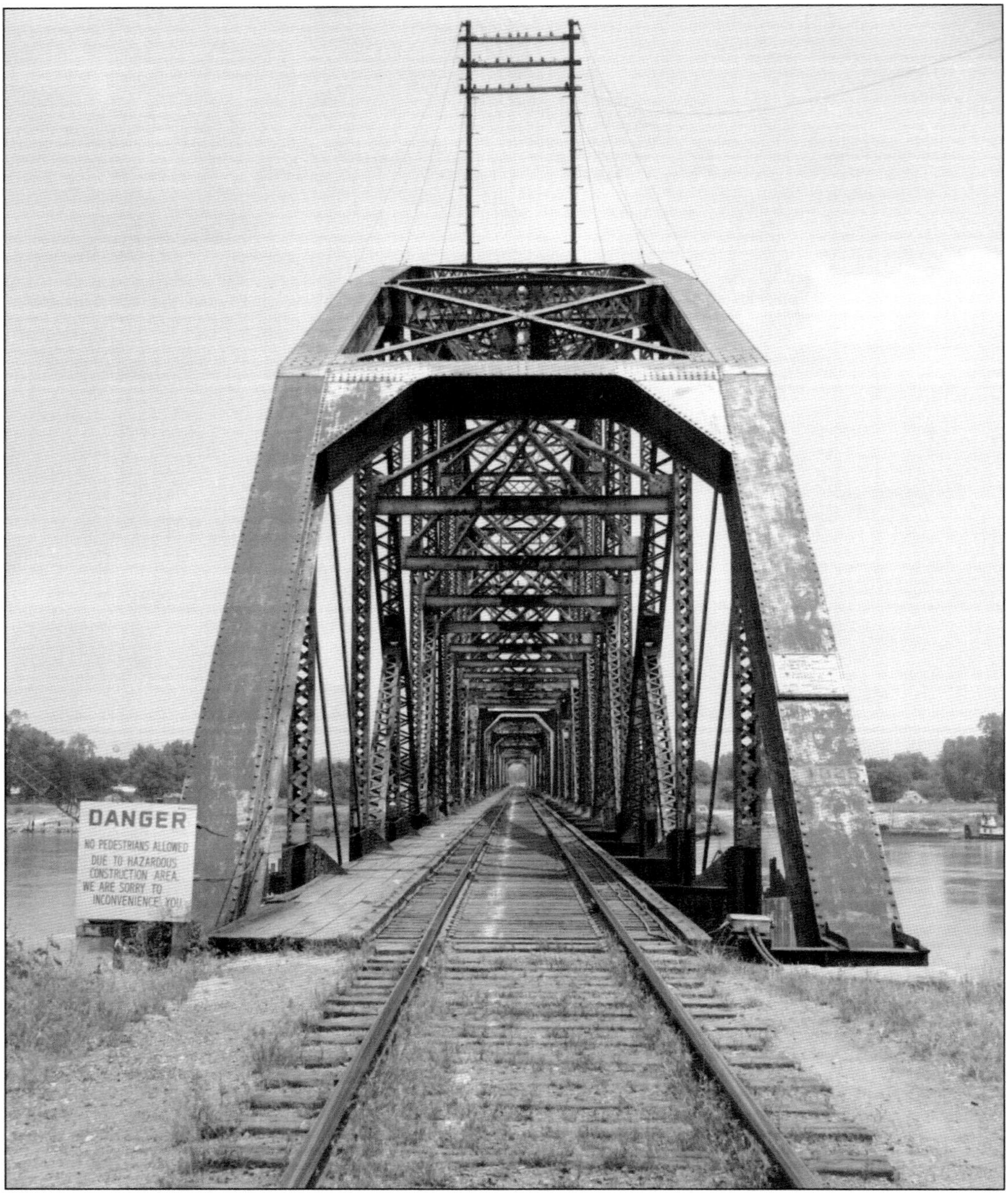

This May 23, 1970, photograph was taken with a view looking across the Arkansas River bridge from the south entrance. The sign to the left reads, "Danger. No pedestrians allowed due to hazardous construction area. We are sorry to inconvenience you." (Courtesy of Bill Pollard; photograph by Clifton Hull.)

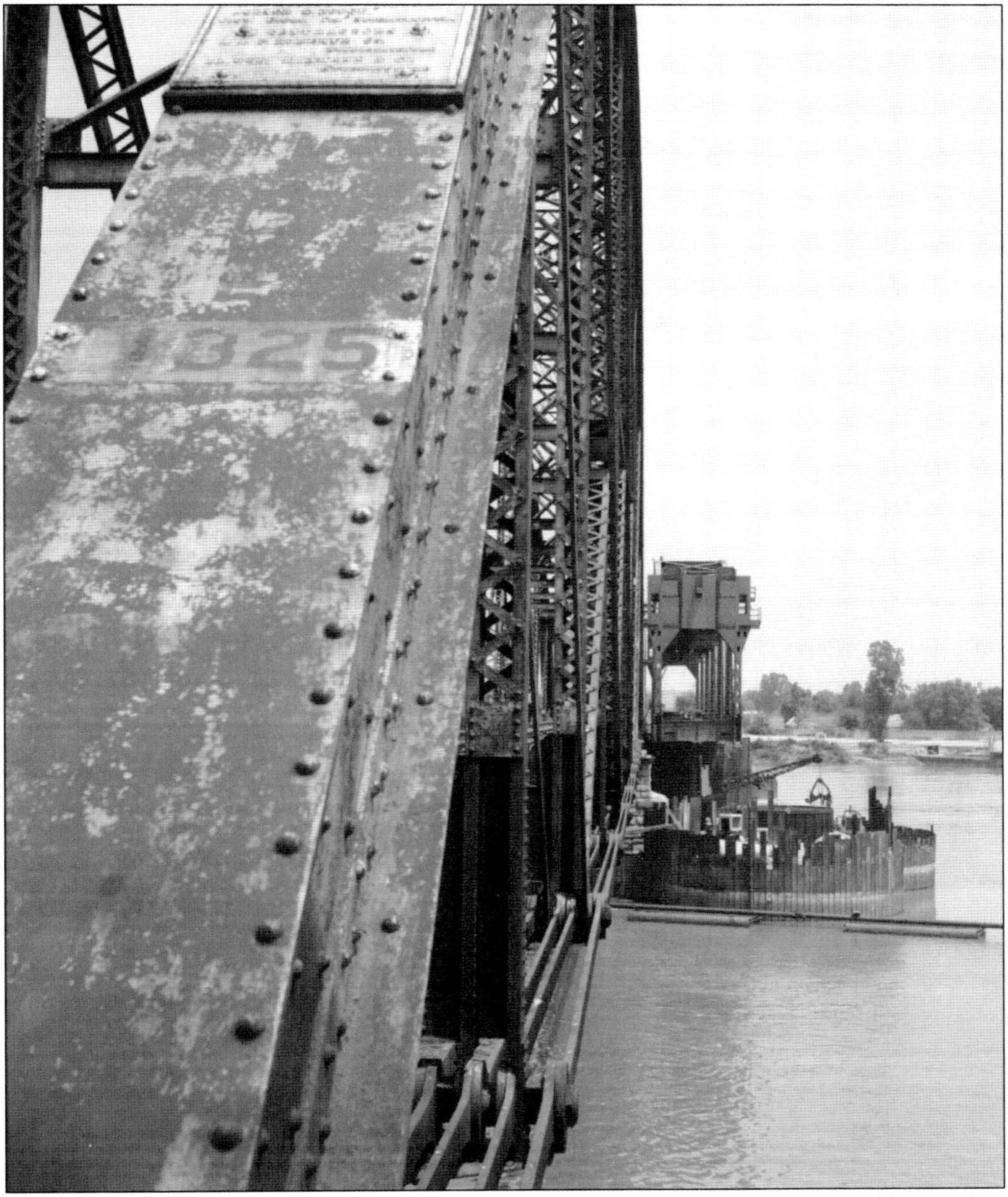

Here, pier protection cells are being constructed in the Arkansas River, which would help define the navigation channel for barge traffic. The lift span that would soon replace the swing span is visible beside the bridge, waiting to be lifted into place. The numeral 1325 indicates the bridge number in Rock Island's bridge inventory system, with the bridge being 132.5 miles from Memphis. Also, note the bridge's dedication plaque toward the top; in the 1990s, it disappeared while the bridge was not in use. (Courtesy of Bill Pollard; photograph by Clifton Hull.)

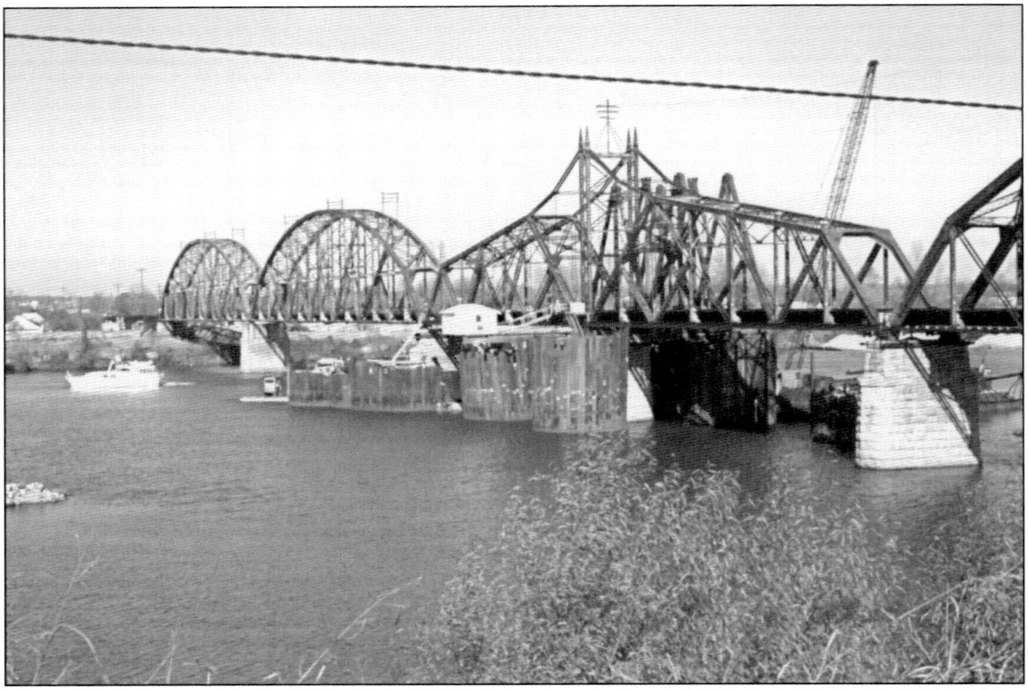

Construction of the pier protection cells is nearly complete, with a crane on the east side of the bridge on a barge in the Arkansas River that was used to lift materials in place. (Courtesy of the UALR Center for Arkansas History and Culture; photograph by Earl Saunders.)

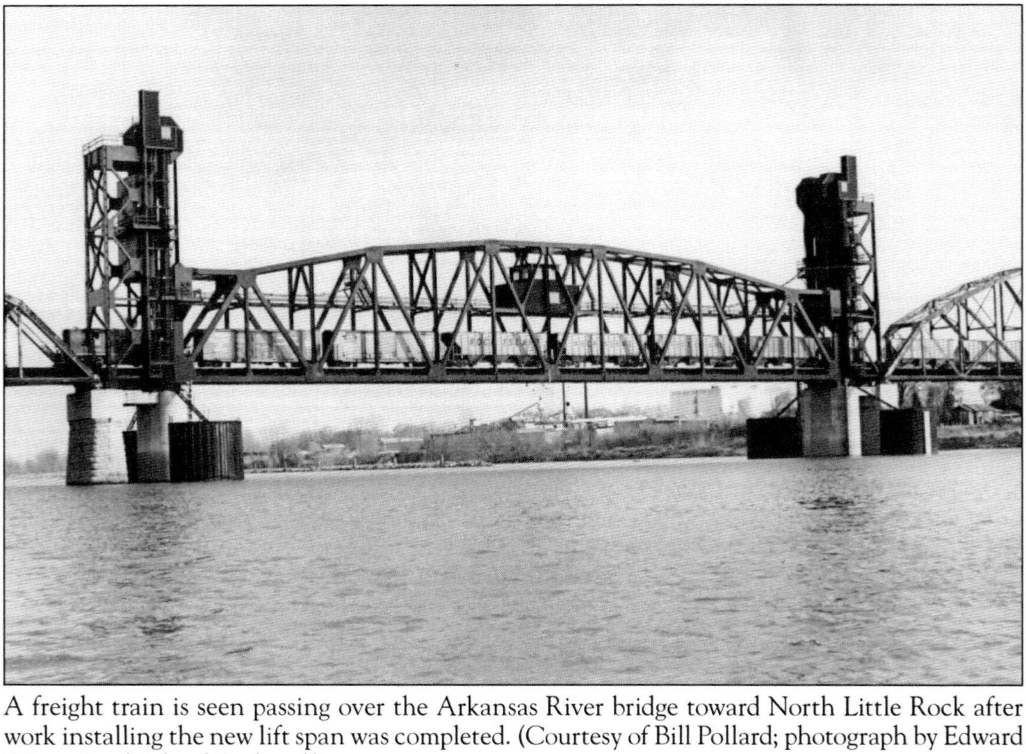

A freight train is seen passing over the Arkansas River bridge toward North Little Rock after work installing the new lift span was completed. (Courtesy of Bill Pollard; photograph by Edward Wojas, Rock Island Railroad.)

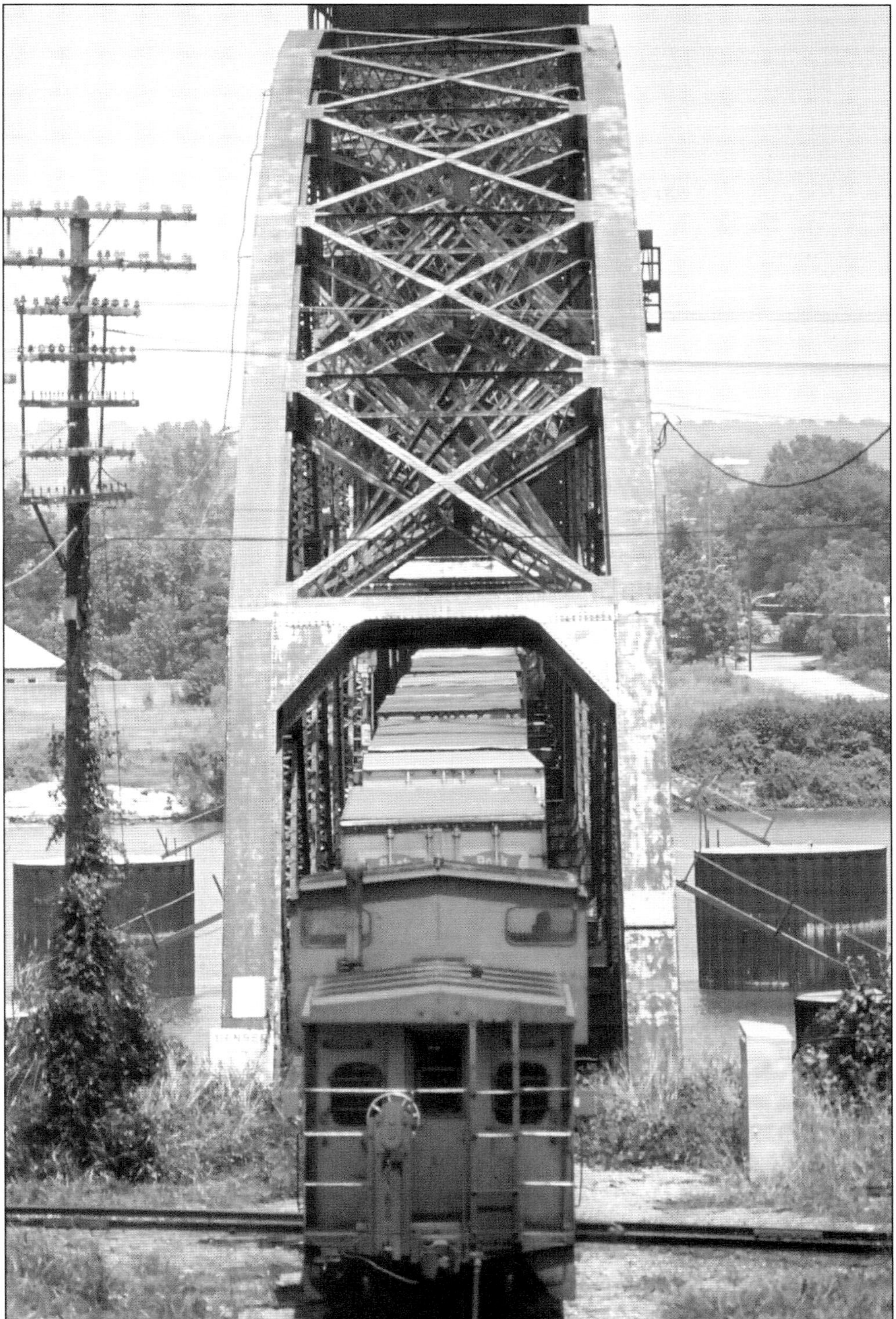

A caboose at the end of a train passes into North Little Rock near the south entrance of the Arkansas River bridge in August 1973. This view is from the perspective of the now removed East Second Street overpass. (Photograph by Bill Pollard.)

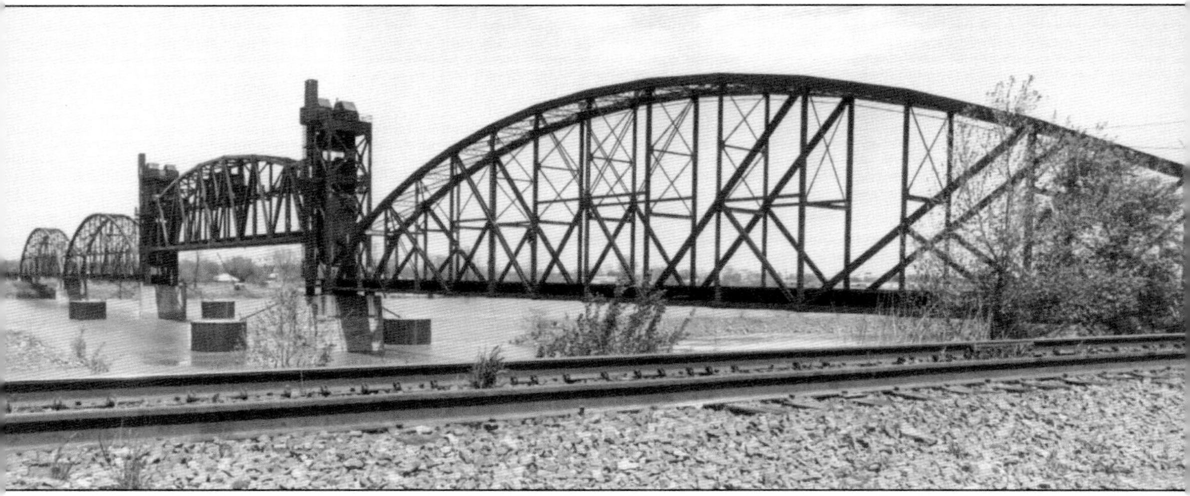

After the Rock Island was shut down in 1980, the Arkansas River bridge continued to be used for a few years by the Little Rock & Western Railway, which was created to operate a stretch of track from Little Rock to Perry. This photograph was taken on April 23, 1983. But in 1984, a spur was built linking the former Rock Island track with the Missouri Pacific (MP) track near Union Station, which allowed access to the MP's Baring Cross Bridge and North Little Rock yard. The nearby crossing where the former Rock Island track crossed the Missouri Pacific was then removed, severing the Little Rock & Western's access to Biddle Yard and the Rock Island Bridge. Railroad historian Bill Pollard estimates that November 1984 was likely when the last train ever crossed the Rock Island Bridge over the Arkansas River. Power was disconnected, except for navigation lights for barges, and the lift span was locked in the "up" position. (*Arkansas Democrat-Gazette* file photograph.)

Five

FREIGHT SERVICE

Handling freight was the bread and butter of the Rock Island, and the key location for assembling and disassembling trains and the serving of equipment for most of its years in Arkansas was Biddle Yard in Little Rock. After assuming control of the Choctaw, Oklahoma & Gulf in 1902, it initially used the rail yard in what is today North Little Rock, but space there was limited. That had originally been a termination point until the Arkansas River bridge was finished in 1899. The Rock Island acquired a large piece of land just a couple of miles down the track south of the Little Rock station in 1907 and steadily began building it up to get above the floodplain. Officially, the railroad moved its yard office there in 1917, but the transition had been under way for a decade before that.

Working on freight trains could be grueling work, switching cars out at different destinations, but many like Joe "Buzzy" Rook, who started as a brakeman with the Rock Island in 1951 out of Little Rock, preferred it to passenger service because he would not be away from home as much. Passenger crews would get on in Little Rock, take trains to Booneville, stay overnight, take a train the next day to Memphis, then come back to Little Rock.

"If I caught the passenger train, I was gone for three days and maybe the fellow right behind me would catch a freight run to Booneville and be back home before I ever left Booneville. And you wouldn't make as much. The passenger rate wasn't as much as the freight rate on pay," Rook said in a 2003 interview.

Over the decades, the diesel locomotives got more powerful and freight trains became longer as the railroad would add more engines to the front of trains to carry more tonnage. And of course, at the end of most trains were cabooses, which evolved from having cupolas sticking out at the top where conductors would ride to having bay windows sticking out of the sides of the cabooses.

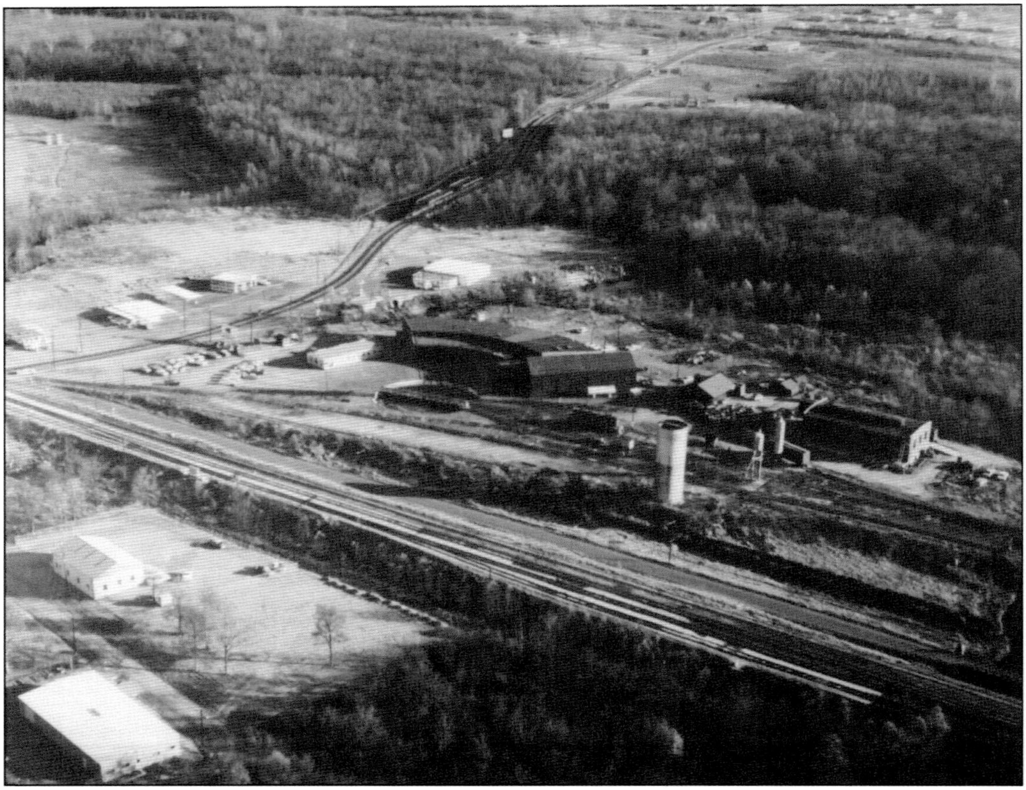

This aerial view shows the eastern edge of Biddle Yard, which included the roundhouse. The long shadows suggest this photograph was taken in the late afternoon; however, the year is unknown. (Clifton Hull Collection, courtesy of Bill Pollard.)

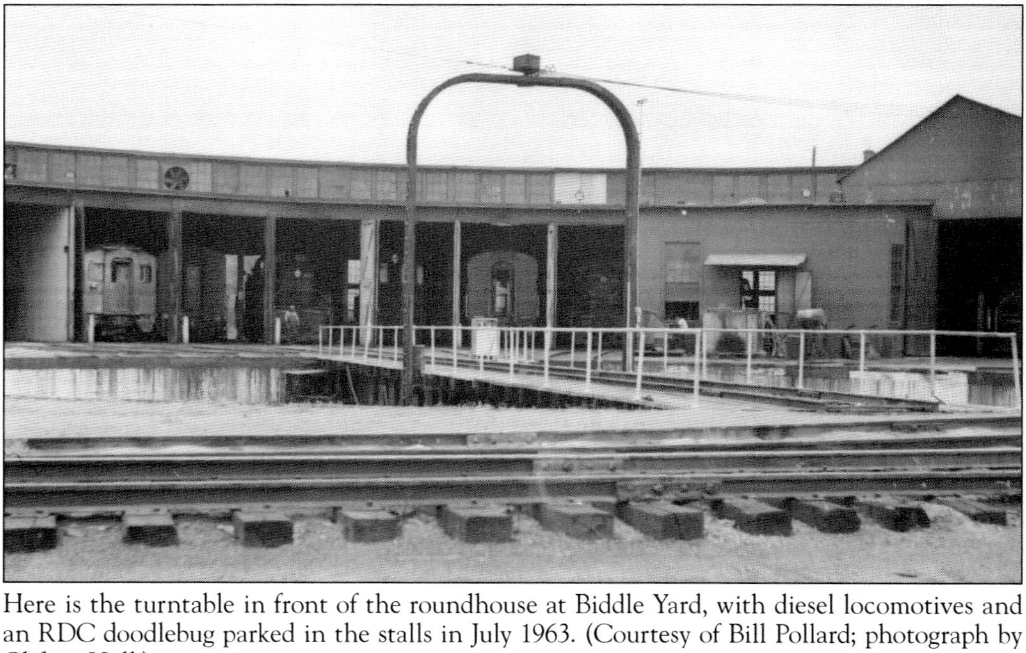

Here is the turntable in front of the roundhouse at Biddle Yard, with diesel locomotives and an RDC doodlebug parked in the stalls in July 1963. (Courtesy of Bill Pollard; photograph by Clifton Hull.)

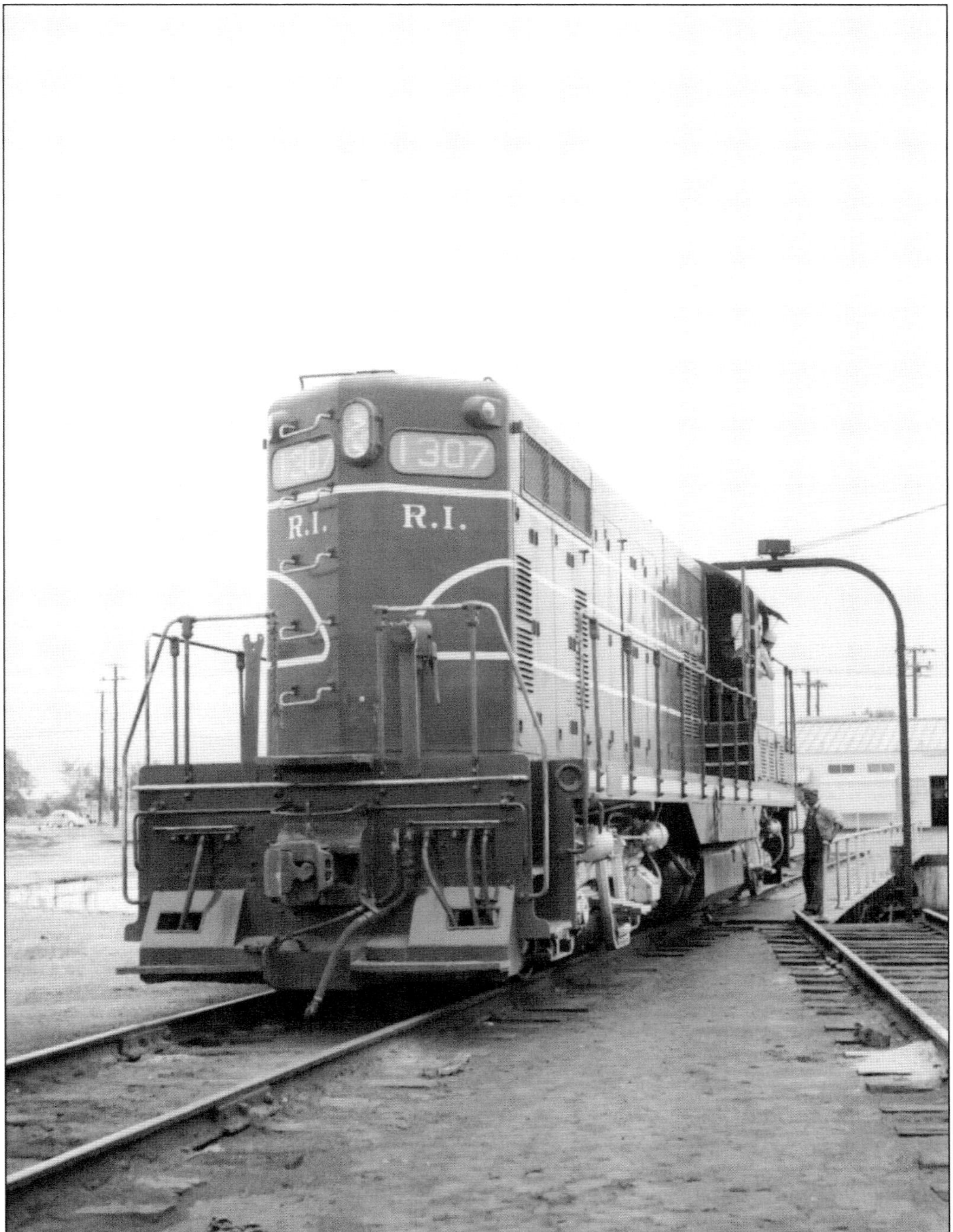

Engine No. 1307, a GP-7, eases off the turntable at Biddle Yard in July 1963 with guidance from an employee on the ground. (Courtesy of Bill Pollard; photograph by Clifton Hull.)

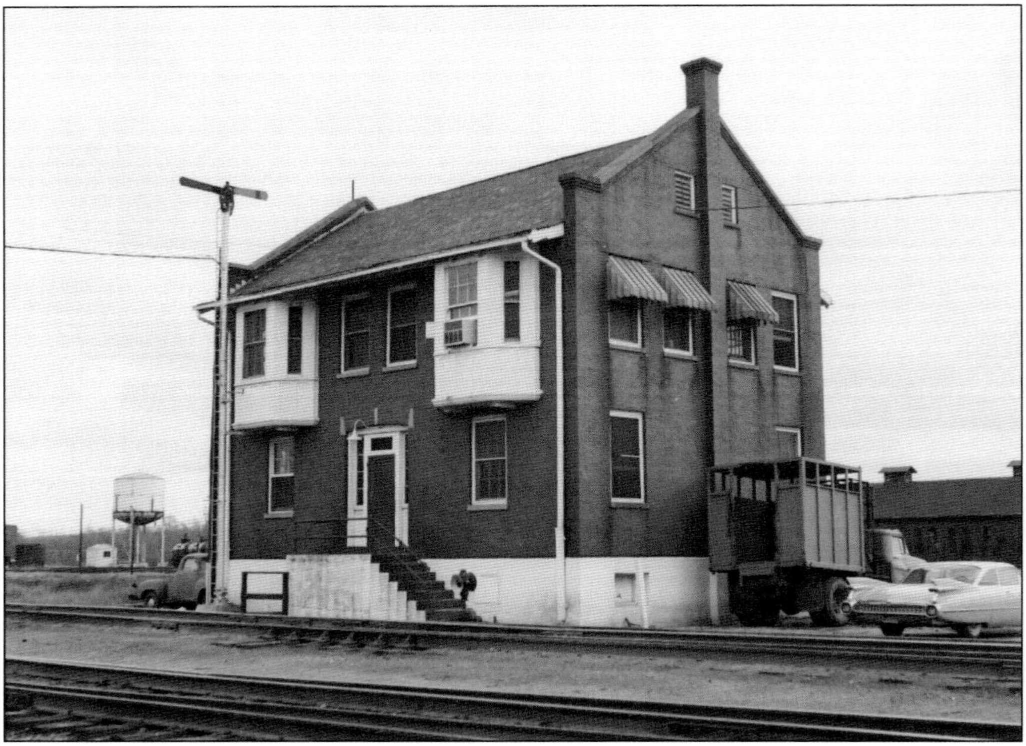

The Biddle Yard office was built in 1912. In this 1961 photograph, note the semaphore train order signal with blades in the "stop" position for both directions. This signal was removed in the 1960s. (Courtesy of Bill Pollard; photograph by Clifton Hull.)

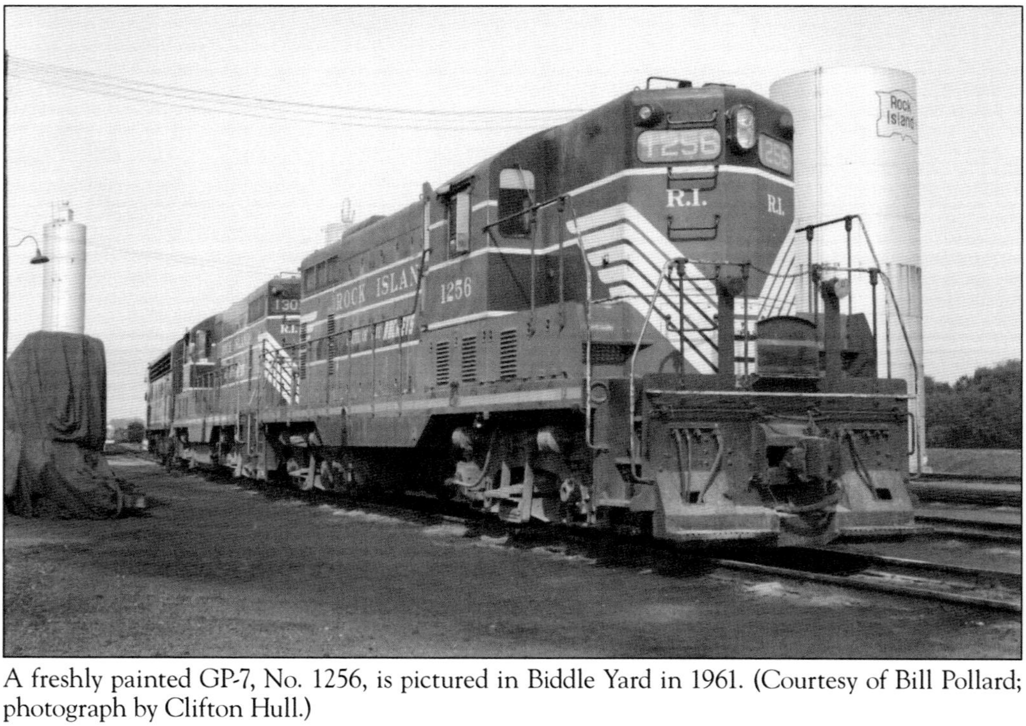

A freshly painted GP-7, No. 1256, is pictured in Biddle Yard in 1961. (Courtesy of Bill Pollard; photograph by Clifton Hull.)

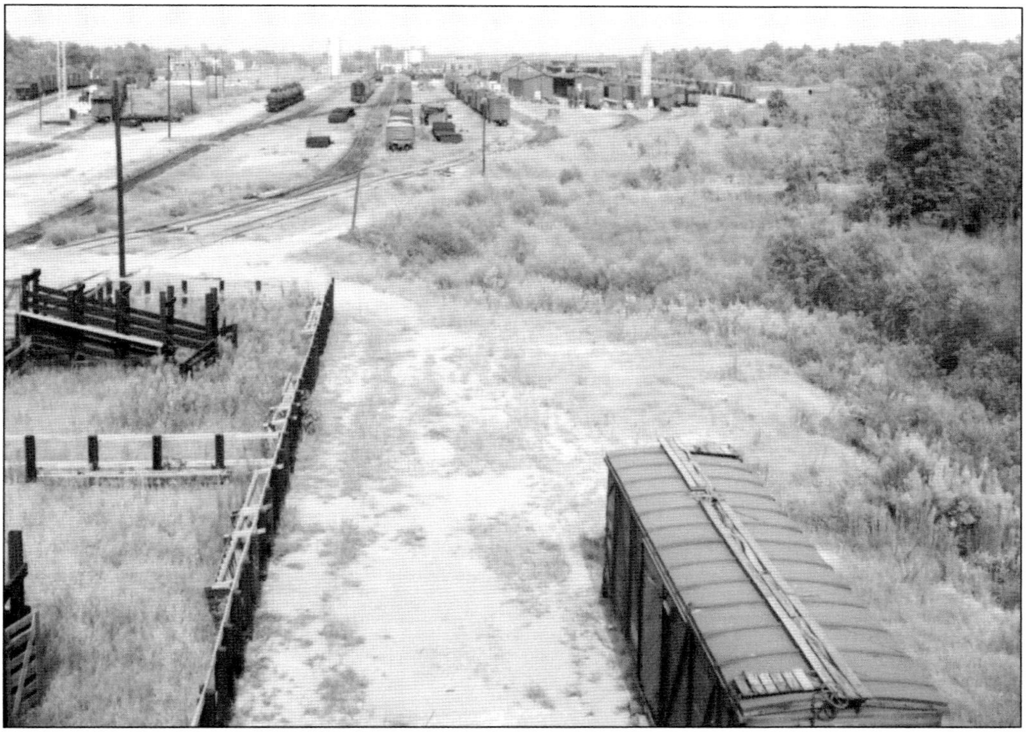

Taken from the Arch Street overpass in August 1963, this photograph of the western end of Biddle Yard shows the old stock pens in the foreground. (Courtesy of Bill Pollard; photograph by Clifton Hull.)

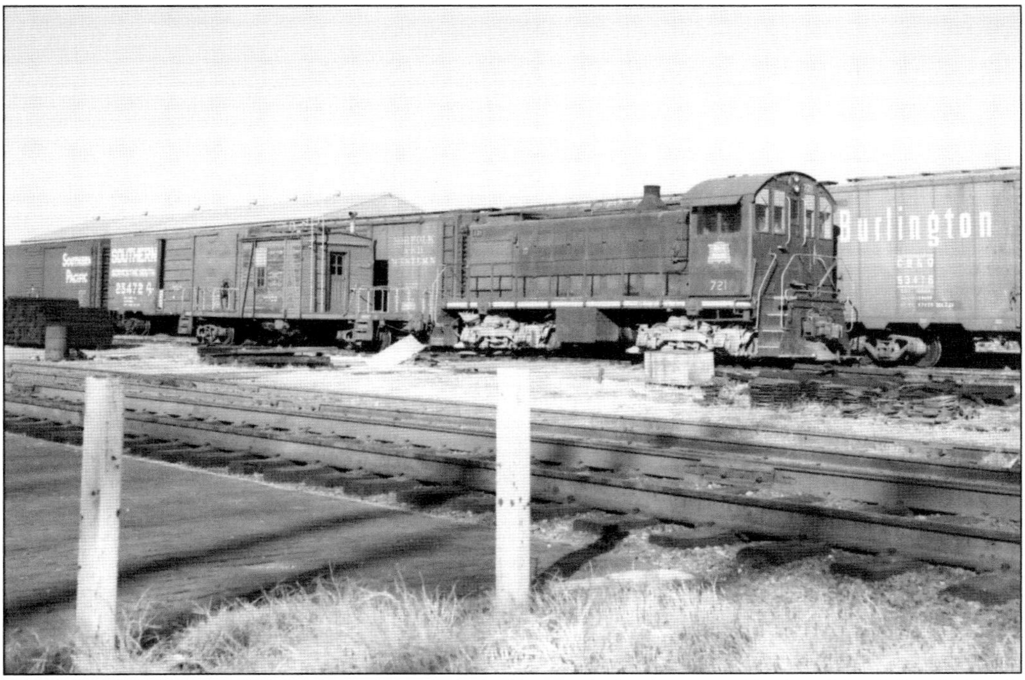

This switch engine and transfer caboose are working in the Argenta Yard in North Little Rock in January 1964. (Courtesy of Bill Pollard; photograph by Clifton Hull.)

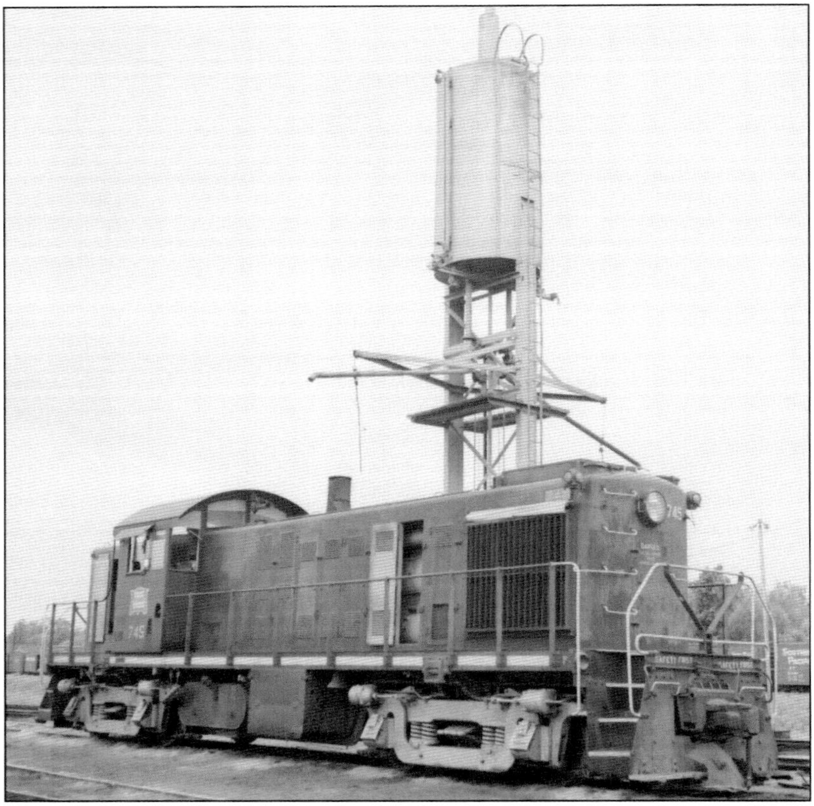

Alco No. 745 is at the fuel standpipe in Biddle Yard in July 1963. (Courtesy of Bill Pollard; photograph by Clifton Hull.)

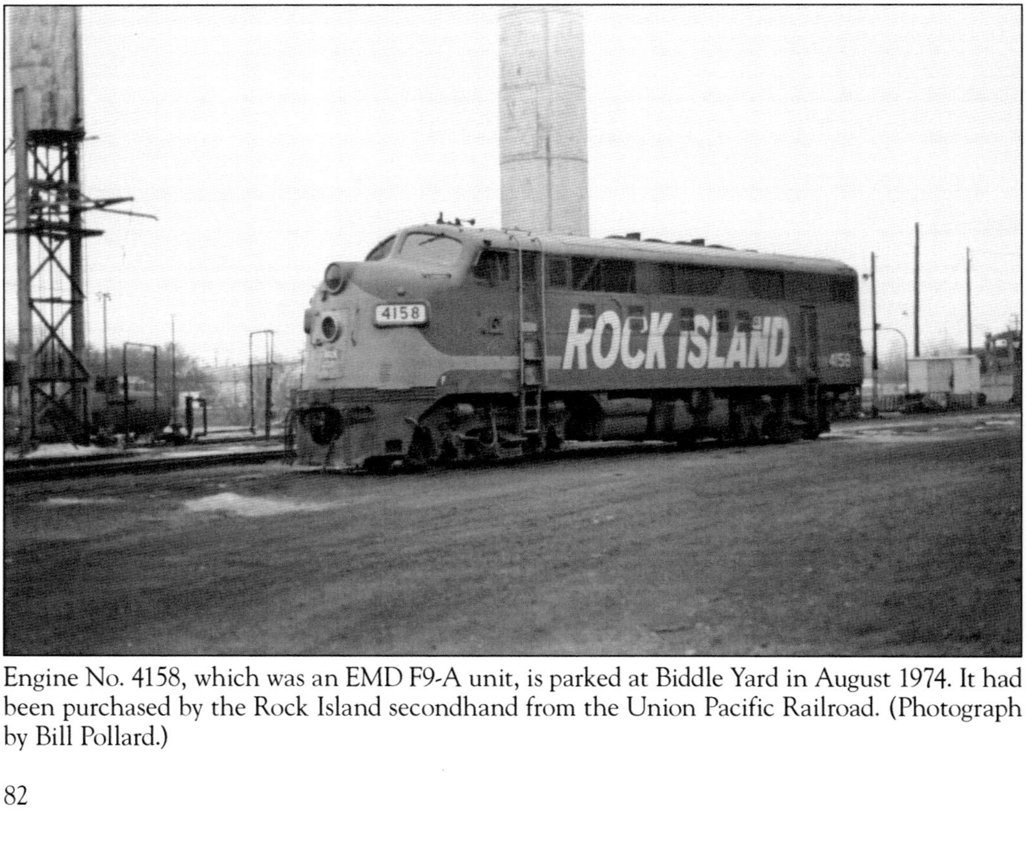

Engine No. 4158, which was an EMD F9-A unit, is parked at Biddle Yard in August 1974. It had been purchased by the Rock Island secondhand from the Union Pacific Railroad. (Photograph by Bill Pollard.)

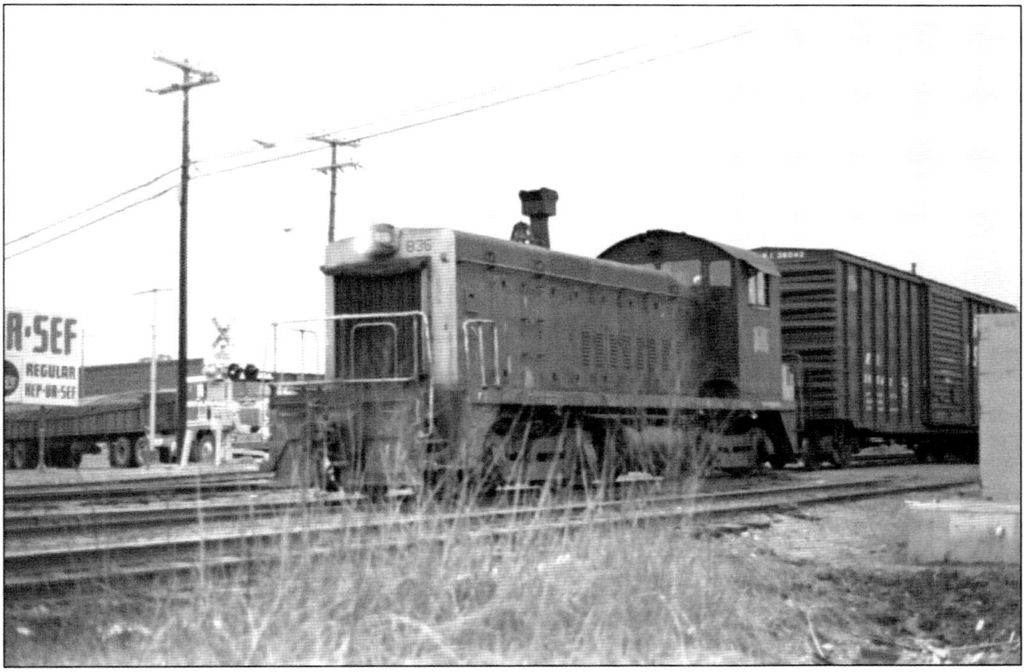

Switcher No. 836 leads a group of cars through the Confederate Boulevard crossing entering Biddle Yard in April 1974. (Photograph by Bill Pollard.)

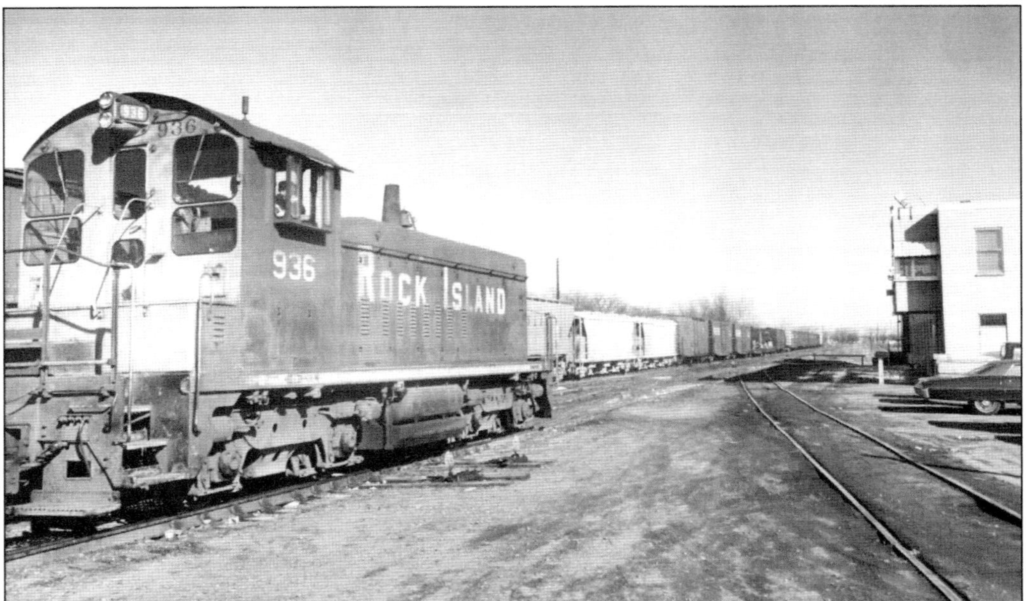

Switcher No. 936 is pictured on January 15, 1975, with the Biddle Yard control tower visible to the right. It was housed in a building that was constructed in 1967 directly next to the yard office to help consolidate employees who had worked in the Little Rock passenger station to Biddle Yard. (*Arkansas Democrat-Gazette* file photograph; photograph by Steve Keesee.)

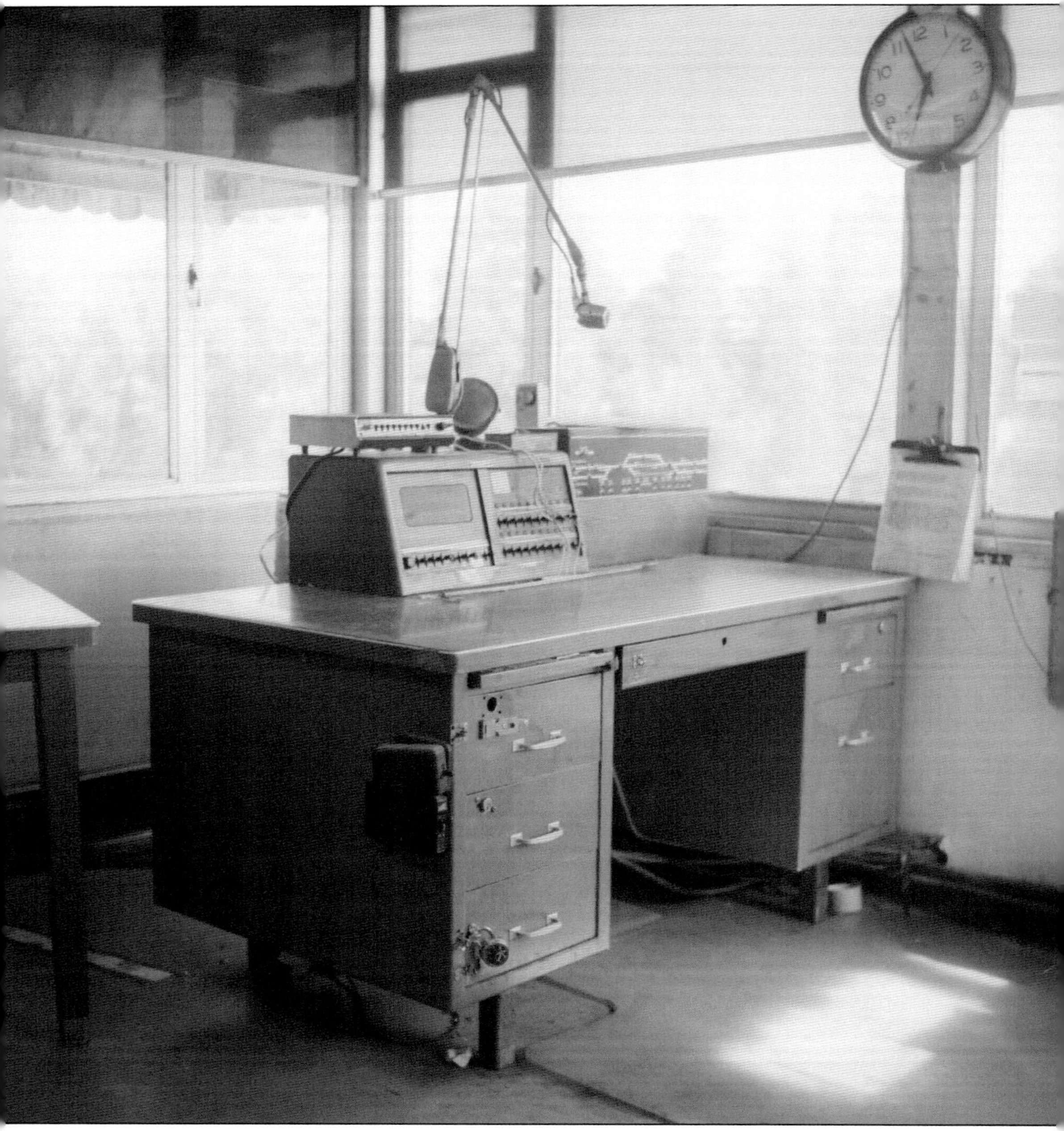

Once the nerve center for activity in Biddle Yard, the control tower is quiet in this photograph from October 1982, after the Rock Island's shutdown. The track diagram and control panel on the desk governed traffic on all the Rock Island main lines between the Arkansas River bridge and Hot Springs Junction at the west end of Biddle Yard. This was in the more modern office building constructed in 1967. (Courtesy of Bill Pollard; photograph by Clifton Hull.)

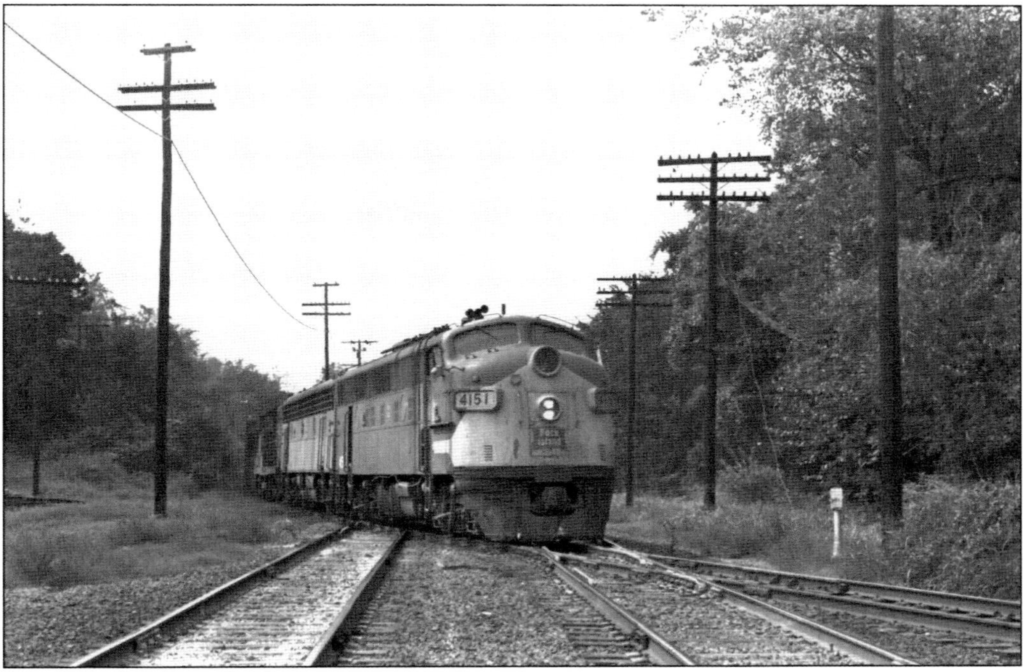

Just a few miles outside of Biddle Yard, a westbound freight is drawn by Engine No. 4151 at HH crossing. That is near the Third Street overpass where the Rock Island passes over the Missouri Pacific's double-track main line just south of the competitor's Union Station in 1972. HH was a Missouri Pacific timetable designation. All junction points received letter designations. (Photograph by Bill Pollard.)

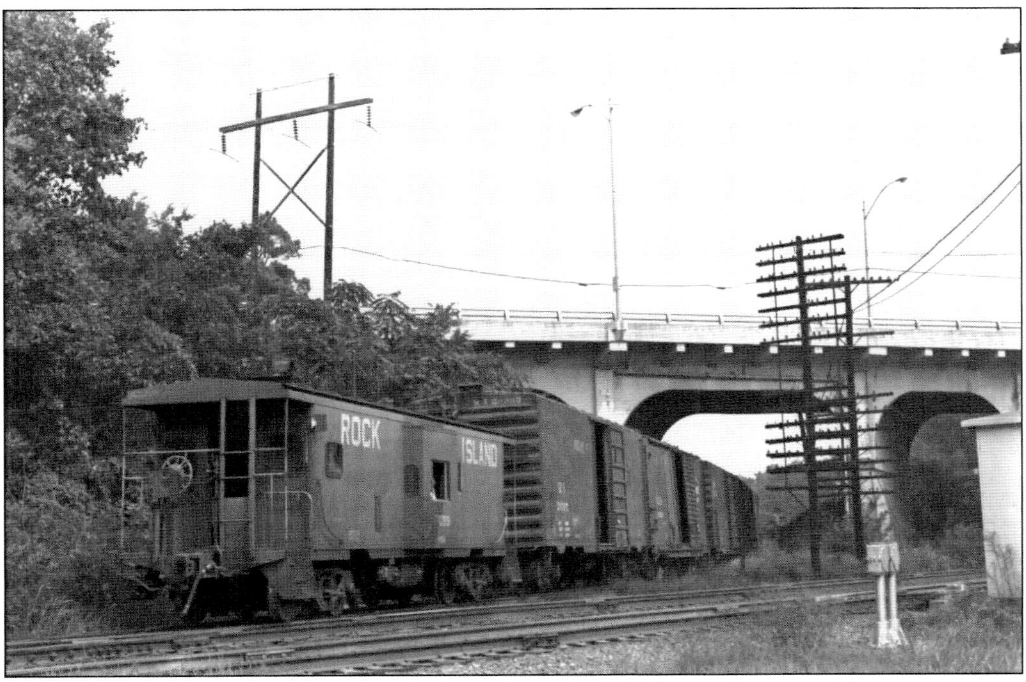

The bay-window Caboose No. 17099, built in November 1966, is at the rear of the train moving west in 1972. (Photograph by Bill Pollard.)

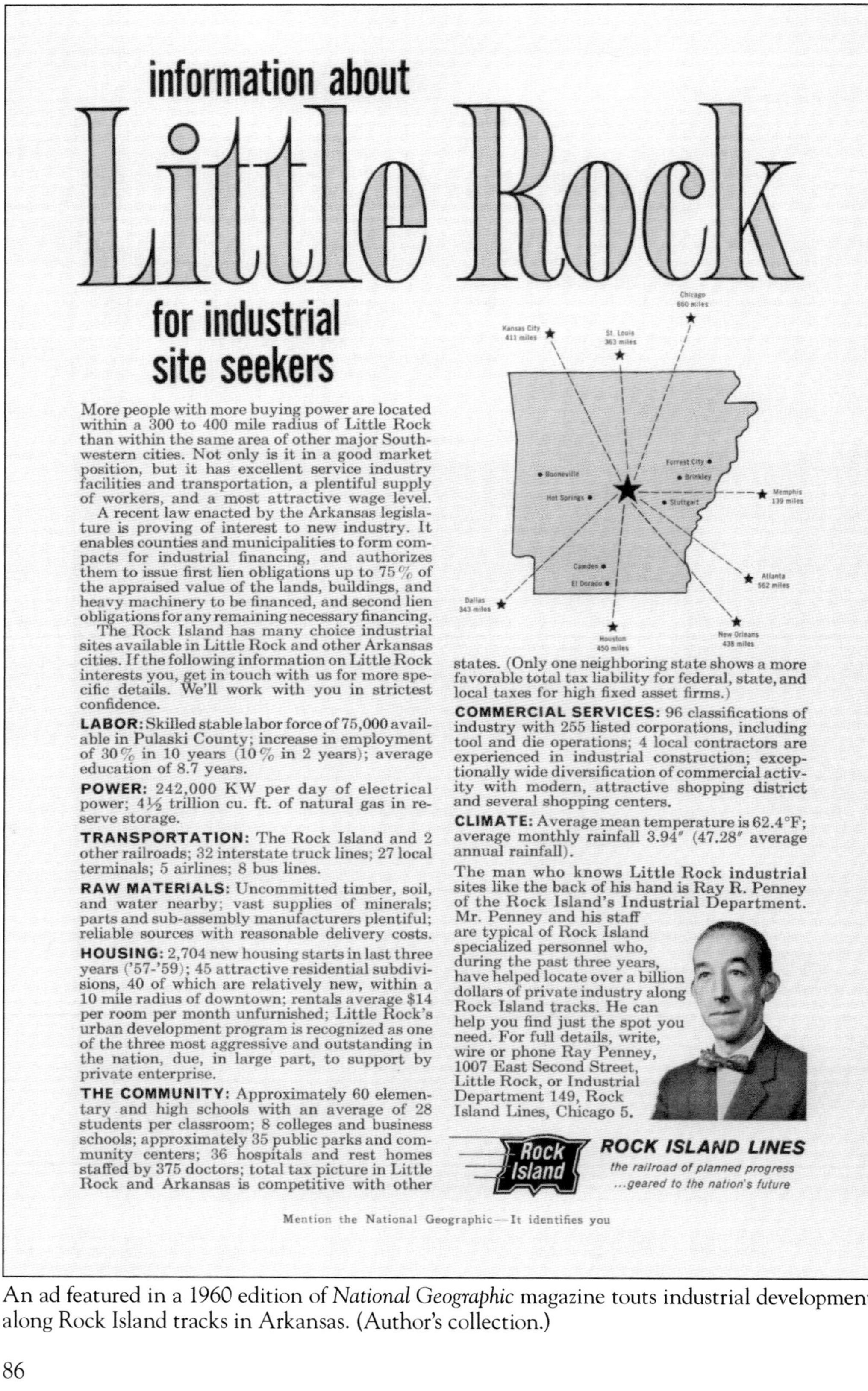

information about

Little Rock

for industrial site seekers

More people with more buying power are located within a 300 to 400 mile radius of Little Rock than within the same area of other major Southwestern cities. Not only is it in a good market position, but it has excellent service industry facilities and transportation, a plentiful supply of workers, and a most attractive wage level.

A recent law enacted by the Arkansas legislature is proving of interest to new industry. It enables counties and municipalities to form compacts for industrial financing, and authorizes them to issue first lien obligations up to 75% of the appraised value of the lands, buildings, and heavy machinery to be financed, and second lien obligations for any remaining necessary financing.

The Rock Island has many choice industrial sites available in Little Rock and other Arkansas cities. If the following information on Little Rock interests you, get in touch with us for more specific details. We'll work with you in strictest confidence.

LABOR: Skilled stable labor force of 75,000 available in Pulaski County; increase in employment of 30% in 10 years (10% in 2 years); average education of 8.7 years.

POWER: 242,000 KW per day of electrical power; 4½ trillion cu. ft. of natural gas in reserve storage.

TRANSPORTATION: The Rock Island and 2 other railroads; 32 interstate truck lines; 27 local terminals; 5 airlines; 8 bus lines.

RAW MATERIALS: Uncommitted timber, soil, and water nearby; vast supplies of minerals; parts and sub-assembly manufacturers plentiful; reliable sources with reasonable delivery costs.

HOUSING: 2,704 new housing starts in last three years ('57-'59); 45 attractive residential subdivisions, 40 of which are relatively new, within a 10 mile radius of downtown; rentals average $14 per room per month unfurnished; Little Rock's urban development program is recognized as one of the three most aggressive and outstanding in the nation, due, in large part, to support by private enterprise.

THE COMMUNITY: Approximately 60 elementary and high schools with an average of 28 students per classroom; 8 colleges and business schools; approximately 35 public parks and community centers; 36 hospitals and rest homes staffed by 375 doctors; total tax picture in Little Rock and Arkansas is competitive with other states. (Only one neighboring state shows a more favorable total tax liability for federal, state, and local taxes for high fixed asset firms.)

COMMERCIAL SERVICES: 96 classifications of industry with 255 listed corporations, including tool and die operations; 4 local contractors are experienced in industrial construction; exceptionally wide diversification of commercial activity with modern, attractive shopping district and several shopping centers.

CLIMATE: Average mean temperature is 62.4°F; average monthly rainfall 3.94" (47.28" average annual rainfall).

The man who knows Little Rock industrial sites like the back of his hand is Ray R. Penney of the Rock Island's Industrial Department. Mr. Penney and his staff are typical of Rock Island specialized personnel who, during the past three years, have helped locate over a billion dollars of private industry along Rock Island tracks. He can help you find just the spot you need. For full details, write, wire or phone Ray Penney, 1007 East Second Street, Little Rock, or Industrial Department 149, Rock Island Lines, Chicago 5.

Rock Island

ROCK ISLAND LINES

the railroad of planned progress ...geared to the nation's future

Mention the National Geographic—It identifies you

An ad featured in a 1960 edition of *National Geographic* magazine touts industrial development along Rock Island tracks in Arkansas. (Author's collection.)

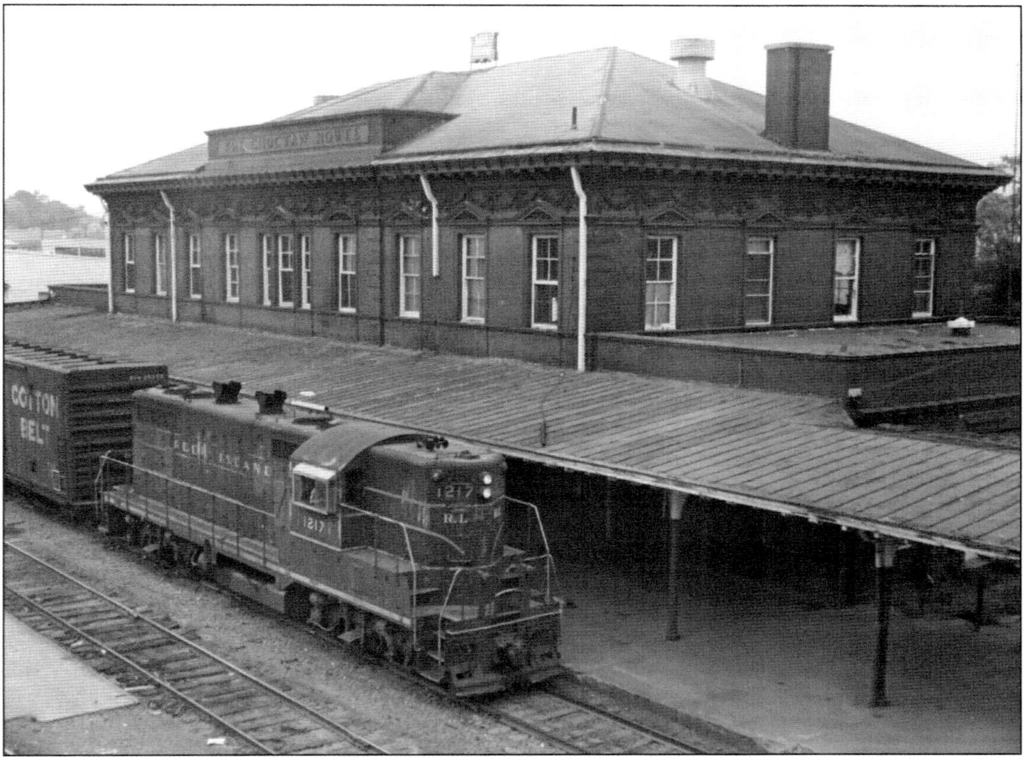

A Stuttgart local, sometimes nicknamed the "Riceland Rocket" for its primary customer there, passes the Little Rock station, which already looks at least partially abandoned in 1972, with wood blocking some windows from the inside on the upper floor. The locomotive is No. 1217, an EMD GP7. (Courtesy of Bill Pollard; photograph by John Martin.)

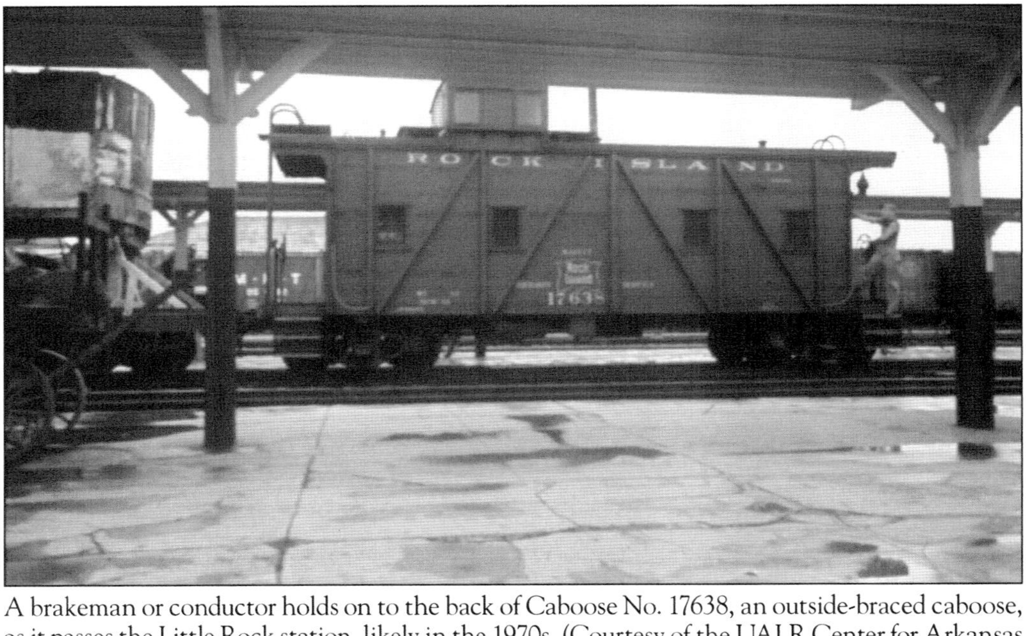

A brakeman or conductor holds on to the back of Caboose No. 17638, an outside-braced caboose, as it passes the Little Rock station, likely in the 1970s. (Courtesy of the UALR Center for Arkansas History and Culture; photograph by Earl Saunders.)

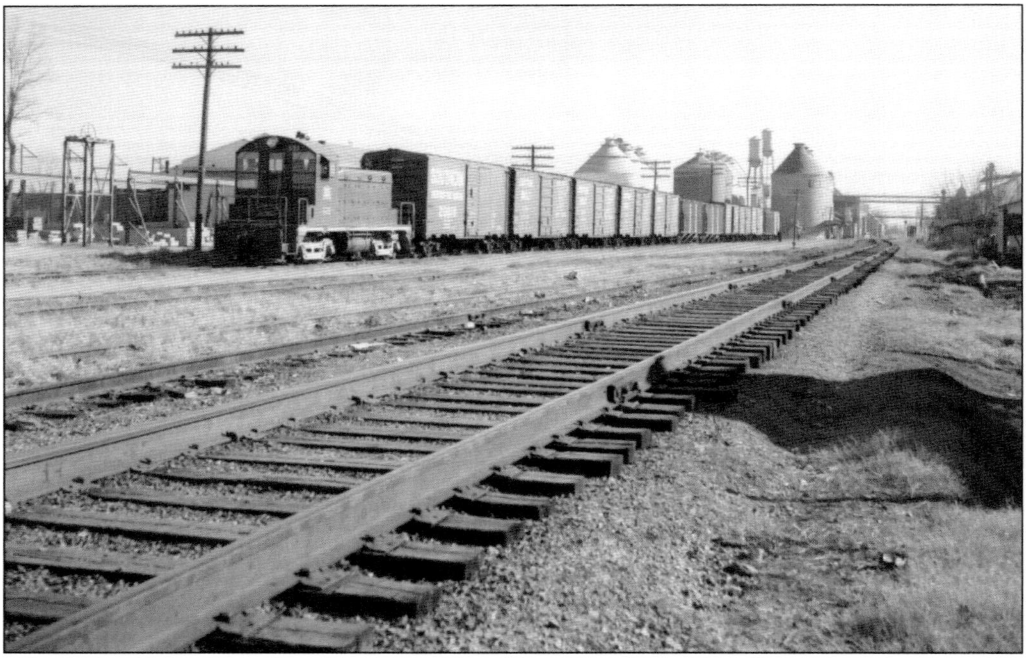

Engine No. 533 is switching cars at the Buckeye Cotton Oil Mill near the North Little Rock depot in January 1964. (Courtesy of Bill Pollard; photograph by Clifton Hull.)

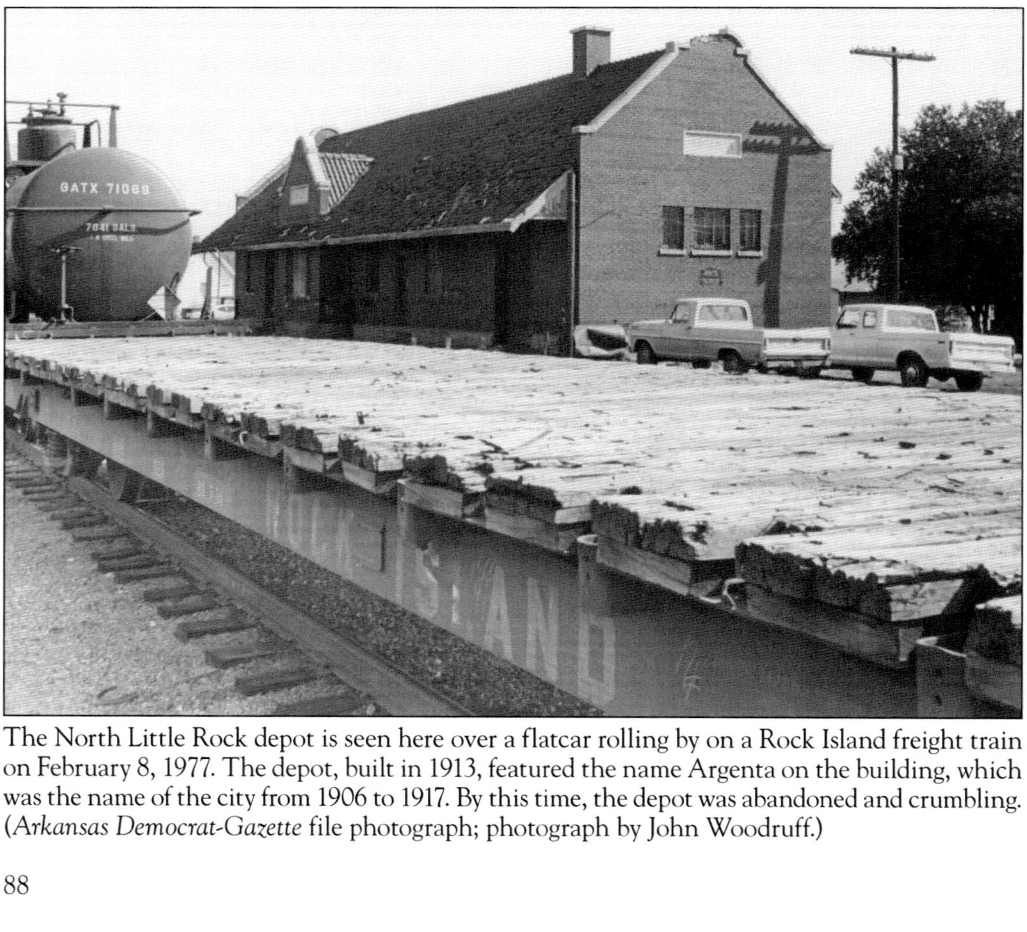

The North Little Rock depot is seen here over a flatcar rolling by on a Rock Island freight train on February 8, 1977. The depot, built in 1913, featured the name Argenta on the building, which was the name of the city from 1906 to 1917. By this time, the depot was abandoned and crumbling. (*Arkansas Democrat-Gazette* file photograph; photograph by John Woodruff.)

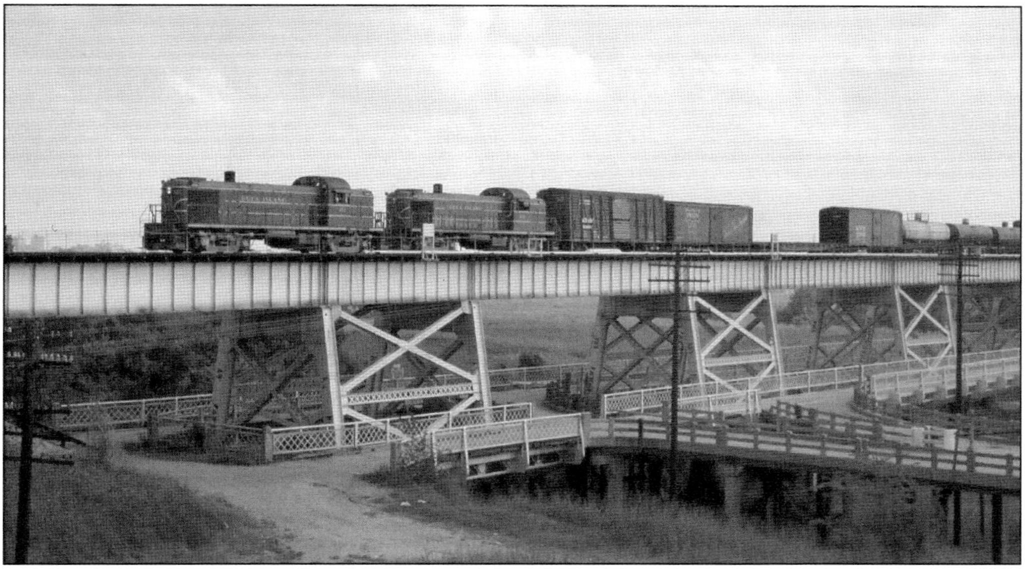

Another impressive bridge used by the Rock Island was the nearly 5,000-foot-long Harahan Bridge, which crossed the Mississippi River between West Memphis, Arkansas, and Memphis, Tennessee. It featured two tracks, as well as a lane for automobile traffic on each side. Pictured here are a pair of Alco RS3 locomotives leading a westbound train into Arkansas, probably in the late 1950s. (Courtesy of Steve Forrest.)

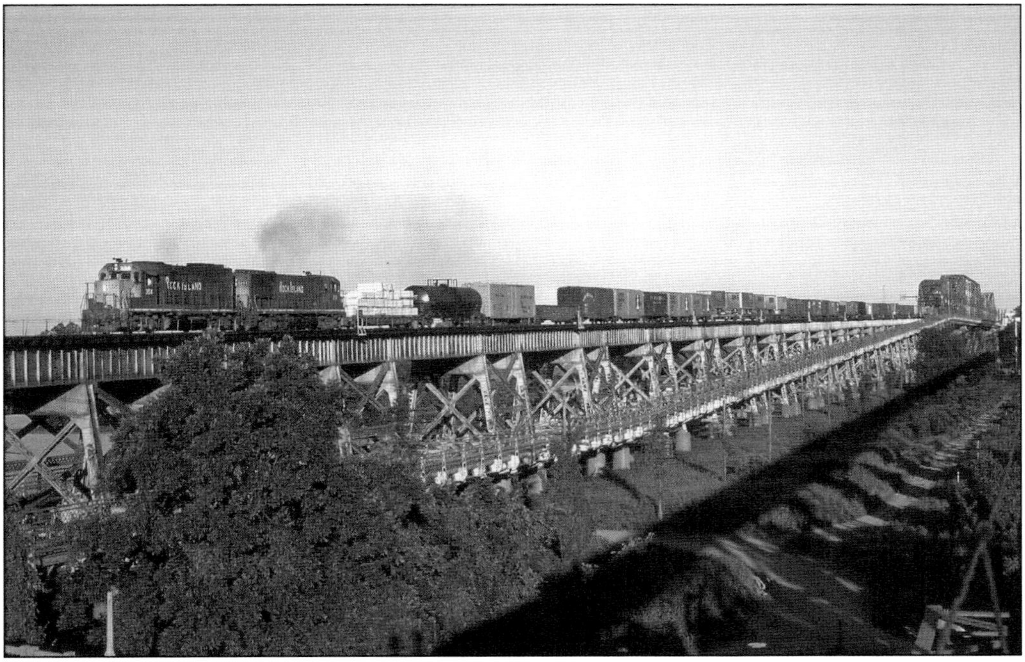

The Harahan Bridge is a cantilevered through-truss bridge featuring a long approach on the western side. Memphis mayor E.H. Crump met with Rock Island officials on February 5, 1912, to discuss the possibility of building the bridge. The Iron Mountain and the Cotton Belt Railroads were also interested and joined to form the Memphis and Arkansas Bridge and Terminal Company. The first train rolled across it on July 14, 1916. Here, a westbound Rock Island train crosses into Arkansas in July 1975. (Photograph by Steve Forrest.)

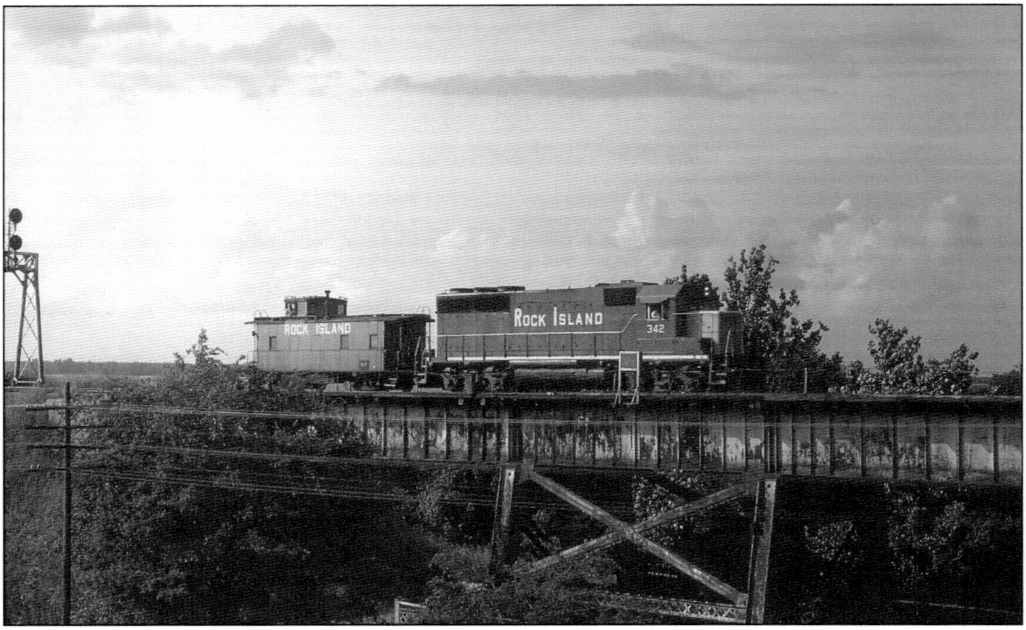

Often, inbound freight crews would yard their train at West Memphis and then bring the caboose and power across the bridge to the Rock Island's East Fourth Street yard in Memphis. Because it was a small yard that was difficult to get in and out of, crews would make multiple trips across the bridge to pick up or deliver segments of trains with connecting railroads. (Photograph by Steve Forrest.)

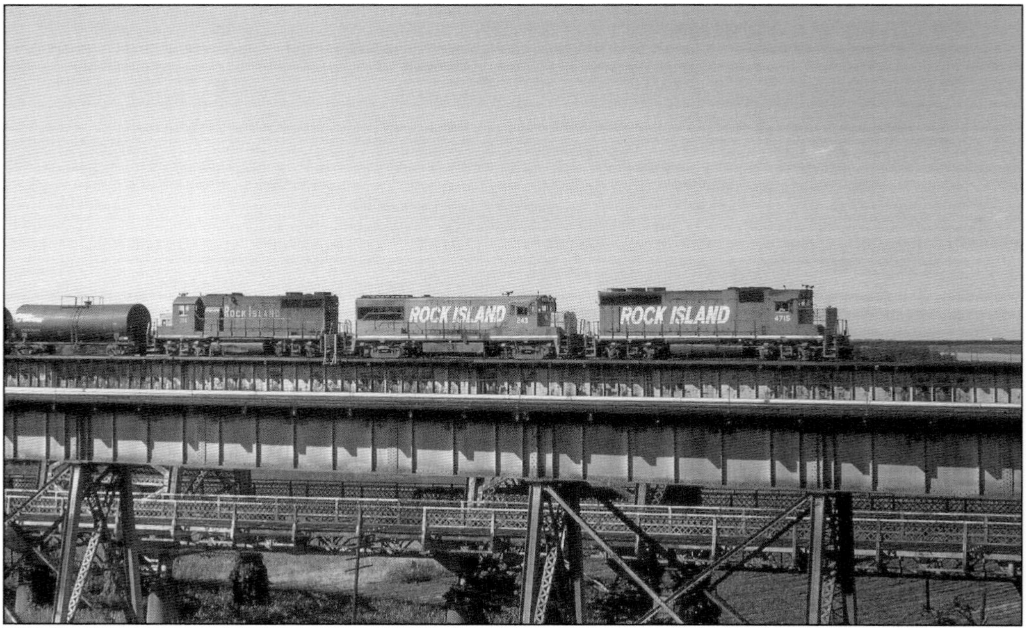

Here, an eastbound freight is on the approach from West Memphis in June 1974. Memphis was the eastern end of the Sunbelt Line of the Rock Island. Because the bridge was shared by several railroads, trains never stopped crossing the Harahan after the Rock Island's shutdown and today it is owned and operated by Union Pacific. The bridge also now features a path for pedestrians and cyclists in what had been a lane for automobile traffic. (Photograph by Steve Forrest.)

Six

Final Years of the Rock Island

With challenges facing the railroad industry in the 1950s and 1960s, which included flat revenue and increasing costs, Rock Island managers decided merging with a larger railroad was their best option for survival. There were talks with several railroads, but eventually, a complicated plan was devised in 1964 for most of the Rock Island to be merged with Union Pacific, while the Arkansas division was to be sold to another carrier. But competitors of the Rock Island vigorously opposed the plan and lobbied hard against it, starting what is said to have been the longest merger case ever considered by the Interstate Commerce Commission, lasting a decade.

As this was being deliberated, the Rock Island deferred making major investments on tracks and equipment. The tracks got to be in such poor shape, especially on branch lines, that derailments were occurring regularly. Even on main lines, slow orders were in place. By the time the merger plan was finally approved in 1974, the Rock Island infrastructure was in such poor condition that the other railroads were no longer interested.

The Rock Island then filed for bankruptcy protection and attempted a reorganization. Part of this strategy included a new image and rebranding the railroad as "The Rock." When new equipment was bought, rebuilt, or repainted, it got the blue-and-white logo, which some disparagingly called "bankruptcy blue."

There were hopes for a turnaround. It had happened before in the railroad industry. The Rock Island, however, had a lot of factors working against it. The final nail in the coffin was a strike by the Brotherhood of Railway and Airline Clerks in August 1979. Employees had by that time been working on expired labor contracts and a dispute over past-due wages finally brought the matter to a head.

As part of an emergency order, the Interstate Commerce Commission eventually ordered the Kansas City Terminal Railway to take over operations. Some creditors wanted the assets liquidated, and on January 24, 1980, Judge Frank McGarr obliged, ordering the shutdown of the railroad to take place two months later.

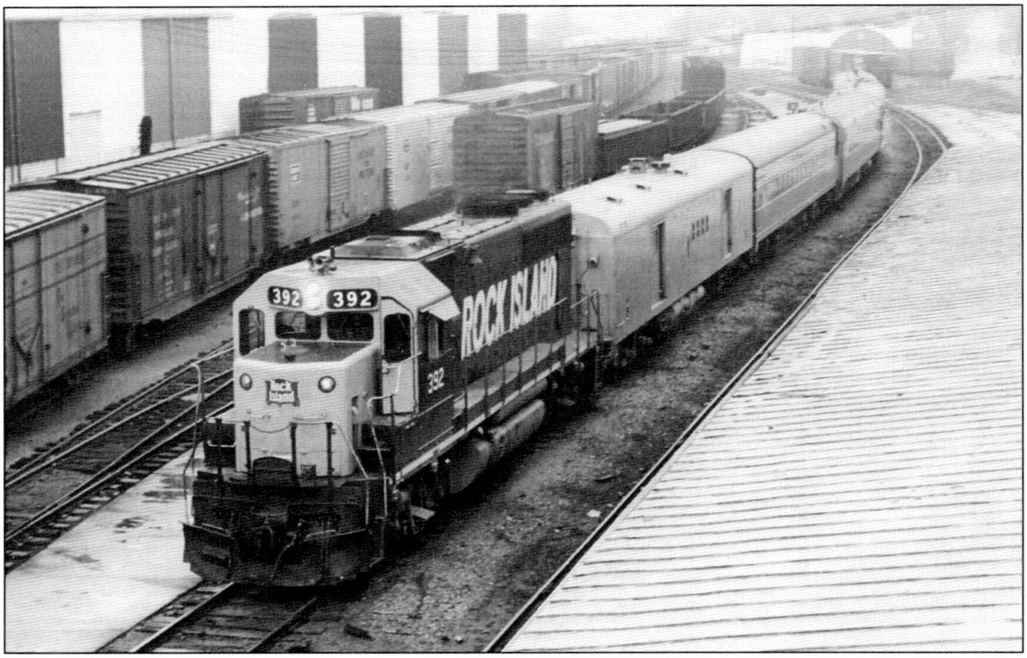

Eight years after regular passenger service stopped on the Rock Island, on February 4, 1975, this train, listed as Passenger Extra No. 392, was carrying some very important guests. Officials with the Sante Fe Railway were inspecting the line while considering acquiring the Arkansas trackage. (Courtesy of Bill Pollard; photograph by John Martin.)

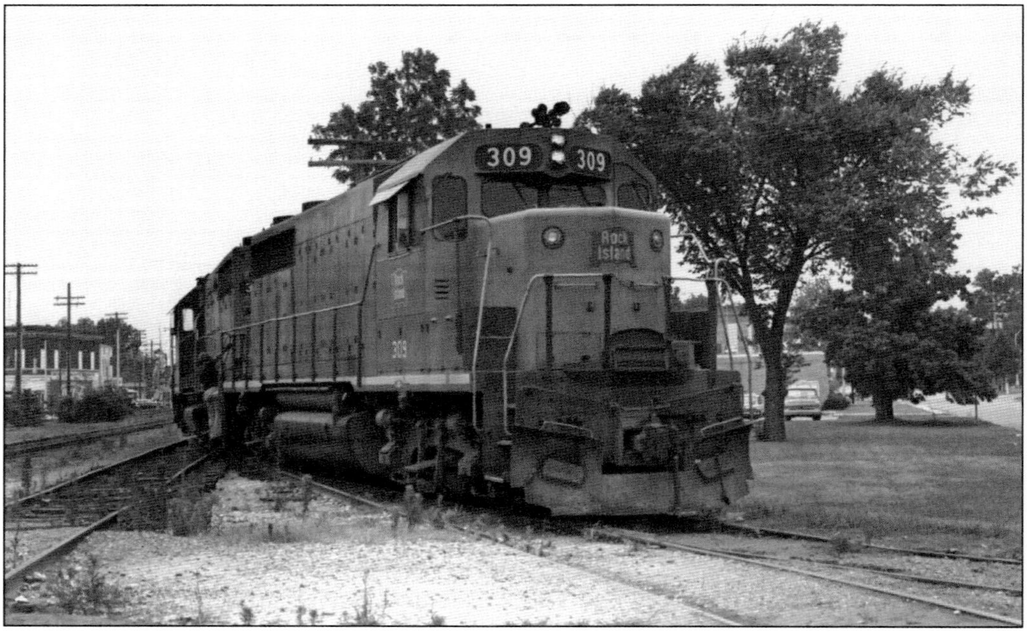

Engine No. 309 leads a freight train in Brinkley, which was a major transfer point with the Cotton Belt Railroad. The Cotton Belt had historically had trackage rights from here to Memphis, which is why that stretch of track never deteriorated: the Cotton Belt invested to keep it maintained. (Photograph by Bill Pollard.)

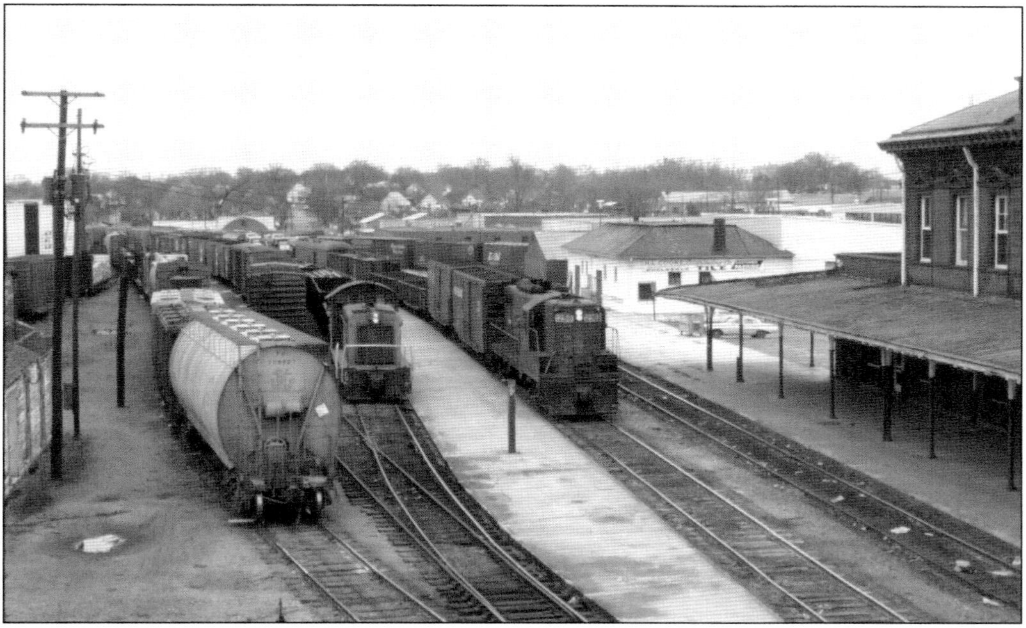

The tracks at the Little Rock station are busy on this day in January 1973 with an eastbound Stuttgart local to the right and a switcher at work to the left. By this time, the station was no longer in use, as it and four city blocks of land had been purchased in 1966 by Hugh B. Patterson, publisher of the *Arkansas Gazette*, who built a large printing plant for the newspaper just south of the station. (Photograph by Bill Pollard.)

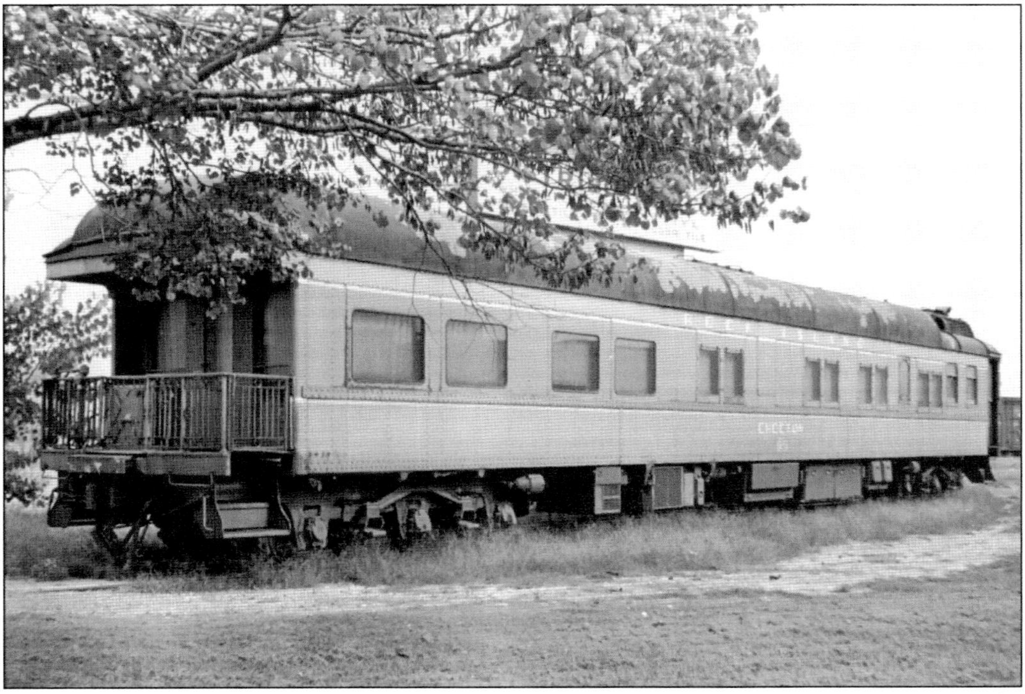

Patterson apparently had a fondness for railroading and purchased Business Car No. 99, the *Choctaw*, for use as a stationary office and conference room. Here, it is parked on a Little Rock siding in 1971. (Courtesy of Bill Pollard; photograph by John Martin.)

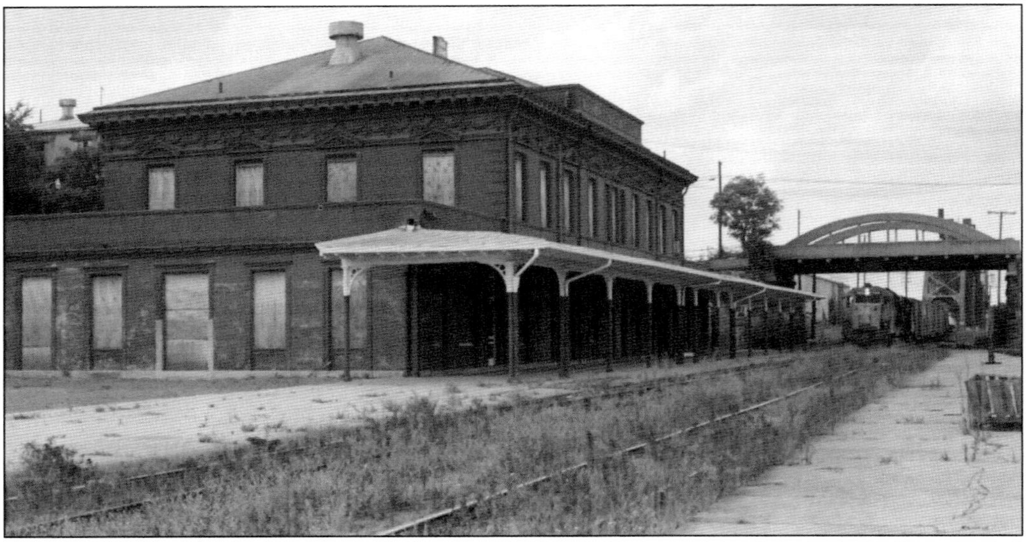

By the time this photograph was taken in 1976, the Little Rock station was boarded up. It may look abandoned, but railroad historian Bill Pollard said in 2015 interview that those at the neighboring newspaper printing plant were watching over it. Pollard said, "The *Gazette* and Hugh Patterson had more than a basic interest in railroad history, and I think they did very good stewardship of that building. Had it not been for the *Arkansas Gazette* taking care of it, keeping it secure, keeping it boarded up . . . I don't think it would have survived to be part of the Clinton (Presidential) Library and those people from the late '60s and early '70s really deserve a lot of credit for preserving that magnificent building."

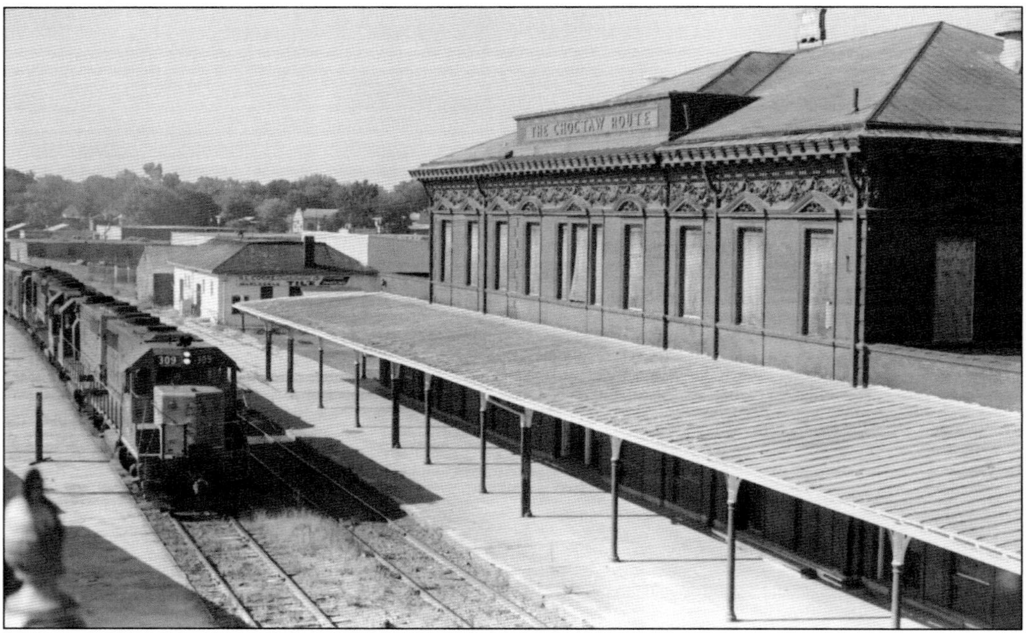

An eastbound freight is seen passing the Little Rock station in 1976. It would remain boarded up until 1990, when it was bought and renovated for restaurant use by the Spaghetti Warehouse chain. But after not getting the kind of revenue hoped, the restaurant closed in 1996 and the building became a nightclub until the property was purchased to become the site where the Clinton Presidential Library would be built. (Photograph by Bill Pollard.)

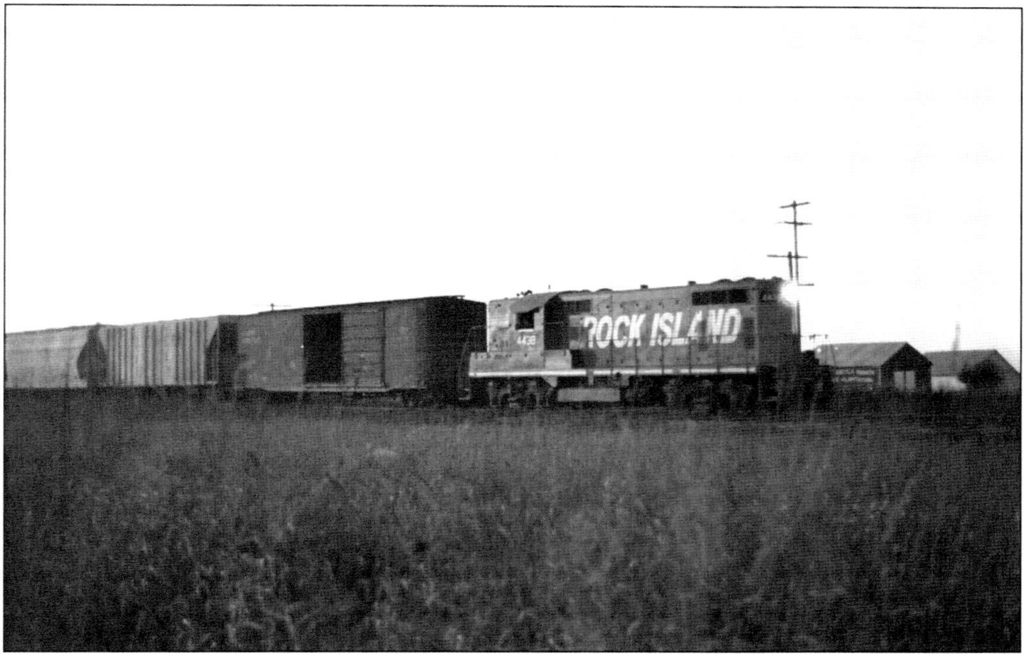

A freight train is headed by Engine No. 4438 at Mesa in 1976. The small town was important to the Rock Island as the place where branch lines separated heading north to Des Arc (though in earlier years it went as far as Searcy) and south to Stuttgart. (Photograph by Bill Pollard.)

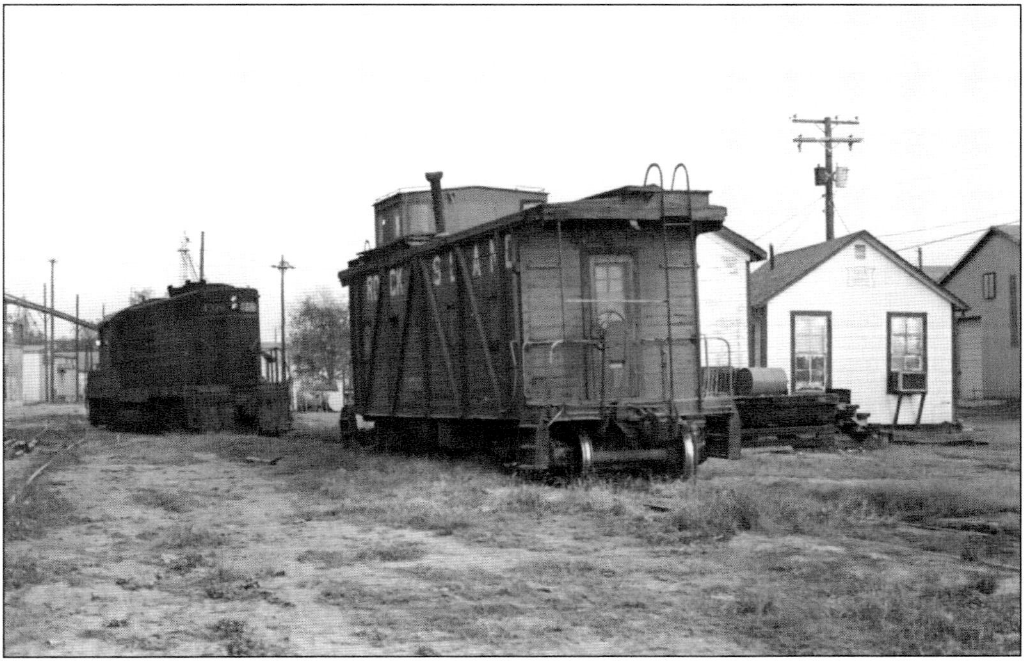

Beginning in 1965, as the Rock Island waited for word from federal regulators on whether it could merge with other railroads, maintenance on tracks, equipment, and facilities was deferred. The approval period for proposed mergers stretched on for a decade, and by the time this photographs was taken in 1975 in Stuttgart, the track is barely visible in the ground. (Photograph by Bill Pollard.)

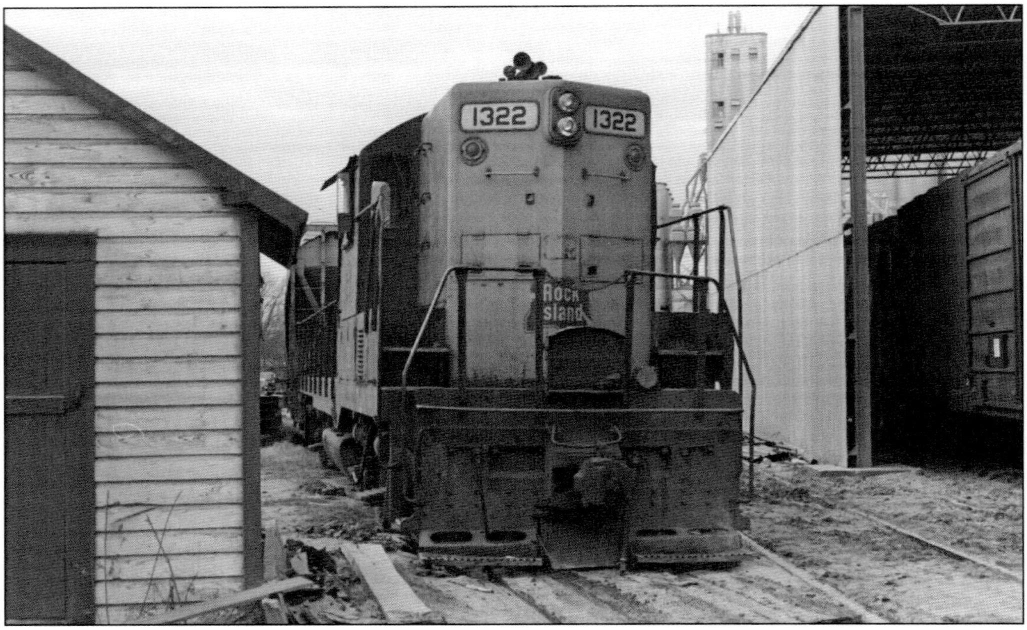

Former conductor Joe "Buzzy" Rook said the Stuttgart branch was one of worst sections of track for the Rock Island in Arkansas. It had a slow order, limiting trains to 10 miles per hour, but it was not even safe at that speed, he said in a 2003 interview. If they went any slower, it would take what seemed like an eternity to get back to Little Rock. There were constant derailments, with the railroad sending a wrecker to rerail the cars. (Photograph by Bill Pollard.)

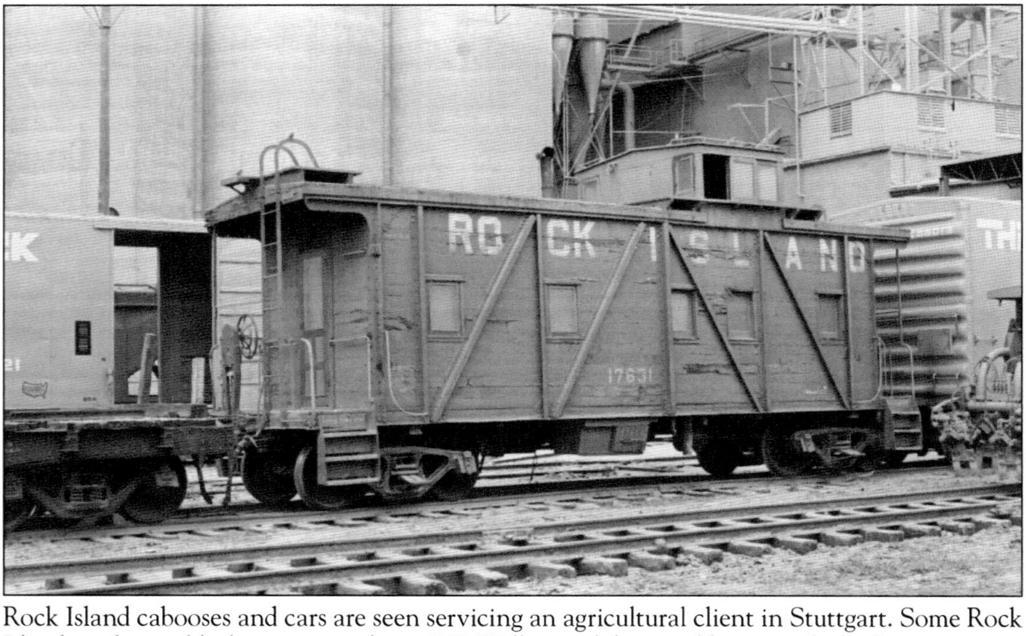

Rock Island cabooses and cars are seen servicing an agricultural client in Stuttgart. Some Rock Island employees, like longtime conductor L.T. Walker, said that in addition to a lack of maintenance, the poor shape of the Stuttgart branch could be blamed on the Cotton Belt diverting its trains onto this line to detour around a Clarendon Bridge repair project. The Cotton Belt carried cars that were heavier than the branch line was designed to accommodate. The mushy ground in east Arkansas was also a factor. (Photograph by Bill Pollard.)

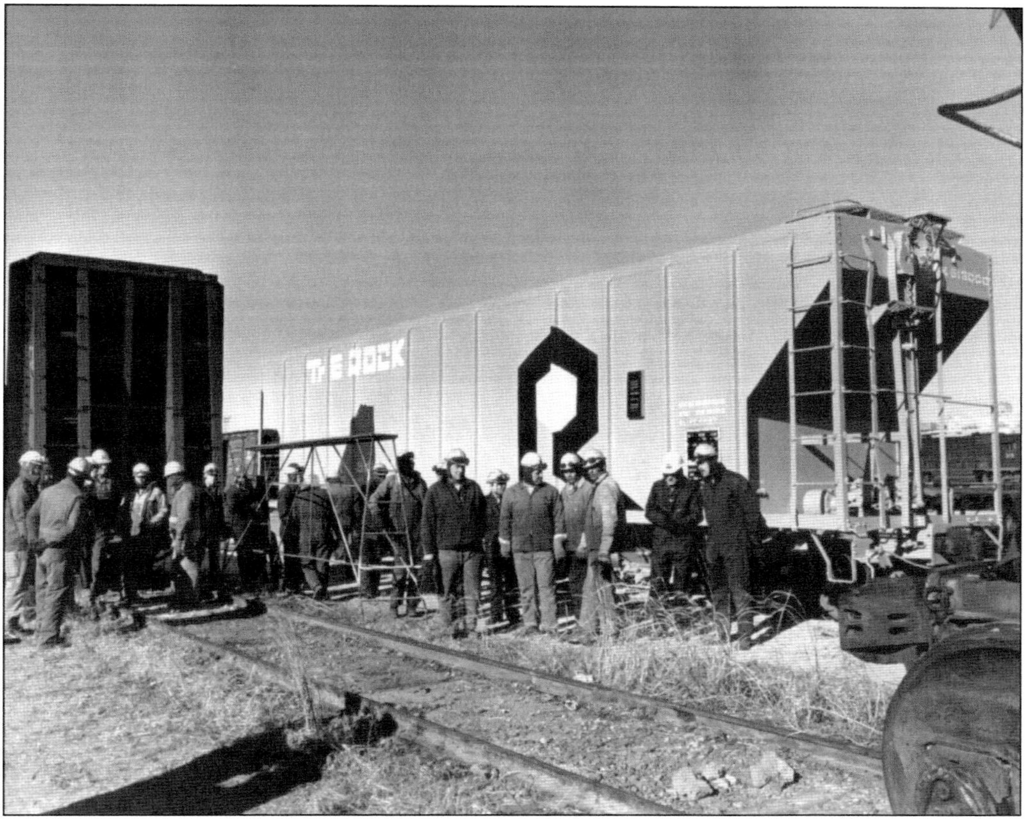

After efforts to merge with other railroads failed, the Rock Island filed for bankruptcy protection in March 1975 and put together a reorganization plan. Management also felt the railroad needed a new image and began rebranding everything "The Rock." The railroad reopened its car repair shop at Little Rock's Biddle Yard, and this photograph from January 8, 1976, shows newly appointed general foreman Clarence Tilton and his crew gathered around the first rebuilt hopper car. (*Arkansas Democrat-Gazette* file photograph.)

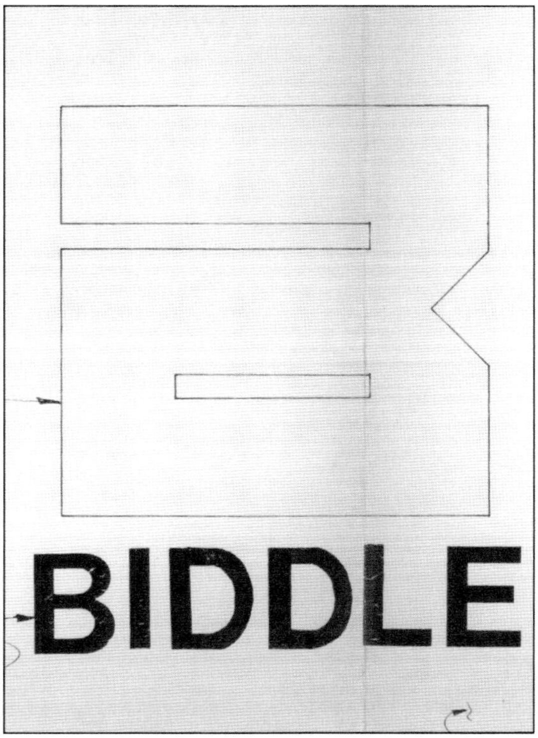

For each railcar built, rebuilt, or painted in Little Rock after the railroad was rebranded "The Rock," the Biddle shop had a special stencil that was used to place a small identifying mark toward the bottom corner of each car. This marking would be seen on cars all over the country for decades after the railroad was shut down. Another shop in El Reno, Oklahoma, had a similar mark for cars built there. (Courtesy of Bill Pollard.)

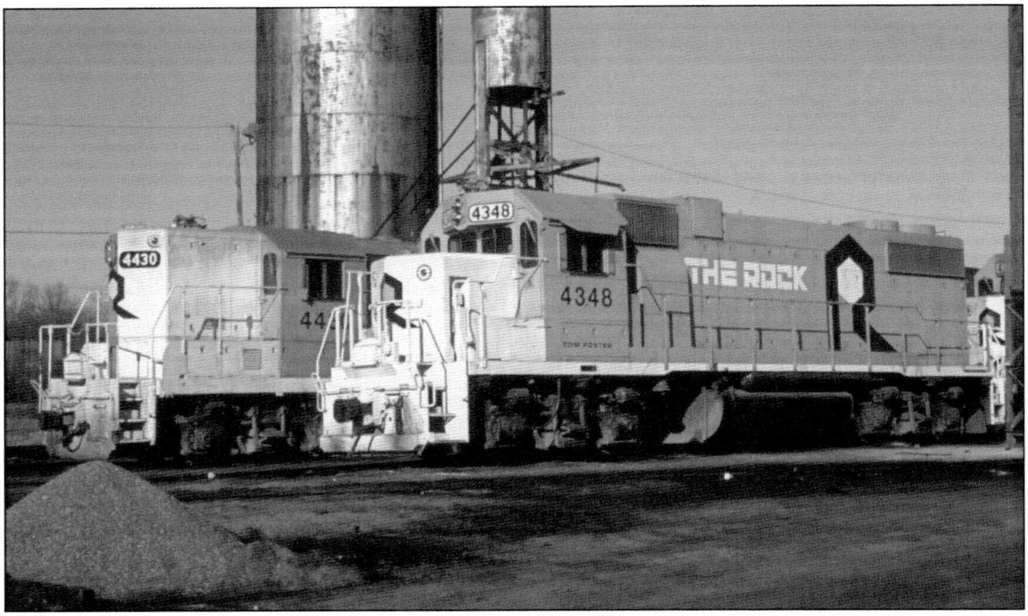

A pair of new GP38-2 diesels is pictured in Biddle Yard after being purchased in the fall of 1976. This batch of engines came in the new blue-and-white paint schemes, and many were named after "friends of the Rock Island," which included political leaders, employees, or cities and states. No. 4348 was named Tom Foster in honor of a longtime employee out of Haskell and Malvern. Soon after No. 4348 was delivered, it was brought to Malvern for a surprise ceremony recognizing Foster's dedication and loyalty to the railroad. Other engines included No. 4335, named in honor of Arkansas governor David Pryor, No. 4320, named for the State of Arkansas, and No. 4343, named for the City of Little Rock. (Courtesy of Bill Pollard.)

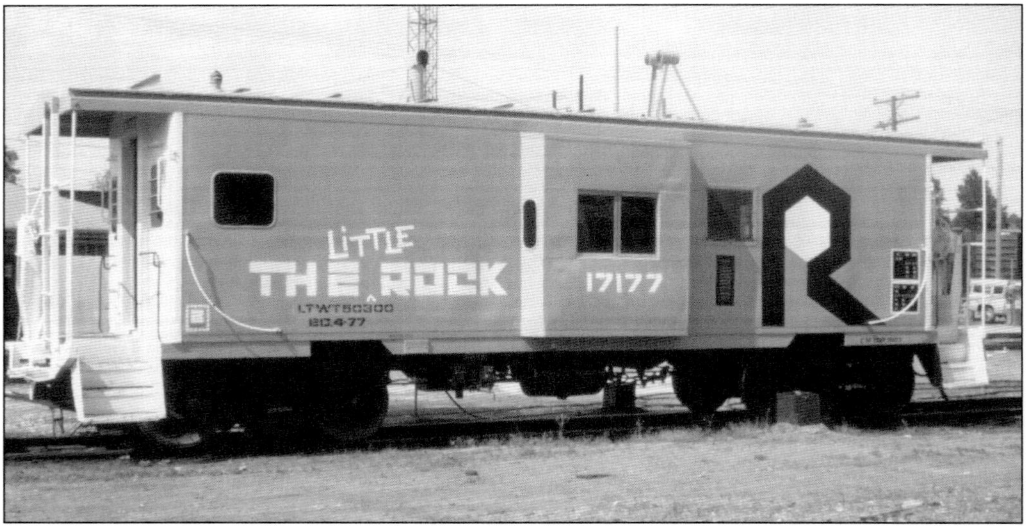

The "Little" Rock was a specific service set up by the Rock Island on an experimental basis to operate Rock Island tracks south of Little Rock. It was an effort to try to make that section profitable with its own management and a degree of autonomy. A couple of dozen locomotives and one caboose were repainted with a slightly modified "The Rock" logo, with "Little" added. Crew sizes for each train were also adjusted based on union agreements to allow more frequent trains than otherwise would be possible with fewer trainmen. (Photograph by Bill Pollard.)

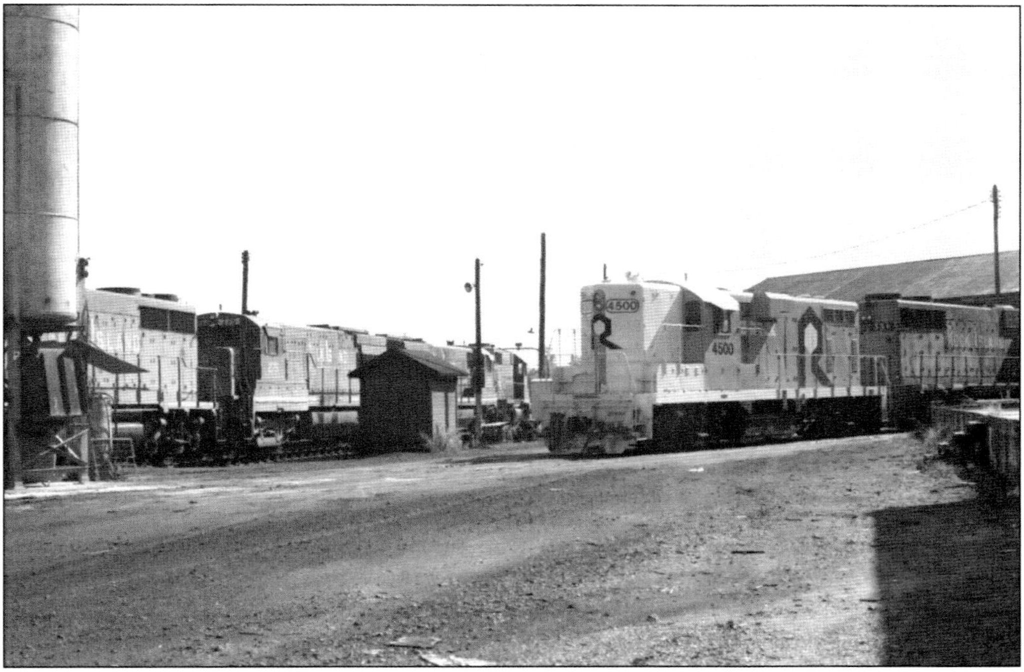

Toward the end of its existence, the appearance of the Rock Island was inconsistent, featuring logos from different eras on its equipment. Here are several generations of locomotives in Biddle Yard in 1976. (Photograph by Bill Pollard.)

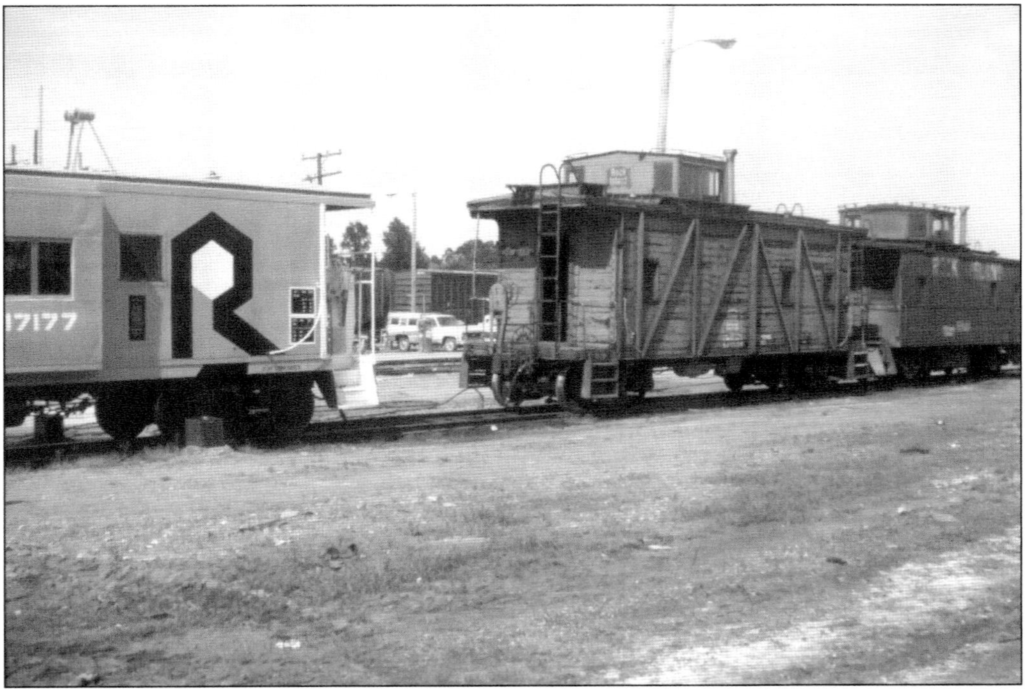

Likewise, here are several generations of cabooses in Biddle Yard in the late 1970s. (Courtesy of the UALR Center for Arkansas History and Culture; photograph by Earl Saunders.)

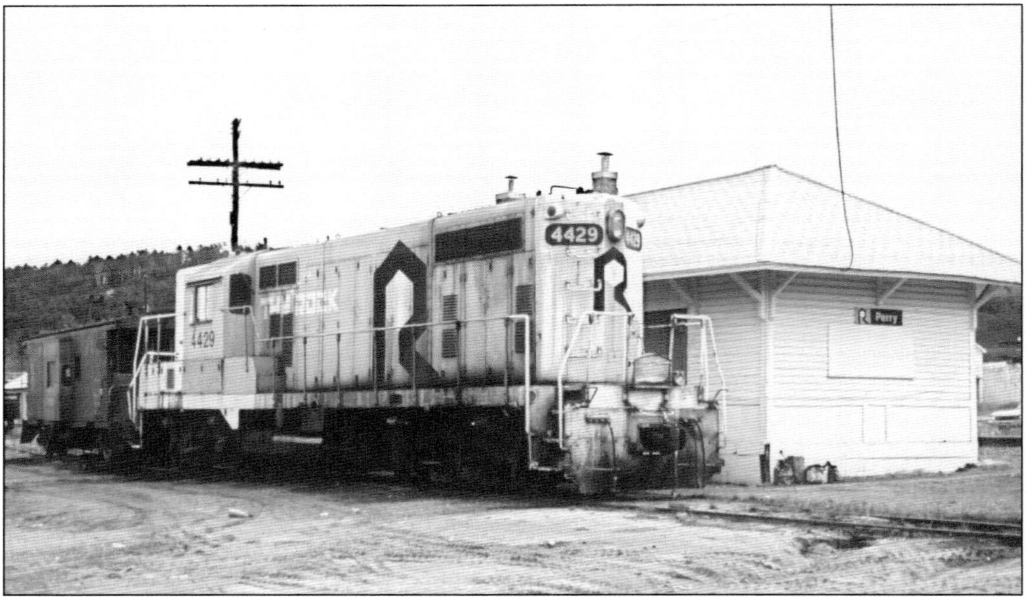

The problem with a blue-and-white logo in a railroad environment was that equipment became dirty very quick. But with the challenges facing the Rock Island, visual aesthetics were probably not a priority at this time. Here, Engine No. 4429, serving at the Perry switcher, is looking pretty grimy along with a caboose at the Perry depot in January 1980, only three months before the railroad would be shut down. (Photograph by Bill Pollard.)

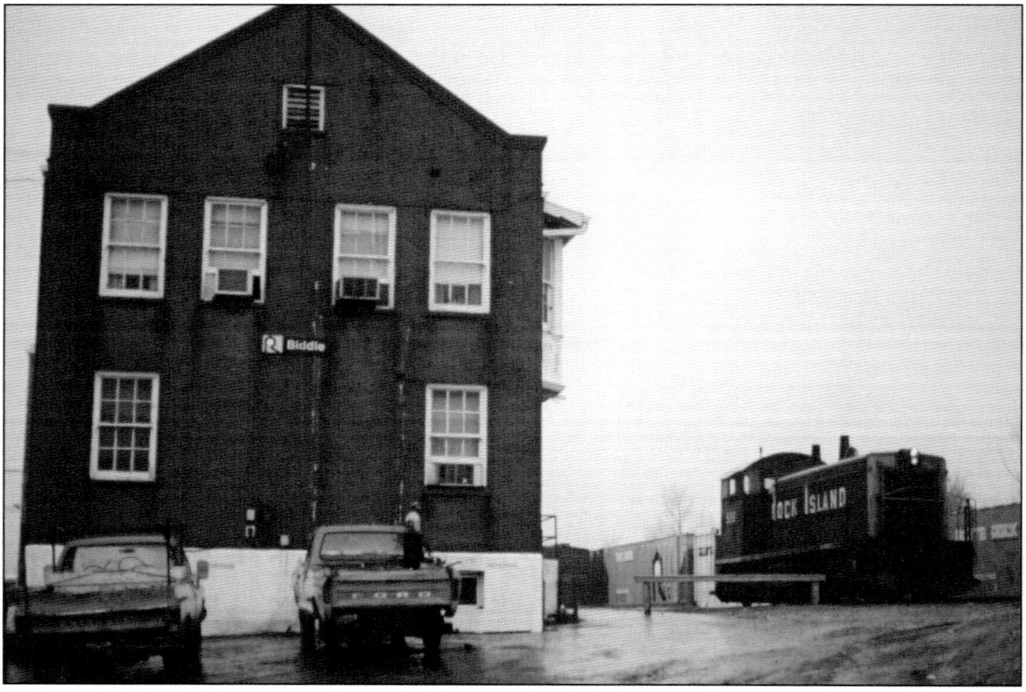

The last day of operations for the Rock Island came on a cold, rainy Sunday in Little Rock on March 23, 1980. Creditors, namely Henry Crown, felt the railroad was worth more dead than alive and had been calling for its assets to be liquidated. A judge finally agreed and set this as the railroad's final day of operations. (Photograph by Bill Pollard.)

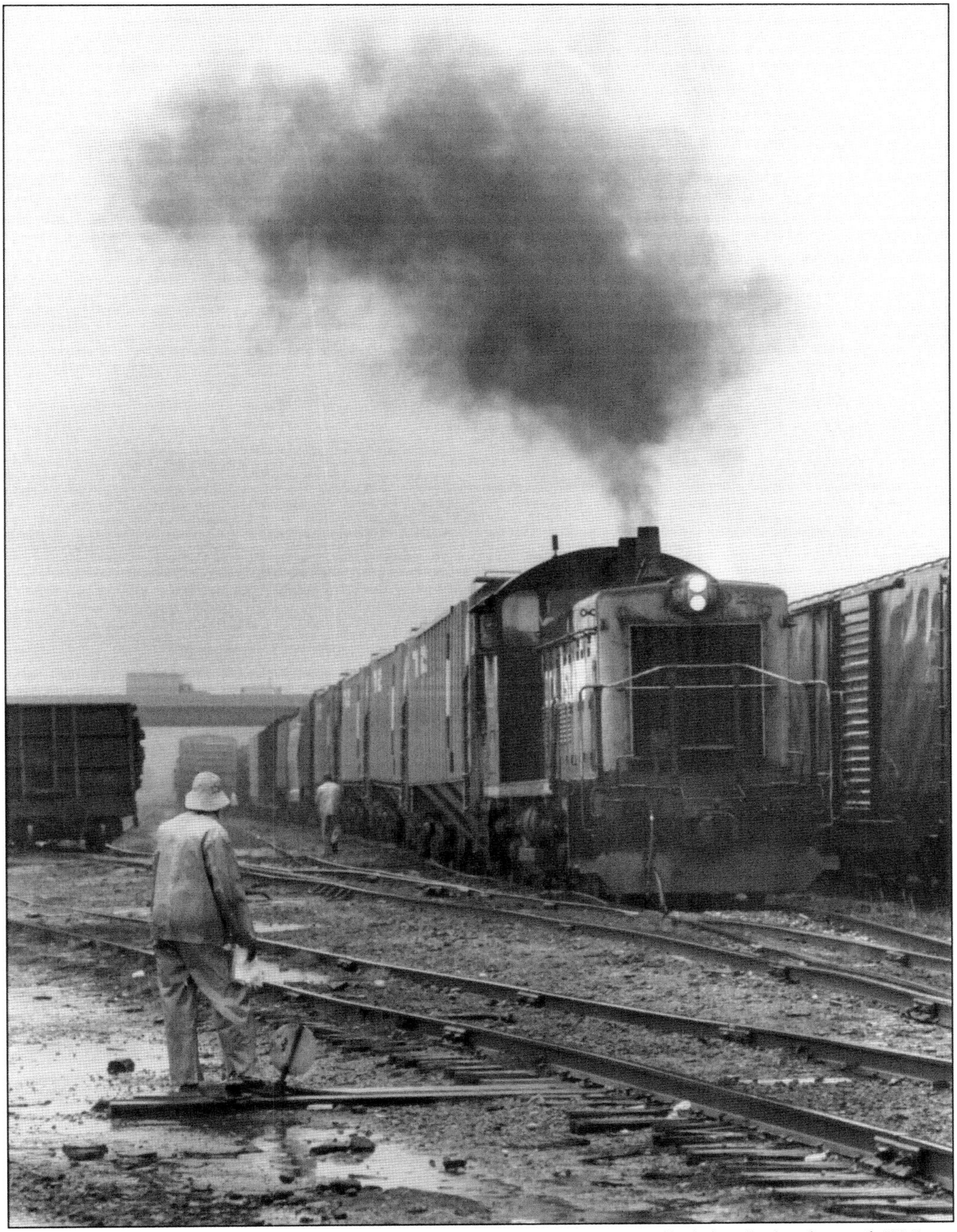

The caption for this photograph that ran in the *Arkansas Gazette* called this "a final switch." Here, a switchman at Biddle Yard lines up the track for a train on that final day, March 23, 1980. Just after midnight, the Cotton Belt Railroad would temporarily assume operations of Rock Island tracks from Memphis to Little Rock and south to Fordyce for a few weeks until May 31. (*Arkansas Democrat-Gazette* file photograph; photograph by John Rossino.)

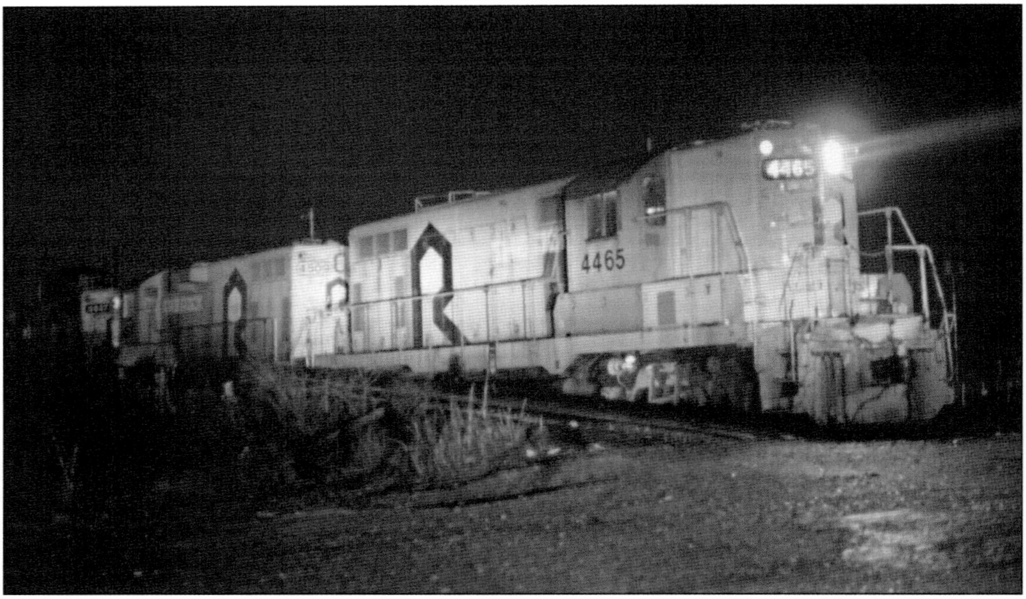

Railroad historian Bill Pollard spent much of that final day taking photographs at Biddle Yard; here, engines for a westbound train are seen waiting at the yard office that night for a crew. The Cotton Belt immediately changed the name of Biddle Yard to the Little Rock Yard. In the following years, all Rock Island structures here were torn down. The Missouri Pacific acquired the yard and had intended to make use of the more modern building constructed in 1967, but a fire during a renovation gutted the building, and it was also razed. (Photograph by Bill Pollard.)

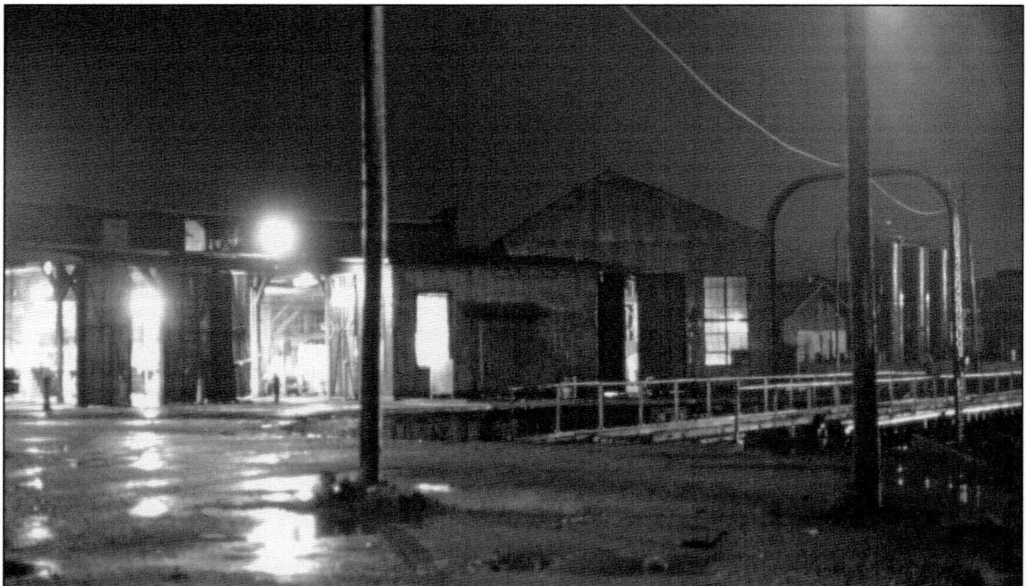

Pollard said the bitterly cold rain and eerie silence added to the misery of the Rock Island's final hours. In this photograph, the roundhouse looks pretty desolate. Most remaining roundhouse and clerical jobs and switch engine assignments were abolished at the end of the second shift. A few Rock Island employees were fortunate enough to be hired by the Cotton Belt. (Photograph by Bill Pollard.)

Seven

After the Shutdown

In most states served by the Rock Island, what had been the main lines of the railroad were preserved by either being acquired by other railroads or in some cases the tracks being bought by the states and leased to other railroads. Despite efforts for that to happen in Arkansas, none succeeded.

A plan was proposed to the Arkansas legislature for the state to buy the right-of-way, but in a vote, it was narrowly defeated. Many former employees of the Rock Island were at the state capitol trying to sway lawmakers, but representatives of competing railroads, namely the Missouri Pacific and Cotton Belt, were pushing against it.

A big shock for many in the state was that, except for a few stretches, the tracks were not taken over by another railroad. The removal of rails on historic routes that had carried trains for more than a century, as well as perhaps millions of passengers, was stark. Railroad stations and bridges that were once landmarks were simply abandoned. Towns that were not served by another railroad were especially hard-hit.

In the months after the Rock Island was shut down, practically every asset was sold or attempts were at least made to sell everything. Bankruptcy sale signs were placed on property such as stations. Two auctions were held at Biddle Yard, as well as at other sites around the country, selling everything from office equipment to depot safes. The rolling stock was moved to large holding yards, with much of the Arkansas equipment sent west to El Reno, Oklahoma. Engines, cabooses, and freight cars were either sold to other railroads or scrapped. It was a grim scene.

But fortunately, a few things did remain; namely, many landmarks around the state, like the Arkansas River bridge and Little Rock depot, were later brought back to life. Both are now part of the Clinton Presidential Library. Other depots built in the 1910s, some of which were also abandoned for a time, have also been preserved. These stand as monuments to a once great railroad. A few stretches of track run trains today, but they represent only a small fraction of what the Rock Island once had in this state.

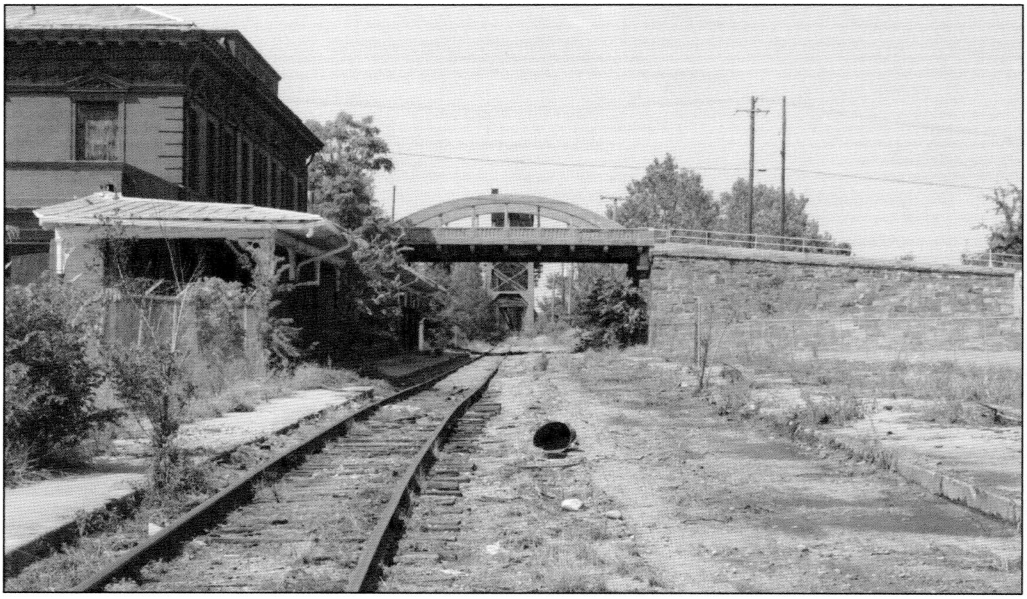

An especially stark scene in the years after the shutdown of the Rock Island was around the old Little Rock passenger station, which had once been such a vibrant place. One track and the Arkansas River bridge continued to be used by the Little Rock & Western Railway until November 1984. These photographs were taken in July 1988 as historic designation was being considered for the Second Street overpass in the distance. (Courtesy of the Library of Congress; photograph by Louisa T. Taft for the Historic American Engineering Record.)

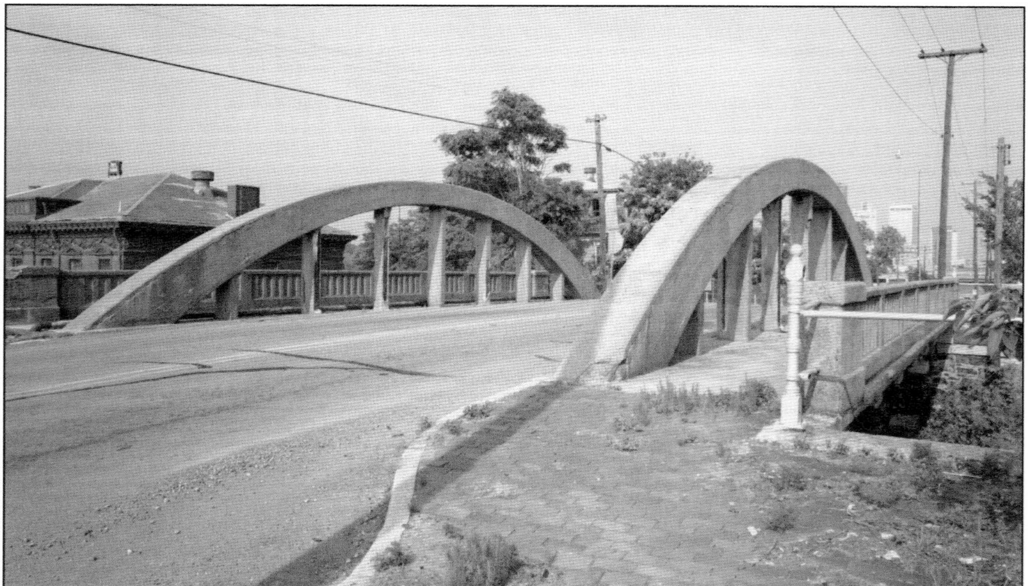

The overpass, which the Rock Island paid to have built in 1915, ended up being torn down in the mid-1990s. The arch was built in a shape similar to the arches of the railroad's Arkansas River bridge. Note that while the railroad had been shut down eight years by this point, the station still features a large Rock Island sign on the roof that includes neon tubing that would have been turned on at night in its passenger days. (Courtesy of the Library of Congress; photograph by Louisa T. Taft for the Historic American Engineering Record.)

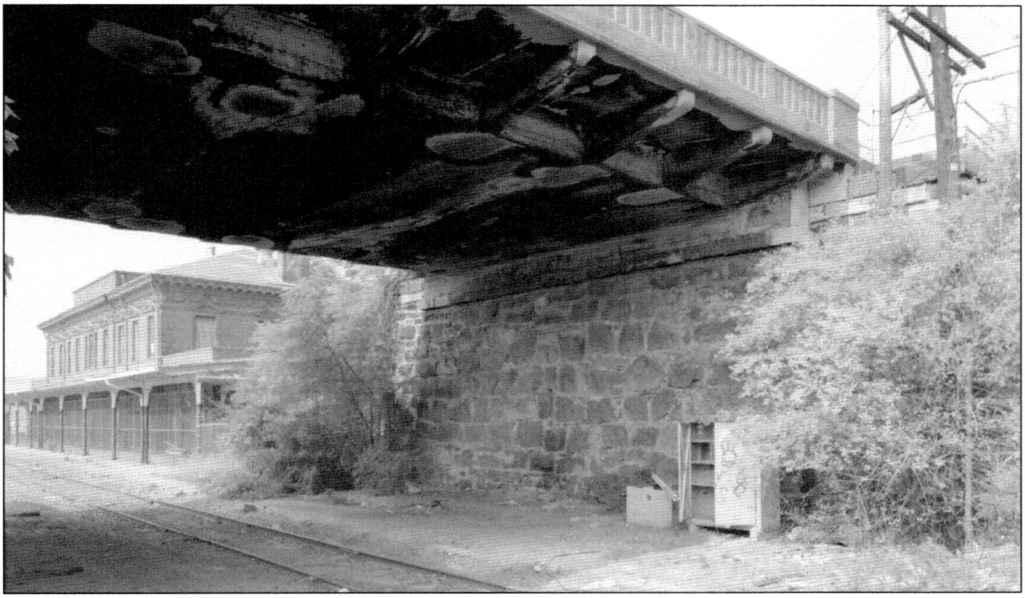

With a view looking south, this photograph was taken from the underside of the Second Street overpass. Note the boarded-up train station in the background. In 1988, a 3.6-acre property including the station and former offices in the George House was for sale for $465,000. By 1990, the station was bought and renovated to become a restaurant that included an old dining car on the track for customers to eat in. (Courtesy of the Library of Congress; photograph by Louisa T. Taft for the Historic American Engineering Record.)

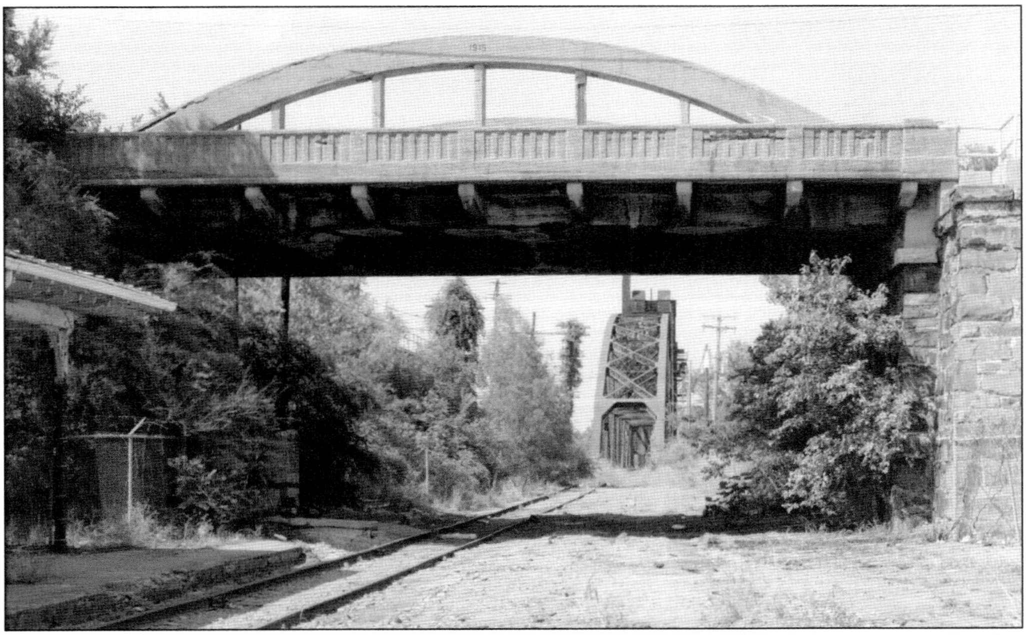

In this closer look at the overpass, one can see the date 1915 stamped into the concrete. By this time in 1988, the track ended just before the bridge. Several miles to the west on Cantrell Road, a similar overpass with curved arches crossed railroad tracks at Little Rock's other train station, which had been the Missouri Pacific's Union Station. (Courtesy of the Library of Congress; photograph by Louisa T. Taft for the Historic American Engineering Record.)

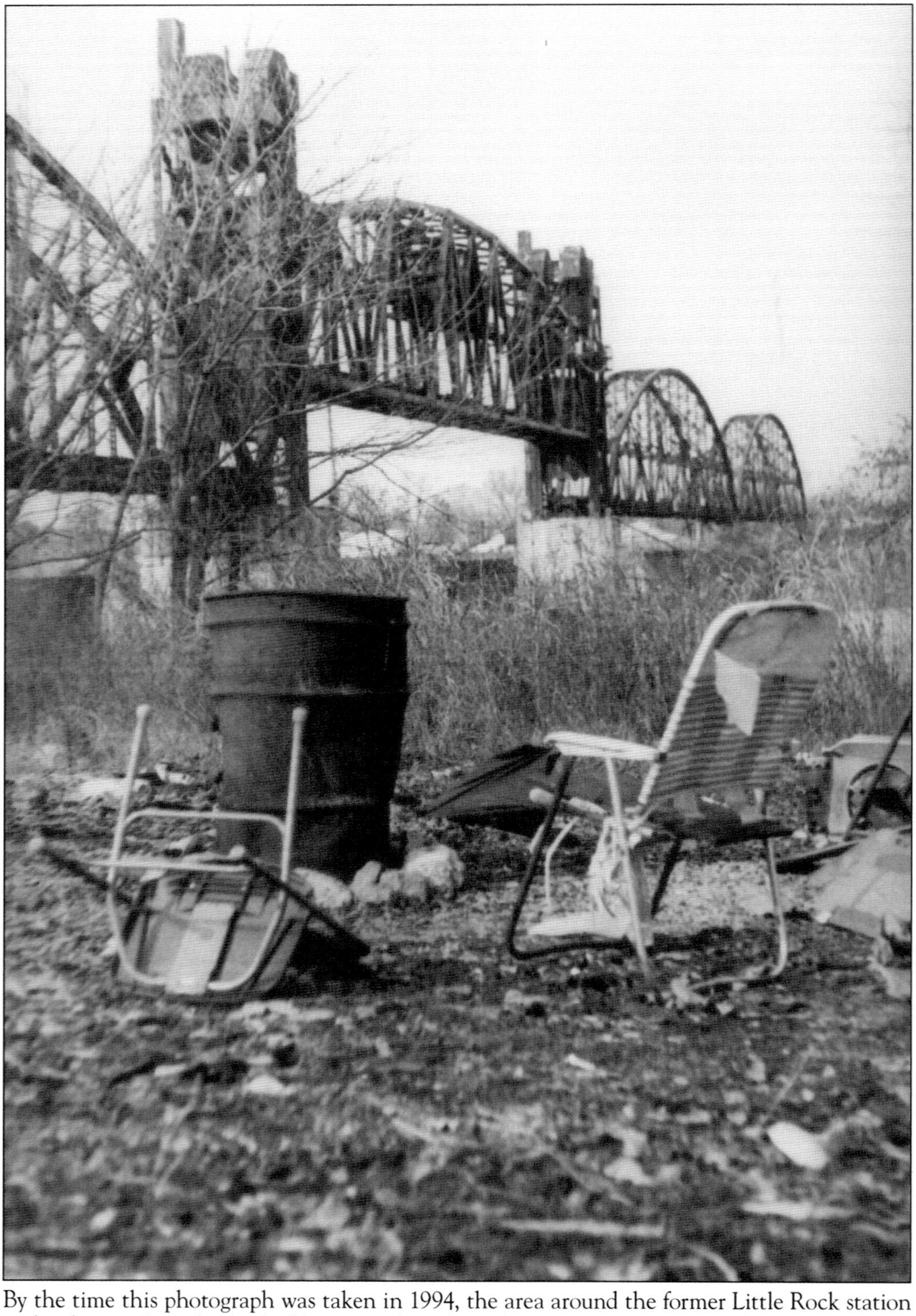

By the time this photograph was taken in 1994, the area around the former Little Rock station and Arkansas River bridge had become a large homeless camp. Mattresses could be found under the Second Street overpass, and here, a 55-gallon oil drum was used for burning material in sight of the unused bridge. (Photograph by author.)

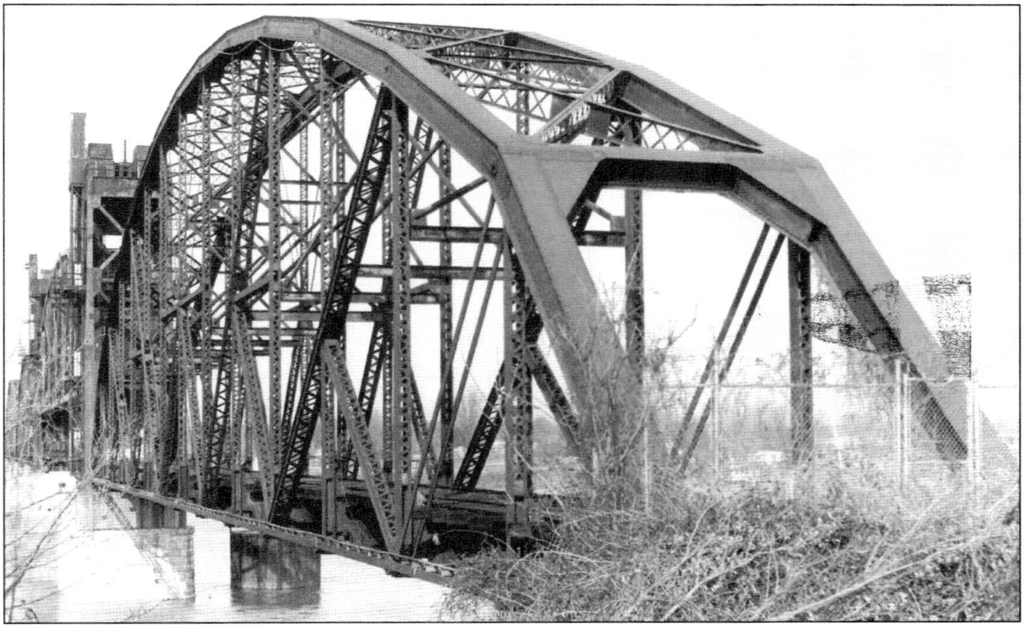

The Union Pacific Railroad ended up with ownership of the bridge, which it did not need because it had two other bridges crossing the Arkansas River at Little Rock, and deemed it a liability. By 1989, a plan was in place for the Rock Island bridge to be dismantled, with its lift span to be used for a bridge in Washington State, while the other spans would be scrapped. Five years later, the bridge was still in place with a fence around it. (Photograph by author.)

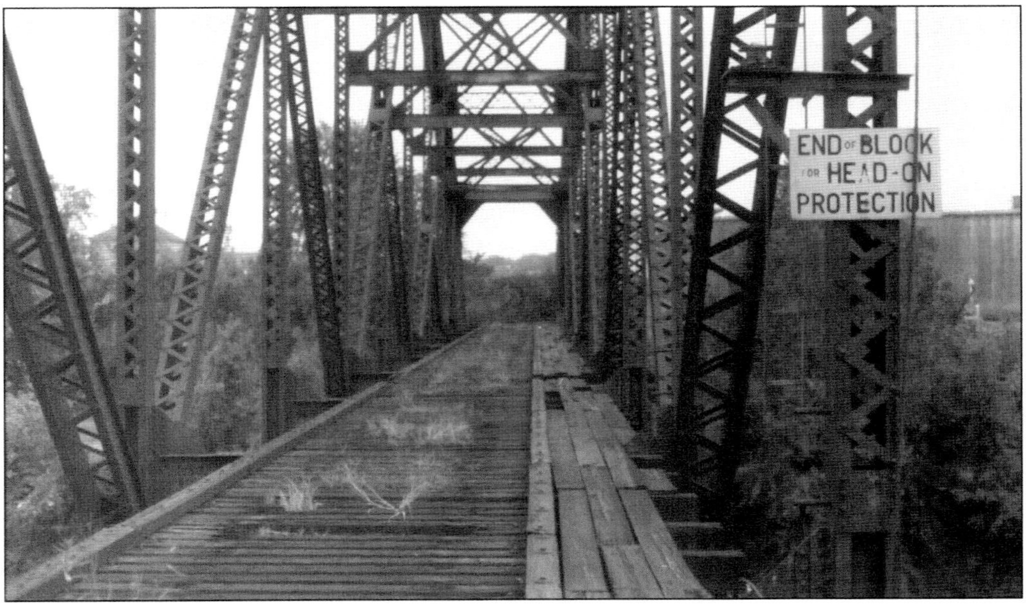

Getting out on the bridge was not difficult, and it is clear from this 1994 photograph that it also was not safe, with boards from the wooden walkway missing, as was a cable that served as a handrail. An official with a local ambulance company said they had many rescues here over the years from people falling from the bridge. The sign to the right is a relic of the railroad warning that it was the end of block signals from here to Biddle Yard. Power to the bridge had been disconnected after it was no longer in use and the lift span was locked in place. (Photograph by author.)

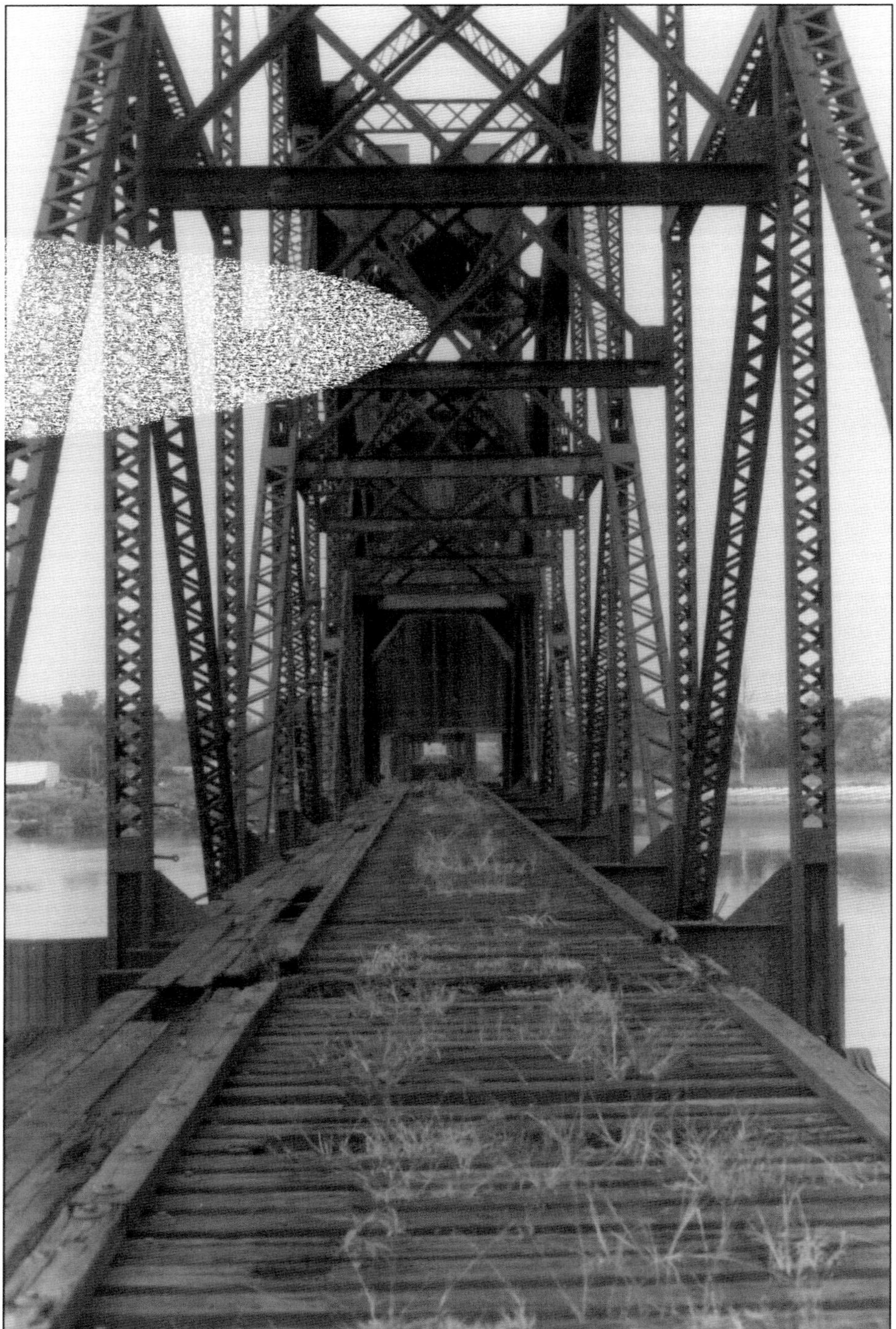

Officials with the cities of Little Rock and North Little Rock and Pulaski County wanted to preserve the Rock Island bridge, calling it an important part of the community's history. They began negotiations with Union Pacific to assume ownership, which the railroad eventually agreed to. But it would be more than a decade before the goal of converting it into a pedestrian and cycling bridge would be realized. (Photograph by author.)

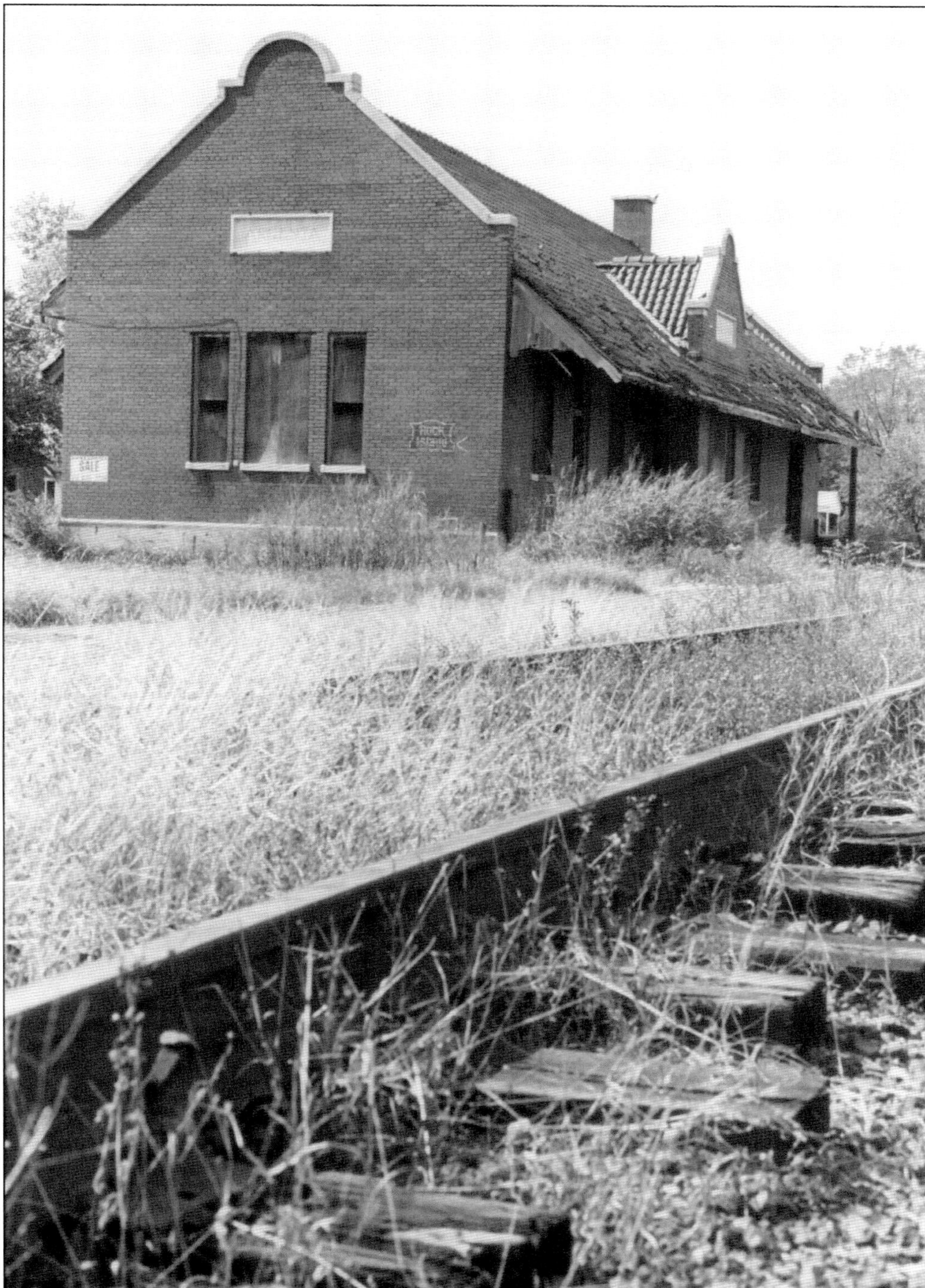

A short distance from the bridge, the North Little Rock depot also sits abandoned in this photograph from November 2, 1981. At that time, the city council had expressed interest in buying the weather- and vandal-ravaged building and authorized the city attorney to begin negotiations with trustees of the bankrupt railroad. But it would be more than 16 years before a renovation finally took place. (*Arkansas Democrat-Gazette* file photograph; photograph by John Woodruff.)

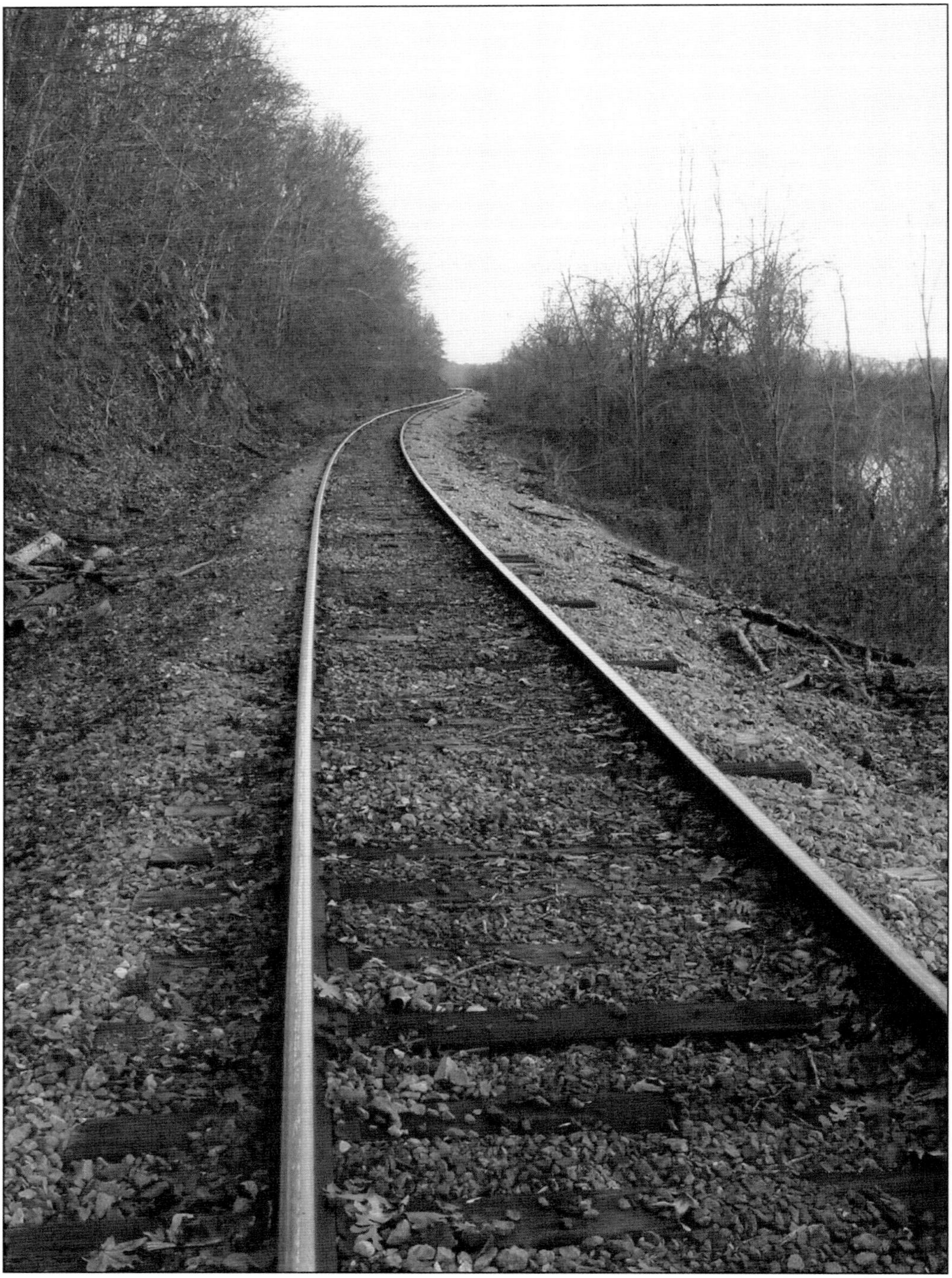

Despite efforts by the state to get another railroad to buy the entire Rock Island system in Arkansas, none did. There was consideration of a proposal for the state to buy the tracks and lease them to other railroads, but that failed in the legislature. Instead, a few sections were picked up by other railroads. A 79-mile segment between Little Rock and Danville became the Little Rock & Western Railway. Here, pictured in 2003, is a scenic section of the track where it briefly runs alongside the Arkansas River west of Little Rock. (Photograph by author.)

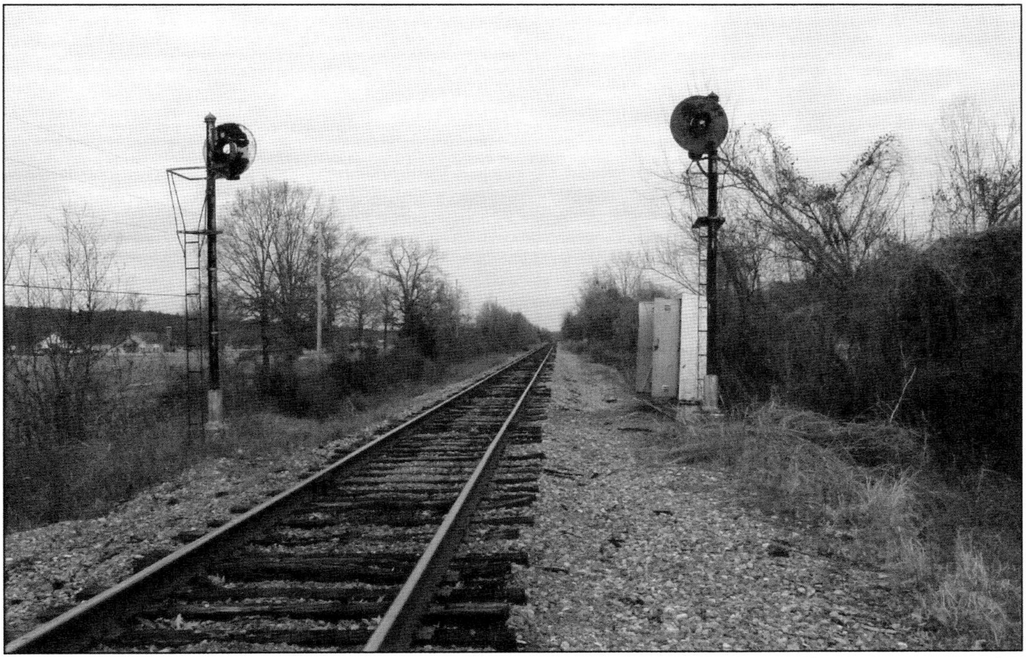

Old block signals from the Rock Island days remain alongside the Little Rock & Western tracks, even though they are no longer in use. This is near the town of Roland in 2004 along what had been part of the old Sunbelt Line linking Memphis, Tennessee, and Tucumcari, New Mexico. (Photograph by author.)

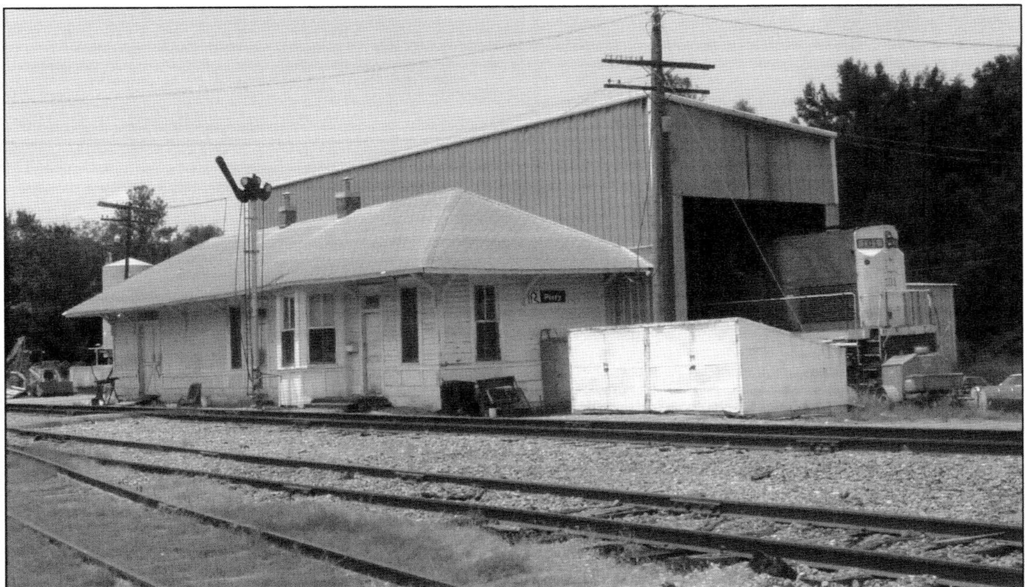

The headquarters for the Little Rock & Western is located in the town of Perry, which uses what was the Rock Island's depot there, still emblazoned with the final "The Rock" logo on the side. The Little Rock & Western built a locomotive servicing shed built behind the depot. Still present in this 2004 photograph is at least part of the original train order signals. As a nod to the original railroad that came through here, the depot is located on Choctaw Avenue. (Photograph by author.)

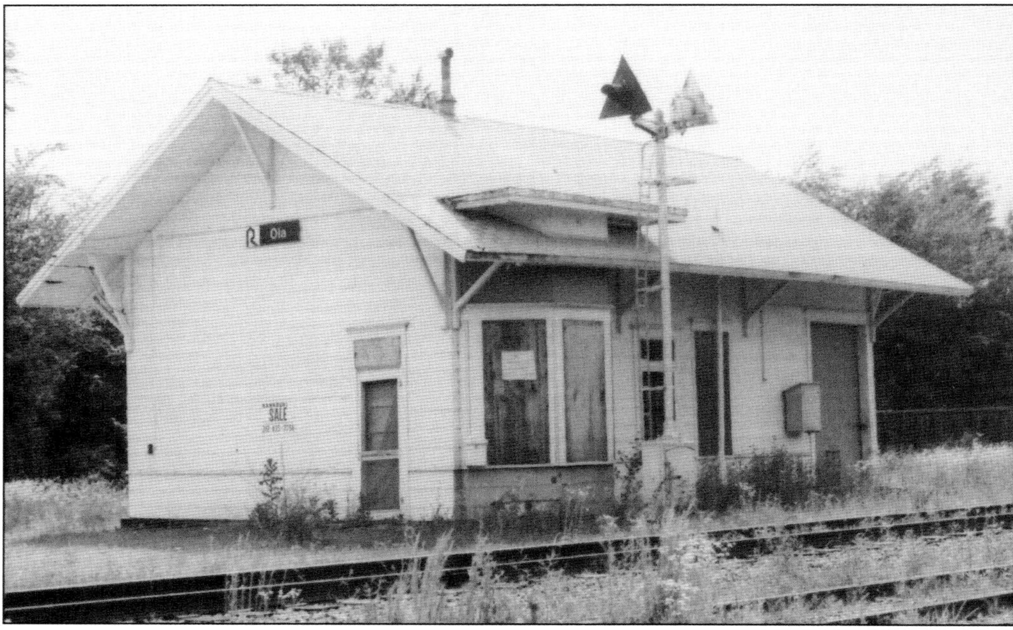

Along the tracks west of Perry was the town of Ola, where the Rock Island had this small depot, seen boarded up in this 1983 postcard image. Still attached to the side at that time is a bankruptcy sale sign, with a phone number. Note that it still features a depot sign with the final logo for "The Rock." (Author's collection.)

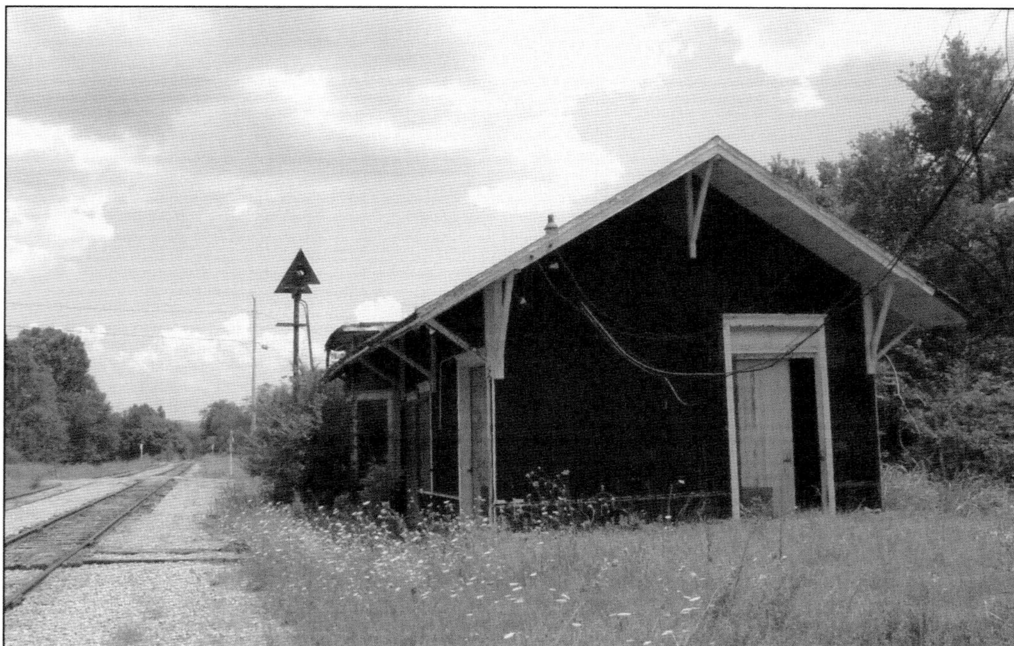

By July 2004, the Ola depot had been painted black to cover graffiti and had just had asbestos removed in advance of its being torn down. Still visible in this photograph is the path from the depot to the track for passengers or mail carts. The signal with triangular shaded targets was a newer style of train order signal. This particular signal was rescued, reconditioned, and placed on display at the Arkansas Railroad Museum in Pine Bluff. (Photograph by author.)

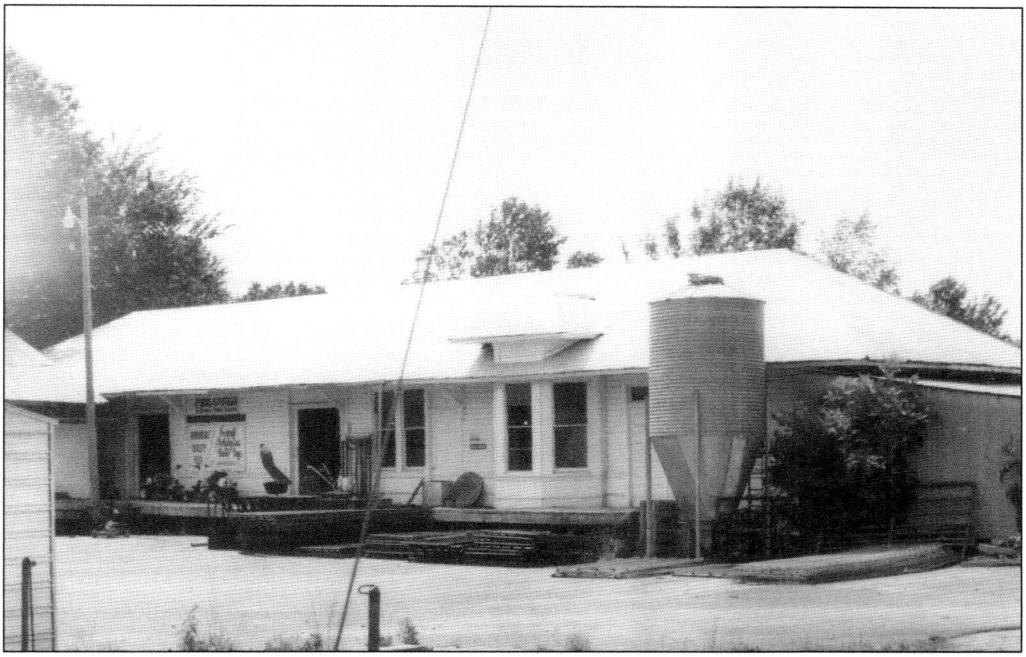

The former Danville depot is featured on this postcard from 1983. This was near where the Little Rock & Western tracks end. (Author's collection.)

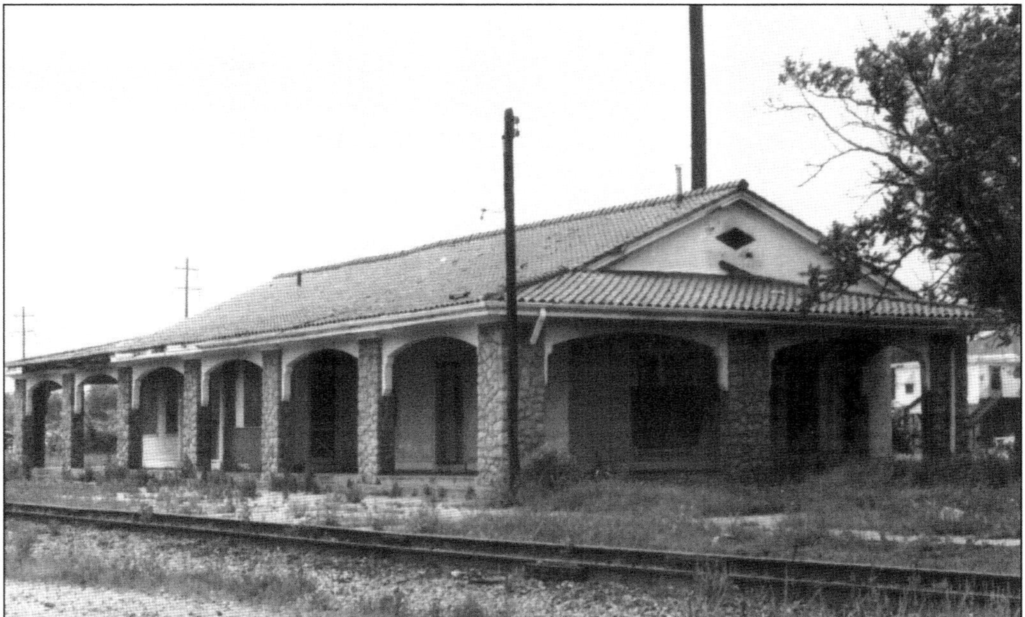

The Booneville depot, pictured here in 1983, was significant as a crew-change point. For trains heading west toward Oklahoma, this is where crews working out of Little Rock got off and would later return east on another train. This unique stone structure, which was abandoned by this time, would eventually be destroyed by a fire. It was near here that Pres. Franklin D. Roosevelt spoke briefly to a crowd of about 3,000 on July 9, 1938, from the back of a train during his whistle-stop campaign for a third term. (Author's collection.)

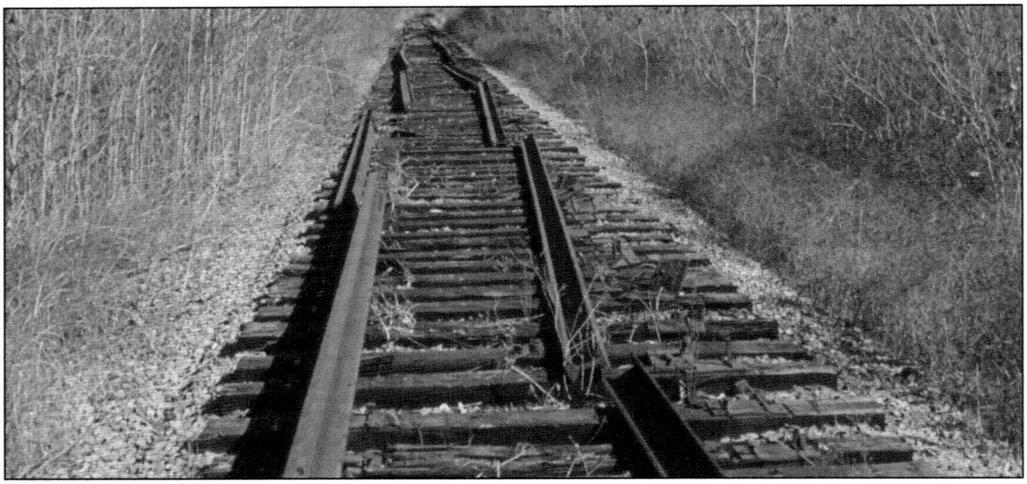

There were pleas from many not to rip out the old Rock Island track with the hope that eventually another railroad would be interested. By March 1982, a contract was awarded to remove more than 3,000 miles of Rock Island track in the United States, including a 36-mile section in Arkansas from Malvern to Sparkman. Four years later in March 1986, this was the scene at Waveland looking east as part of the Sunbelt Line was removed. In nearby Havana, rail historian Bill Pollard noted that rails from a siding reading "Carnegie 1899" were undoubtedly from when the railroad was first built through by the Choctaw, Oklahoma & Gulf. He assumes it was probably part of the original CO&G main line and was later relegated for use in the siding. "If I had any way to secure a section of that rail, I would have done so . . . it was gone by the time I went back a few weeks later." (Photograph by Bill Pollard.)

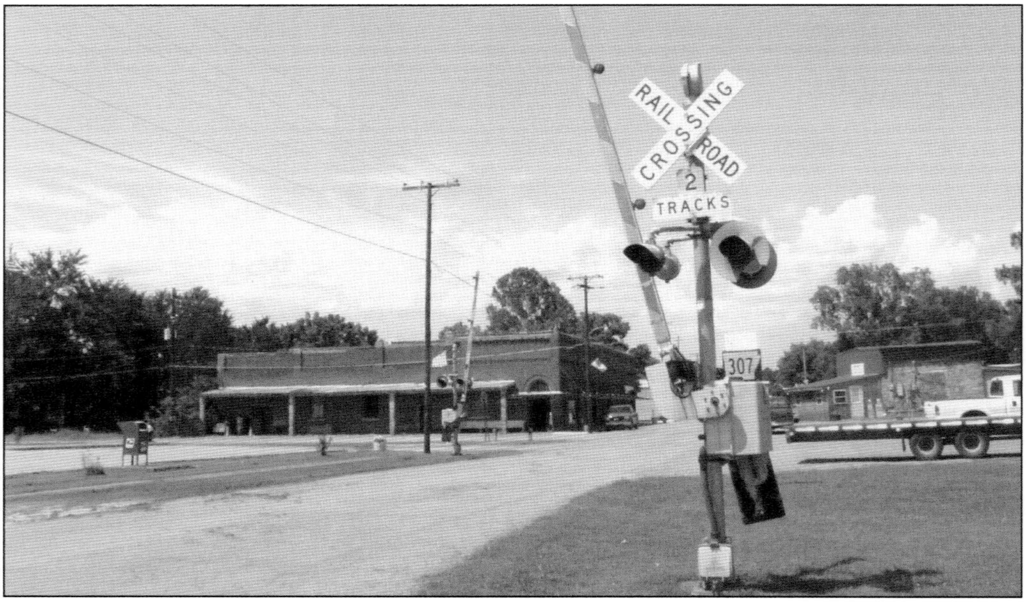

While the tracks may have been taken out, many communities have kept reminders of places that were once part of a national transportation vein. In this photograph from July 2004 in Belleville, despite the presence of railroad crossing gates, tracks are no longer there. Perhaps millions of people moved through this spot during the nearly 70 years passenger trains ran through here. Many other communities in Arkansas also have railroad crossing signs still in place where rails are long gone. (Photograph by author.)

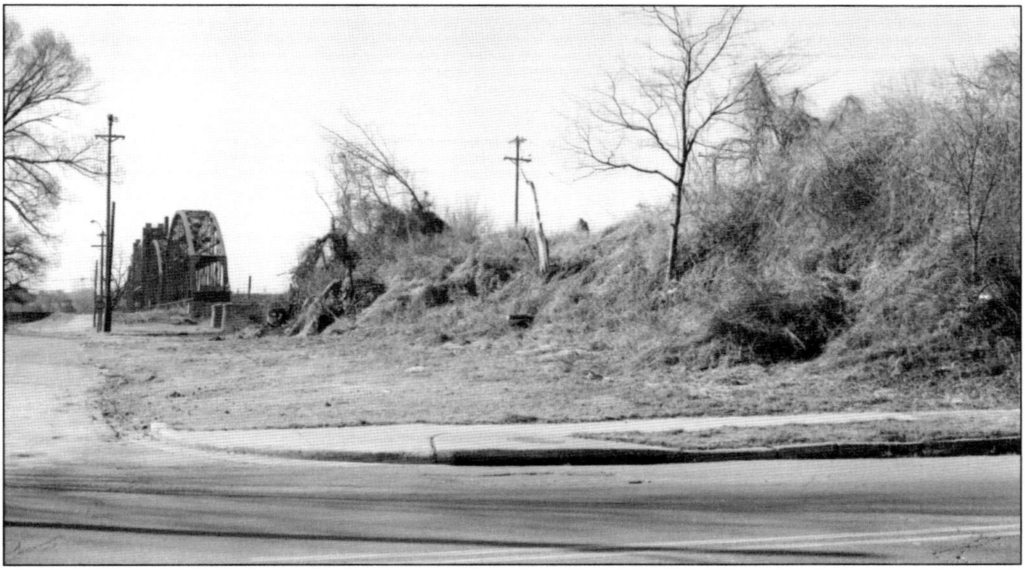

In March 1991, the roughly nine-foot-high embankment for the Rock Island's track in North Little Rock leading to the Arkansas River bridge was removed by heavy, earth-moving equipment. Photographer Clifton Hull said in his caption that the removal process revealed the upper two feet were composed of cinders from early coal-burning locomotives. This roadbed would have been created in the late 1890s. (Courtesy of Bill Pollard; photograph by Clifton Hull.)

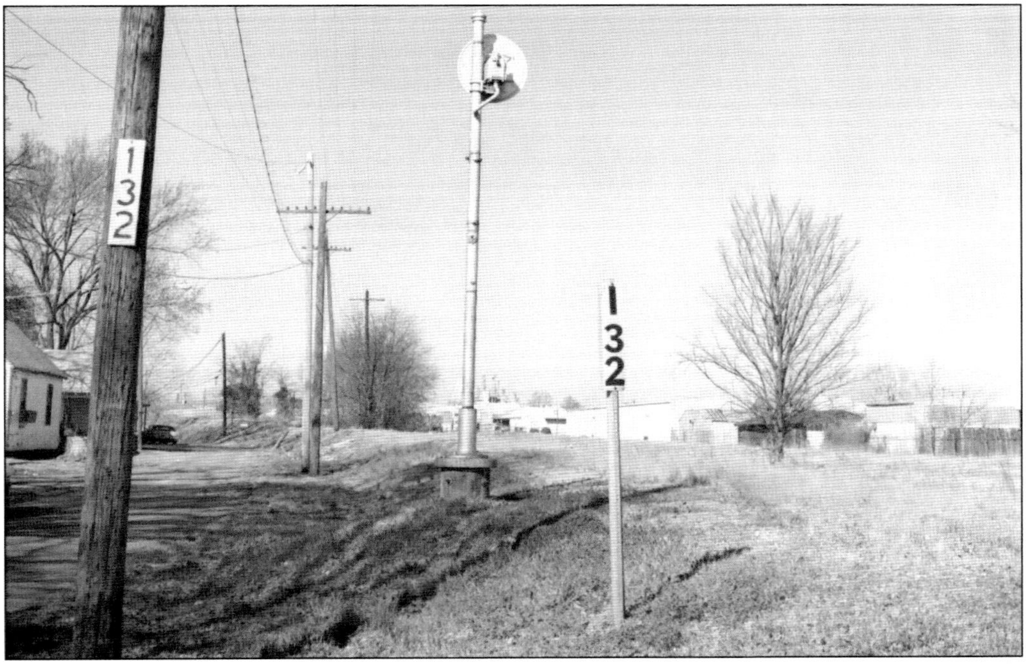

Most of the Rock Island's tracks through North Little Rock were taken up by April 1988. While documenting the removal of the bridge's embankment three years later, Clifton Hull also visited the nearby depot area, noting the visible remains of the railroad. It had been 11 years at that point since the Rock Island was shut down, but the sign noting milepost No. 132 remains, though with no track. This was 132 miles from Memphis Central Station. (Courtesy of Bill Pollard; photograph by Clifton Hull.)

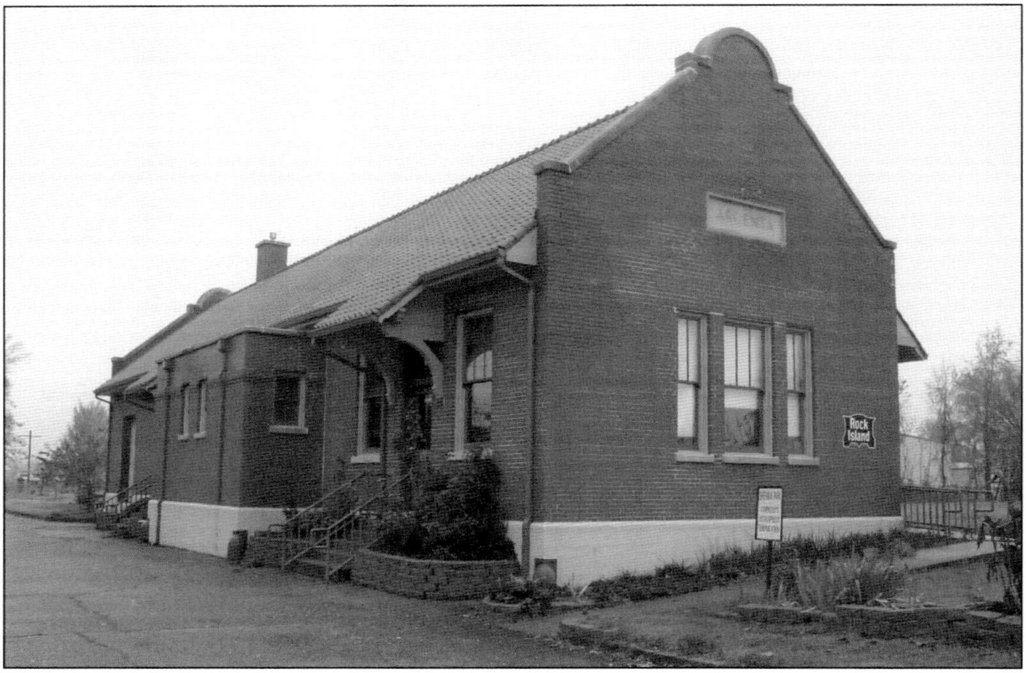

After sitting abandoned and deteriorating for decades, the depot in North Little Rock on East Fourth Street was renovated in 1998 at a cost of nearly $300,000. Longtime Rock Island conductor L.T. Walker put on his old passenger service uniform to speak at the ceremony that May cerebrating completion of the renovation. It now houses the nonprofit Sherman Park Community Development Corporation. This photograph was taken in December 2004. (Photograph by author.)

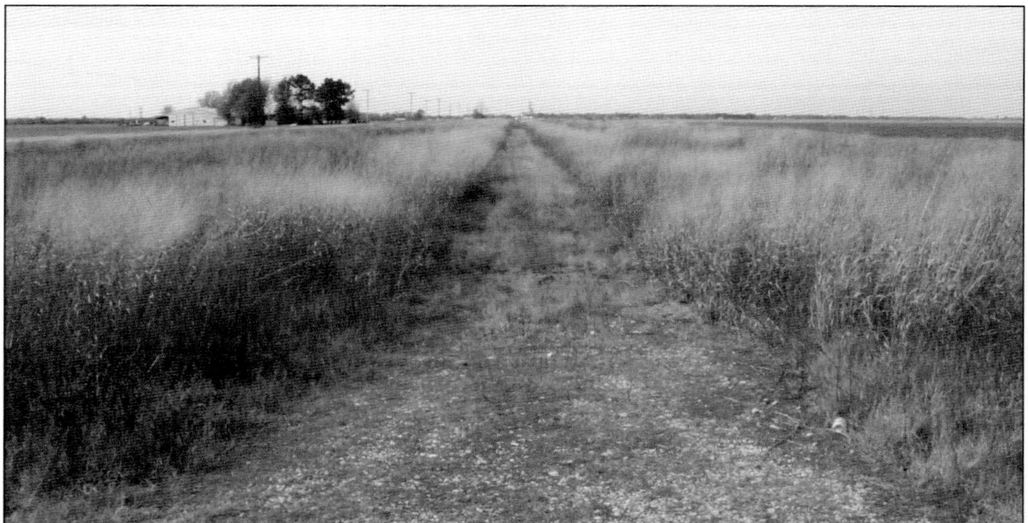

About two decades after the Rock Island track in this area near the Lonoke-Prairie County Line was removed, the spot where trains ran for more than a century is still evident in the tall grass in this photograph taken in 2004. An industrial building in the distance, built along the tracks, served the agricultural community in Carlisle. This right-of-way had been part of the original Memphis & Little Rock Railroad, which was the first chartered in the state. The Nature Conservancy bought much of this land to preserve native plants. (Photograph by author.)

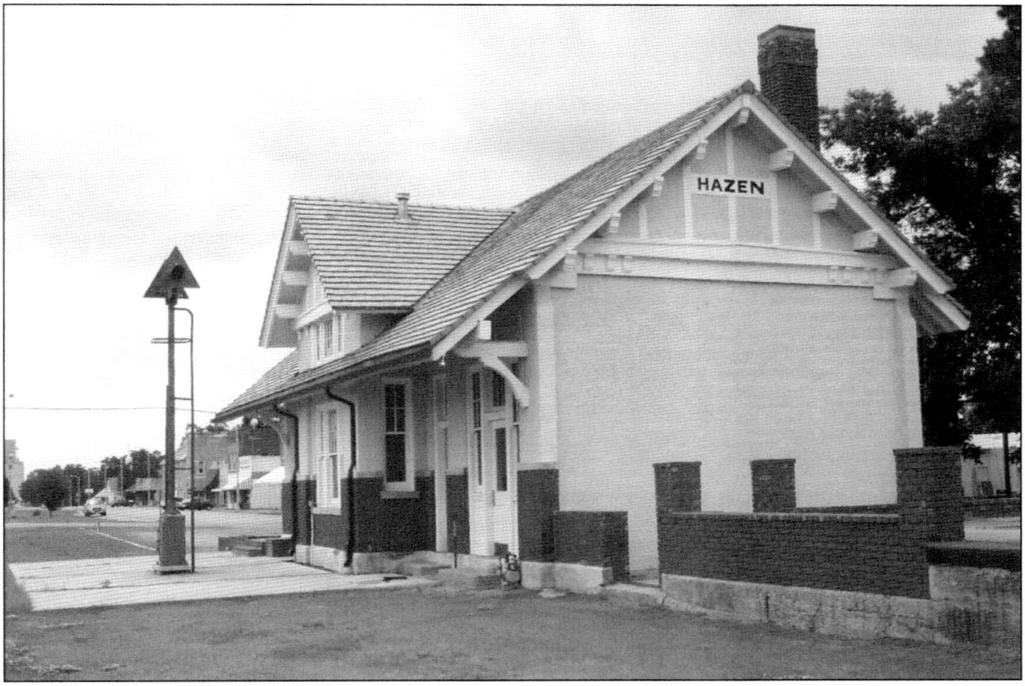

Here is the depot at Hazen, which was built by the Rock Island in 1915. It was added to the National Register of Historic Places in 1987 and, as evident in this 2004 photograph, has been beautifully restored. (Photograph by author.)

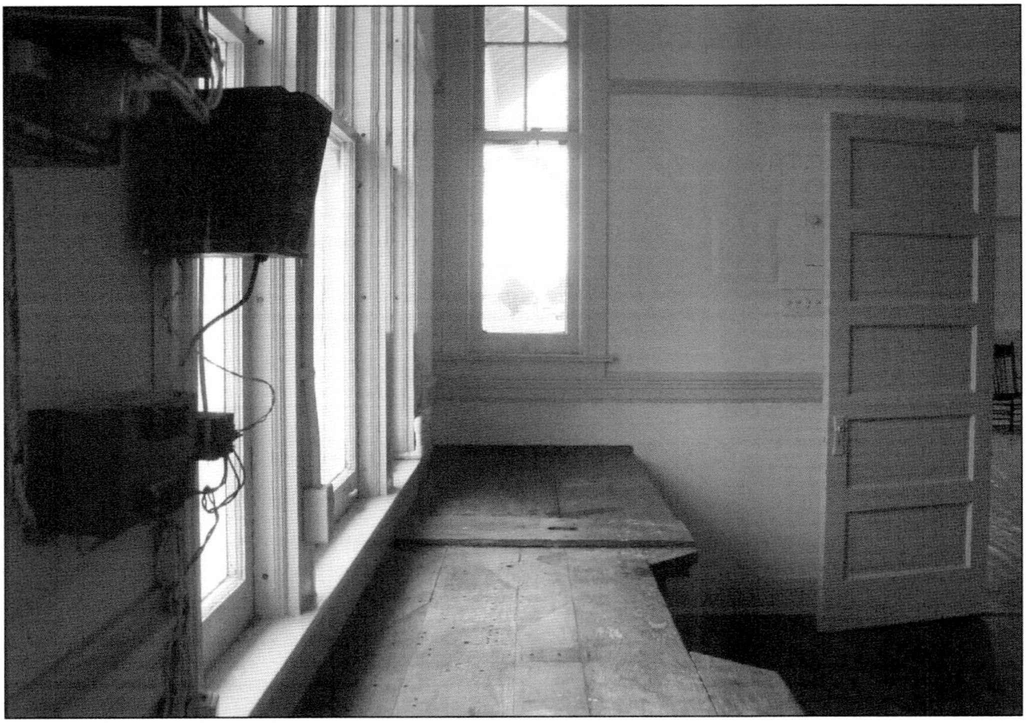

The projected telegrapher's booth in the Hazen depot looks in this 2004 as it likely did during the years it was in use by the railroad. (Photograph by author.)

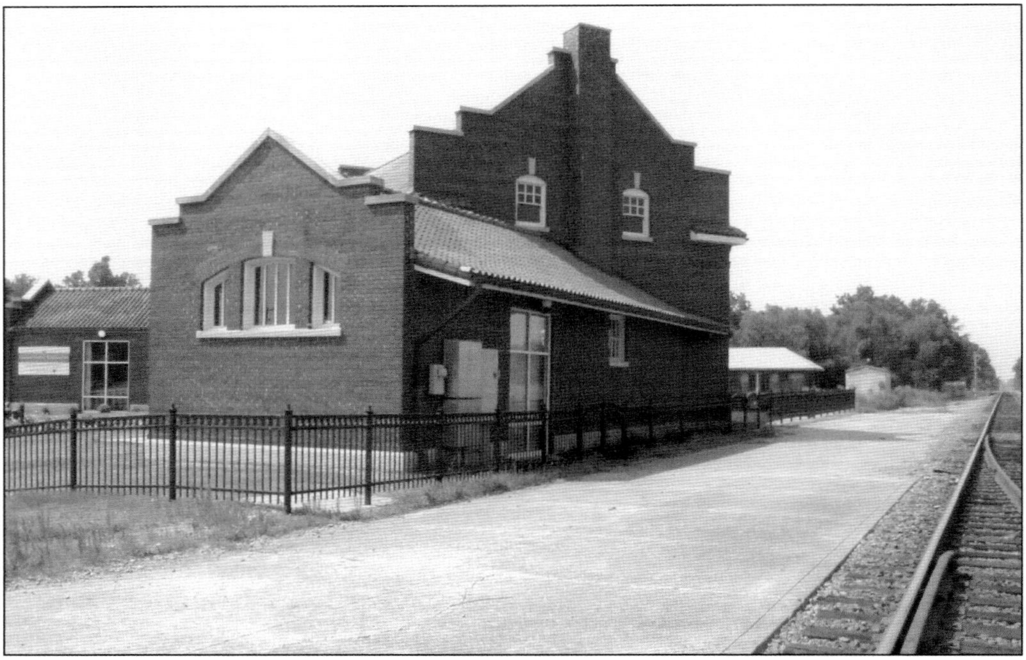

Union Station at Brinkley was in rough shape, boarded up and abandoned for many years, but by July 2005, it had been restored as a museum highlighting the city's railroad history. The Rock Island shared this building with the Cotton Belt, which ran trains north from here to St. Louis and south to Texas. (Photograph by author.)

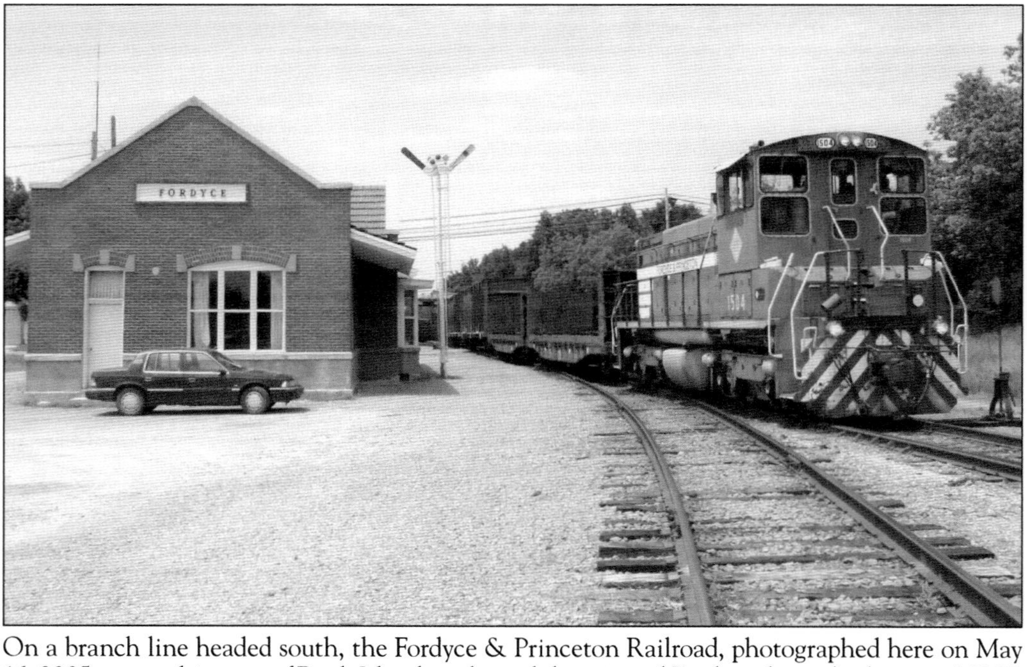

On a branch line headed south, the Fordyce & Princeton Railroad, photographed here on May 16, 2005, was making use of Rock Island tracks and the original Fordyce depot, built around 1925. The old semaphore train order signal also remains here. The track branching off to the left of this photograph connects with the Union Pacific here. Also, the engine in use here, F&P No. 1504, is an old Rock Island switcher that used to be No. 941. (Photograph by author.)

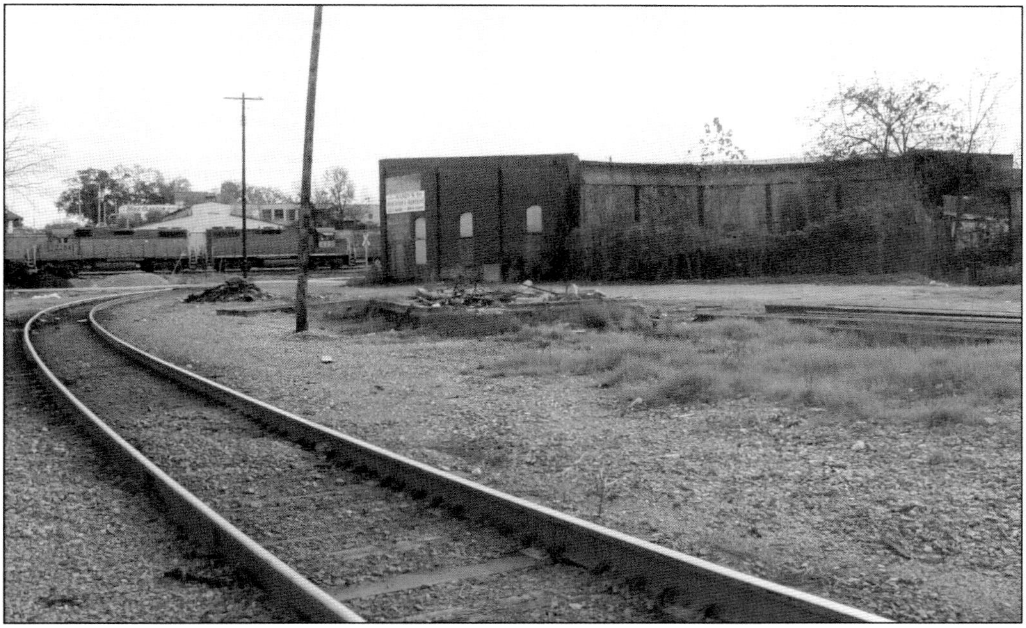

The Rock Island and Missouri Pacific had competing service to Hot Springs, both with branch lines splitting off heading toward the resort town. The Missouri Pacific had a straighter, more direct route, but the Rock Island benefited from having a lot of industries alongside its line. The building in the background is the five-stall roundhouse of Rock Island predecessor Hot Springs Railroad, known as the "Diamond Jo" Line. Below, their two lines meet, with the Missouri Pacific crossing over the Rock Island's track near Hot Springs. This photograph was taken in 2007, with the Rock Island's former track being used by the Arkansas Midland Railroad. The Missouri Pacific's track had been removed and, as of this publication, the former right-of-way was being considered for a rails-to-trails program linking Little Rock and Hot Springs. (Photographs by author.)

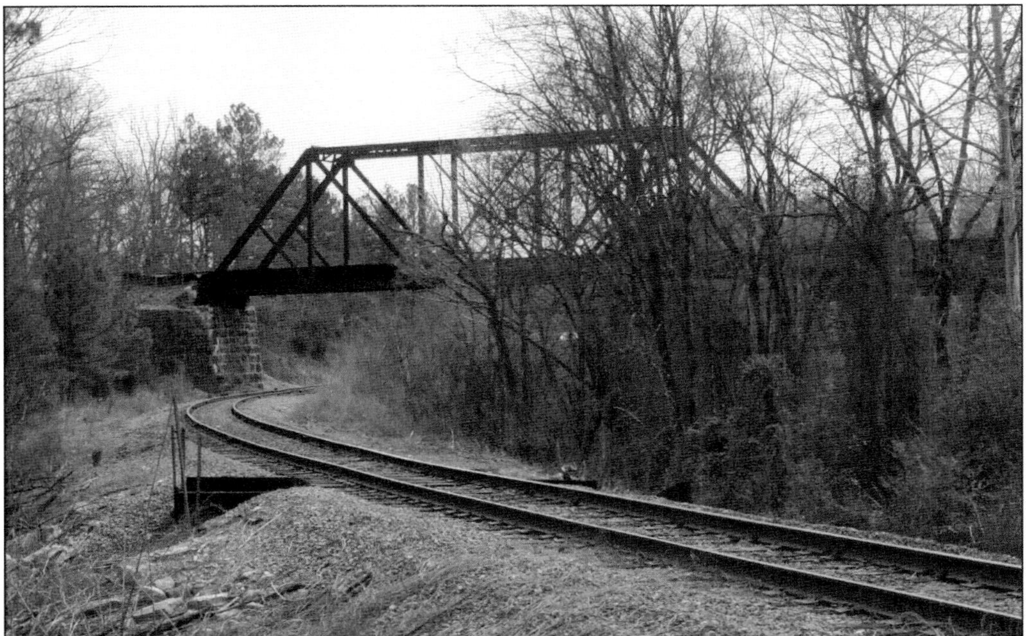

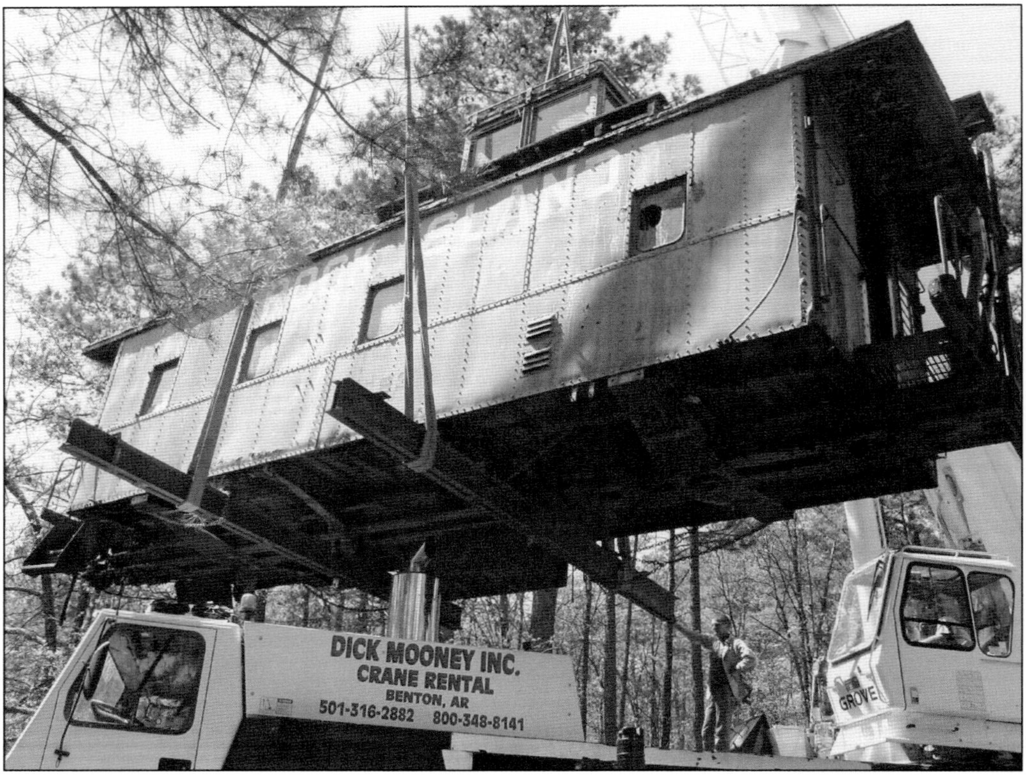

Rock Island Caboose No. 17883, which was sold after the 1980 liquidation of railroad property, was being moved in 2004 from one private home to another just west of Little Rock. Here, a crane has lifted the frame of the caboose, built in the 1930s, from its trucks to be placed on a trailer. (Photograph by author.)

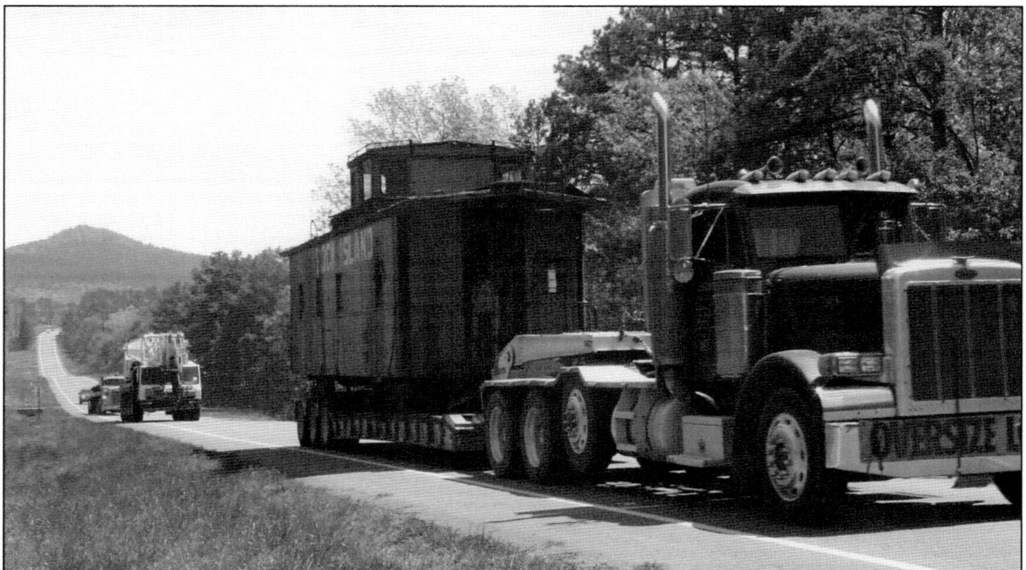

It was quite a scene as the caboose is then transported by truck on Highway 10, with Pinnacle Mountain in the background. (Photograph by author.)

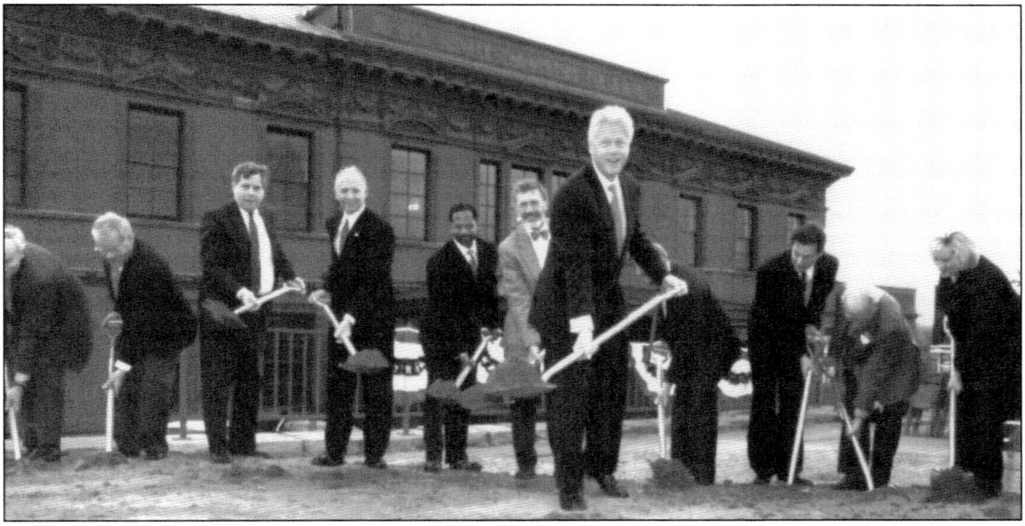

As US president Bill Clinton's second term in office came to a close and after some debate about where to build his presidential library, it was eventually decided that the library would be built in Little Rock along the Arkansas River on the grounds that had belonged to the Rock Island. The complex would incorporate the railroad's passenger station and the Arkansas River bridge. Clinton had been governor of Arkansas when the railroad shut down in 1980. A ground-breaking ceremony to build Clinton's presidential library was held on December 5, 2001, with the old train station looking grand as a backdrop for the ceremony. Former president Bill Clinton shoveled the first scoop of dirt, formally marking the beginning of construction. (Courtesy of Skip Rutherford.)

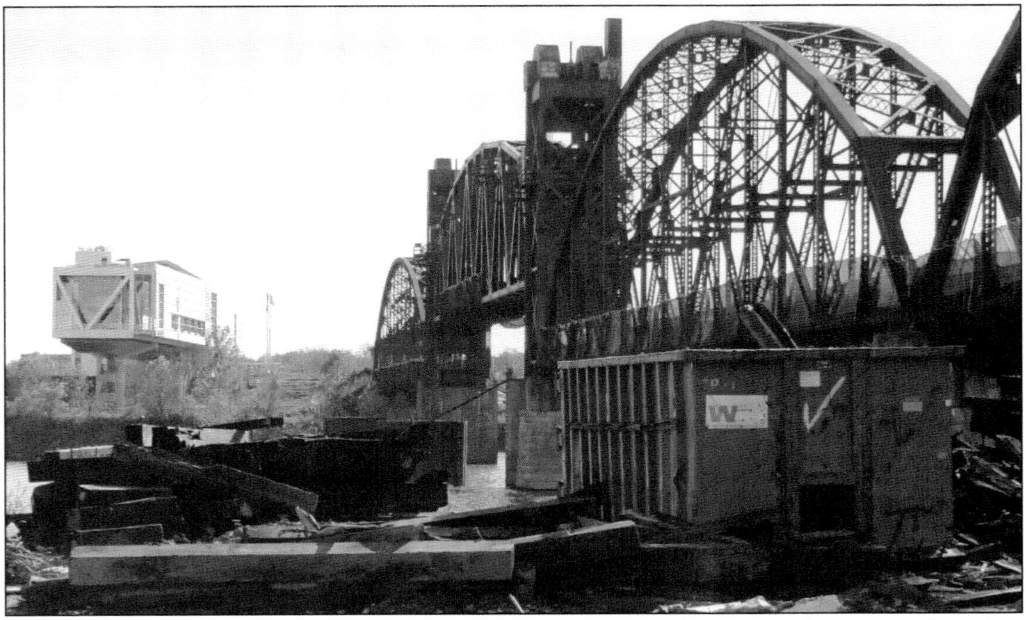

It was hoped that the Rock Island bridge would be converted into a pedestrian and cycling bridge in time for the 2004 opening of the presidential library, but the cost of embarking on the restoration was more than had originally been anticipated. It took several years of fundraising to amass the $11 million eventually needed to complete the project. Here, on November 28, 2010, with the presidential library on the other side of the Arkansas River, rotting timber was being removed from the bridge. (Photograph by author.)

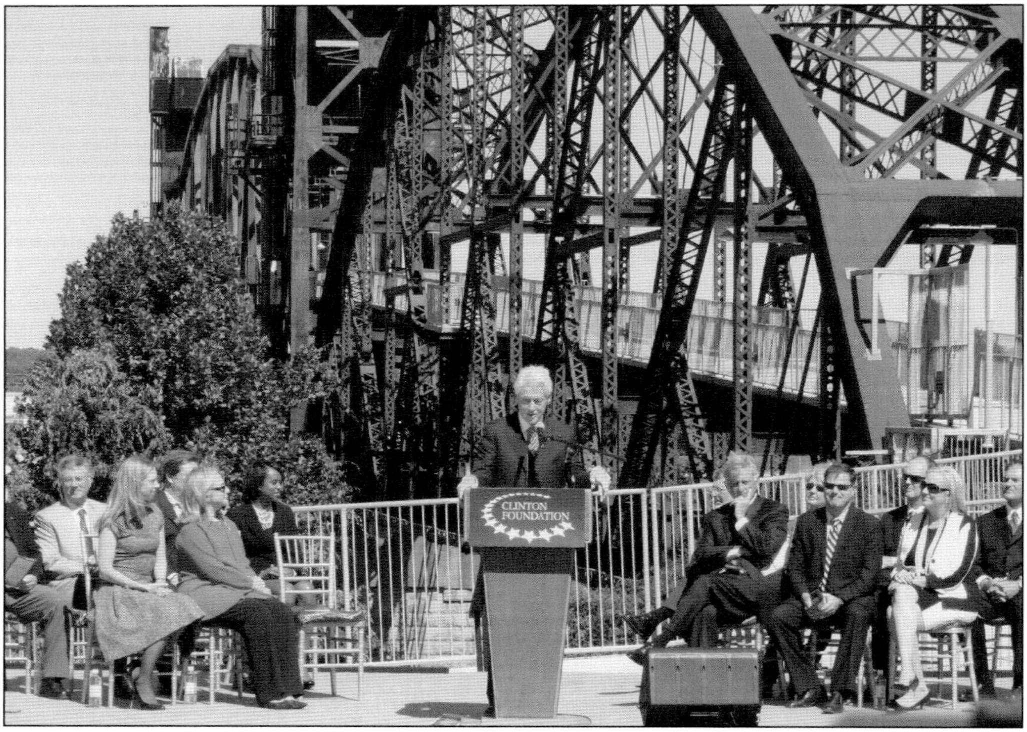

At the bridge dedication ceremony on September 30, 2011, the Clinton family made their arrival by walking across the bridge. Then, the former president spoke, with the Rock Island Bridge, which was renamed the Clinton Presidential Park Bridge, as a backdrop. (Photograph by author.)

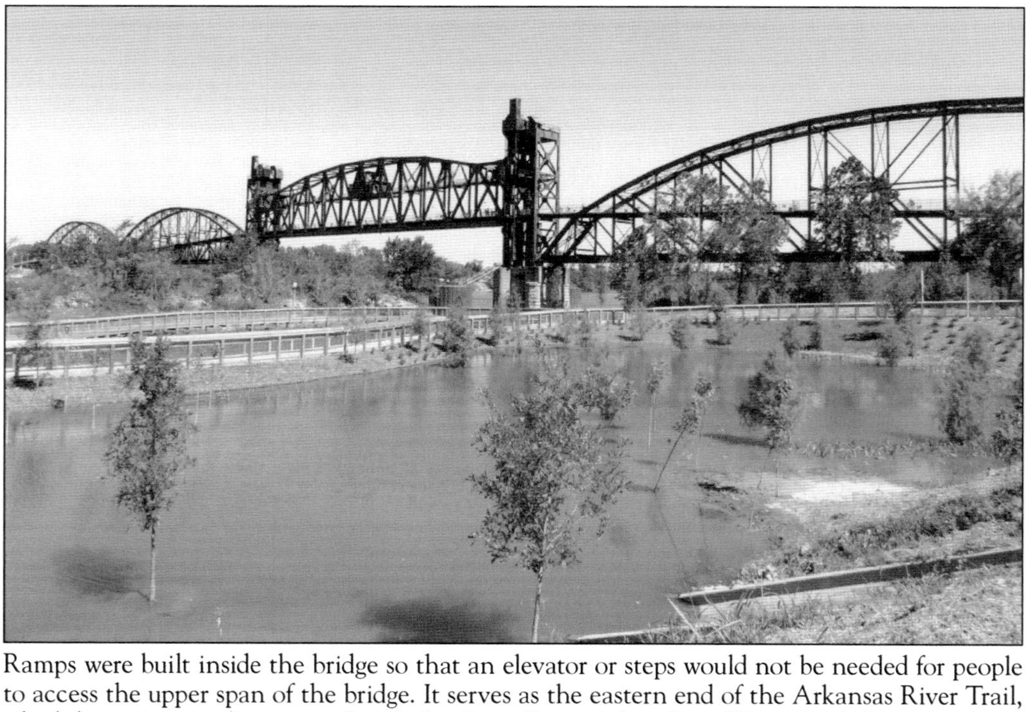

Ramps were built inside the bridge so that an elevator or steps would not be needed for people to access the upper span of the bridge. It serves as the eastern end of the Arkansas River Trail, which has proven to be extremely popular for walking and cycling. (Photograph by author.)

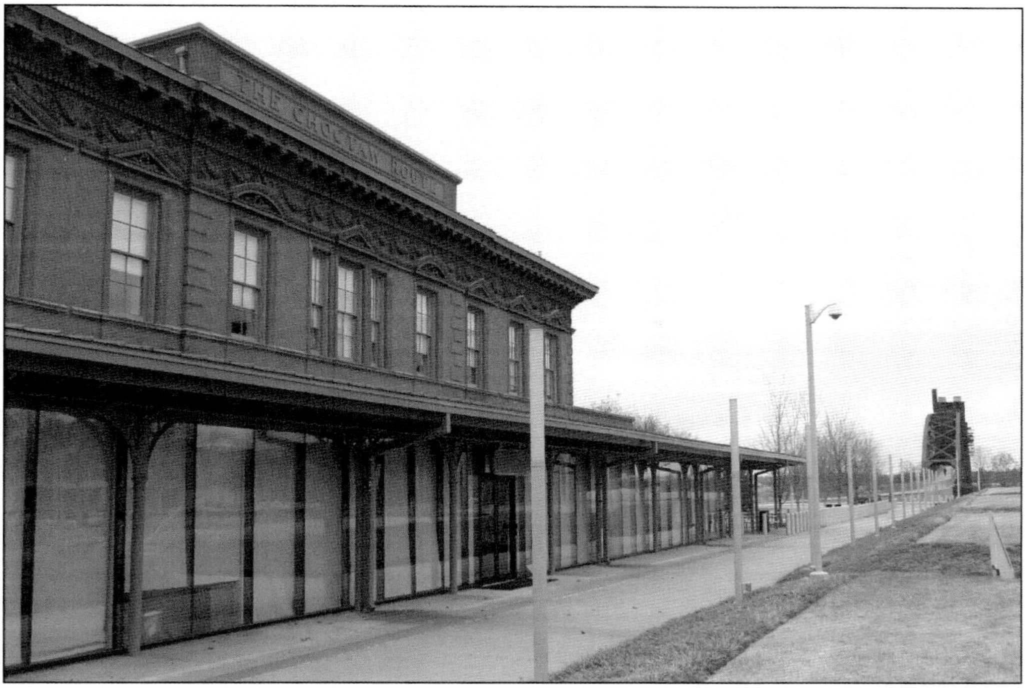

The old passenger station would be renovated to become the home of the William J. Clinton Foundation and the University of Arkansas Clinton School of Public Service, which is the educational arm of the presidential library. The station is now called Sturgis Hall, in recognition of a major renovation grant from the Roy and Christine Sturgis Trust. The large Clinton Presidential Center building was constructed next door. A sidewalk, shown here in December 2015, follows the same path between the bridge to the station as a track once did. (Photograph by author.)

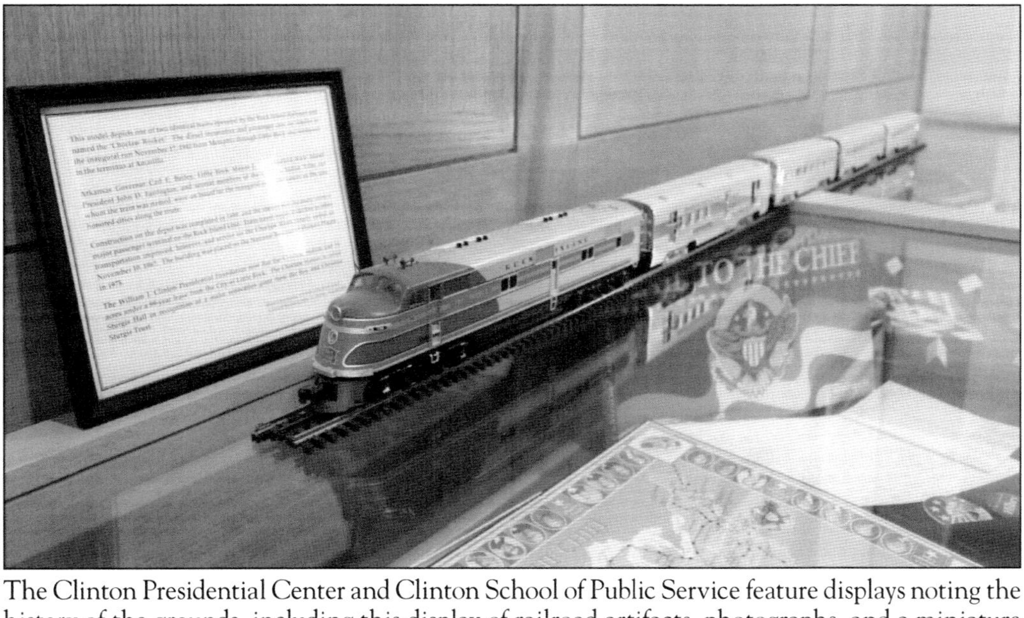

The Clinton Presidential Center and Clinton School of Public Service feature displays noting the history of the grounds, including this display of railroad artifacts, photographs, and a miniature train identical to the Rock Island's Choctaw Rocket that ran through Little Rock in the 1940s and 1950s, between Memphis, Tennessee, and Amarillo, Texas. (Photograph by author.)

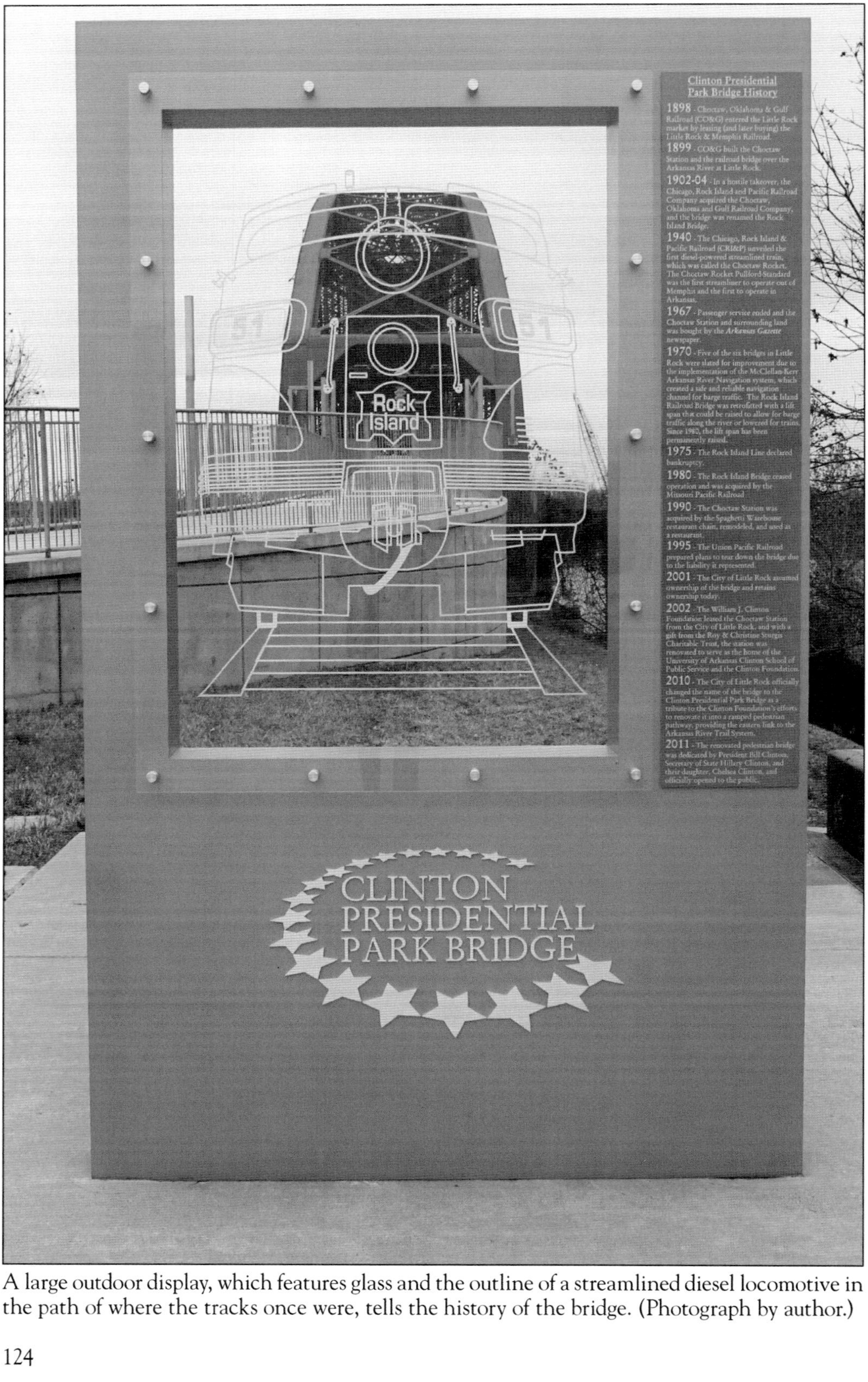

A large outdoor display, which features glass and the outline of a streamlined diesel locomotive in the path of where the tracks once were, tells the history of the bridge. (Photograph by author.)

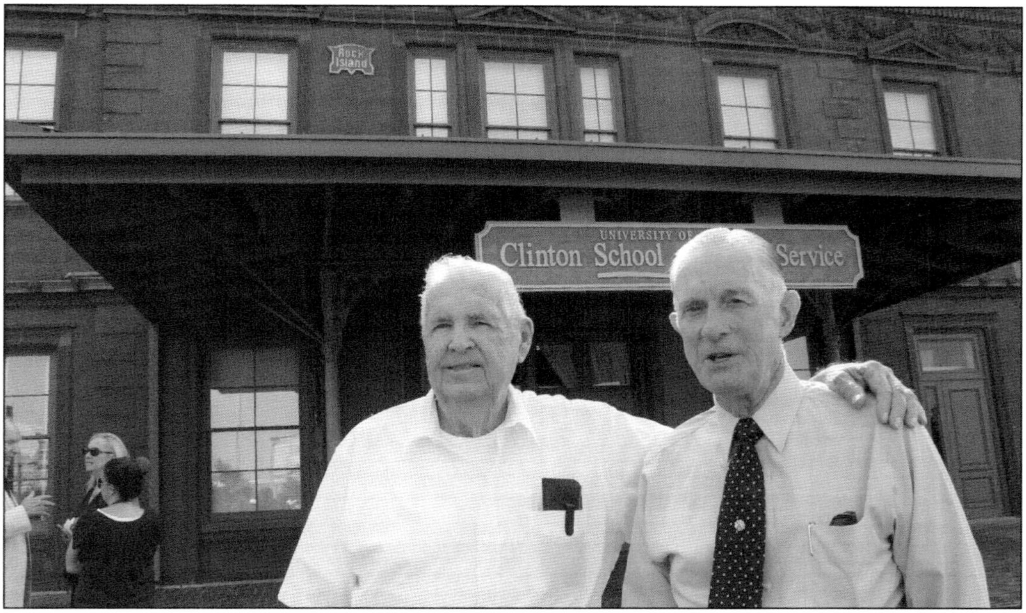

The large neon Rock Island sign, which was on top of the passenger station for decades, is said to have blown off during a storm in the 1990s. Former Rock Island employees regretted the building no longer having a symbol of the railroad, so in 2016, Guy Winters (left), who had a brass sign that had hung at a depot in Colorado Springs, Colorado, offered it to the library if it would be featured prominently. At the ceremony on August 29, 2016, it was formally dedicated. Standing with Winters afterward was Jerry Oates, president of a group of former Rock Island employees, with the sign above. (Photograph by author.)

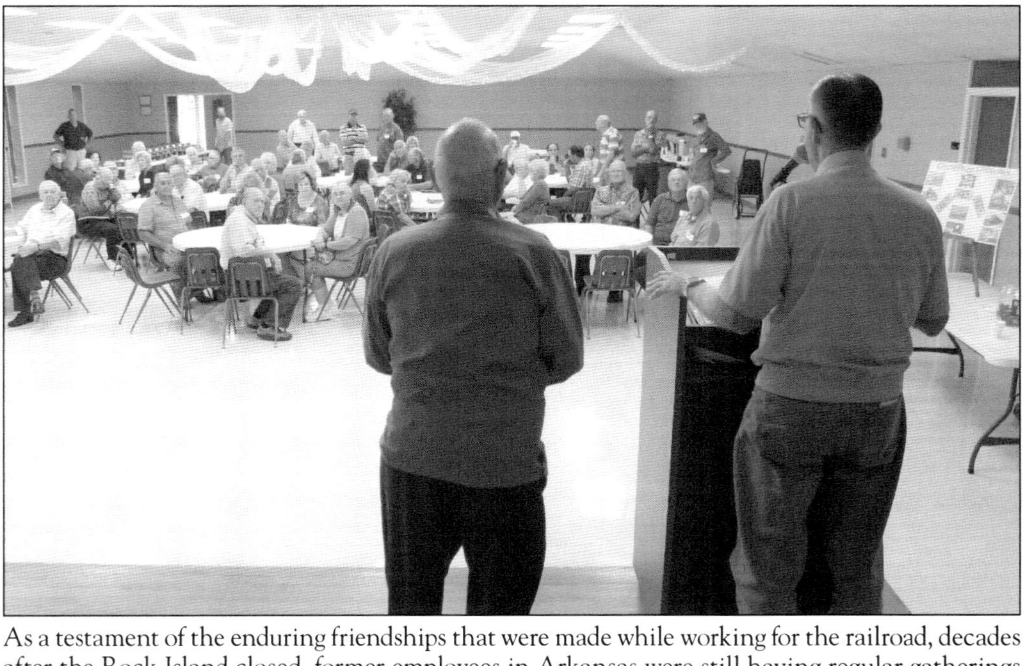

As a testament of the enduring friendships that were made while working for the railroad, decades after the Rock Island closed, former employees in Arkansas were still having regular gatherings to catch up. This photograph was taken at September 27, 2016, at an annual reunion drawing people from all around the region. (Photograph by author.)

Bibliography

Dean, Jerry. "Rock Island at End of Line; Cotton Belt Takes Throttle." *Arkansas Gazette* March 24, 1980.

Frantz, Susan. "Morale Is Low as Rail Subsidies End." *Arkansas Gazette* March 23, 1930.

Goen, Steve Allen. *Down South on the Rock Island, 1940–1969.* La Mirada, CA: Four Ways West Publications, 2002.

"Group to Ask Clinton to Help Save Rail Lines." *Arkansas Gazette* February 14, 1985.

Hull, Clifton E. *Railroad Stations and Trains through Arkansas and the Southwest.* Hart, MO: White River Productions, Inc., 1997.

Jones, Luke. "A Mighty Good Road." *Arkansas Business* July 30, 2012.

Schneider, Gregory L. *Rock Island Requiem: The Collapse of a Mighty Fine Line.* University Press of Kansas, 2013.

"Seventieth Anniversary." *Rock Island* October 1922.

Stout, Greg. *Route of the Rockets, Rock Island in the Streamlined Era.* Hart, MO: White River Productions, Inc., 1997.

Trimble, Mike. "Rock Island Employees Weigh Family Budgets; Many Agree to 'Loan.'" *Arkansas Gazette* March 9, 1975.

www.encyclopediaofarkansas.net/encyclopedia/entry-detail.aspx?entryID=5101

INDEX